T0317741

HANDBOOK OF RESEARCH METHODS ON SOCIAL ENTREPRENEURSHIP

Handbook of Research Methods on Social Entrepreneurship

Edited by

Richard G. Seymour

Senior Lecturer, Programme Director, Innovation and Enterprise and Co-Director, Innovation and Entrepreneurship Research Group, The University of Sydney Business School, Sydney, Australia

Edward Elgar
Cheltenham, UK • Northampton, MA, USA

Published by
Edward Elgar Publishing Limited
The Lypiatts
15 Lansdown Road
Cheltenham
Glos GL50 2JA
UK

Edward Elgar Publishing, Inc.
William Pratt House
9 Dewey Court
Northampton
Massachusetts 01060
USA

A catalogue record for this book
is available from the British Library

Library of Congress Control Number: 2011942541

ISBN 978 1 84844 965 7 (cased)

Typeset by Servis Filmsetting Ltd, Stockport, Cheshire
Printed and bound by MPG Books Group, UK

Contents

List of contributors vii
Acknowledgements ix
Introduction by Richard G. Seymour x

PART I CURIOSITY

1 Understanding the social in social entrepreneurship 3
Richard G. Seymour

2 Researching social entrepreneurship 26
Richard G. Seymour

PART II POSTURE

3 Listening to narratives 51
Chris Steyaert and Michel Bachmann

4 Participating in research 79
Mathew Tasker, Linda Westberg and Richard G. Seymour

5 Bounding research settings 106
K. Kumar and Jarrod Ormiston

PART III GATHERING

6 Discourse analysis 127
Fanny Salignac

7 Social network analysis 150
Cynthia Webster and Jennifer Ruskin

8 Surveys and data sets 170
Steven D'Alessandro and Hume Winzar

9 Drawing and verifying conclusions 218
Richard G. Seymour

PART IV VOICE

10 The challenge for researchers 231
Aaron F. McKenny, Jeremy C. Short and G. Tyge Payne

Index 251

Contributors

Michel Bachmann, PhD candidate, Research Institute for Organizational Psychology, University of St Gallen, St Gallen, Switzerland.

Steven D'Alessandro, Senior Lecturer, Department of Marketing and Management, Faculty of Business and Economics, Macquarie University, Australia.

K. Kumar, Professor, Indian Institute of Management Bangalore, Bangalore, India.

Aaron F. McKenny, Division of Management and Entrepreneurship, Michael F. Price College of Business, University of Oklahoma, USA.

Jarrod Ormiston, PhD candidate, Discipline of International Business, The University of Sydney Business School, Australia.

Jennifer Ruskin, Associate Lecturer, Faculty of Business and Economics, Macquarie University, Sydney, Australia.

Fanny Salignac, Lecturer, Centre for Social Impact, Australian School of Business, UNSW, Sydney, Australia.

Richard G. Seymour, Senior Lecturer, Programme Director, Innovation and Enterprise and Co-Director, Innovation and Entrepreneurship Research Group, The University of Sydney Business School, Sydney, Australia.

Jeremy C. Short, Jerry S. Rawls Professor of Management, Rawls College of Business, Texas Tech University, Lubbock, Texas, USA.

Chris Steyaert, Professor, Research Institute for Organizational Psychology, University of St Gallen, St Gallen, Switzerland.

Mathew Tasker, Associate Researcher, Discipline of International Business, The University of Sydney Business School, Australia.

G. Tyge Payne, Associate Professor of Strategic Management and Rawls Professor of Management, Rawls College of Business, Texas Tech University, Lubbock, Texas, USA.

Cynthia Webster, Associate Professor, Department of Marketing and Management, Faculty of Business and Economics, Macquarie University, Sydney, Australia.

Linda Westberg, Associate Researcher, Discipline of International Business, The University of Sydney Business School, Sydney, Australia.

Hume Winzar, Associate Professor, Department of Marketing and Management, Faculty of Business and Economics, Macquarie University, Australia.

Acknowledgements

So here it is at last. . .the beginnings.

I would like to thank everyone involved who got us to this point. There is a huge team of people, many of whom are invisible to the majority of us.

Many thanks go to the editing team at Edward Elgar who have all shown considerable and above-load patience with this work. In particular, thanks to Edward Elgar himself, Francine O'Sullivan, Jennifer Wilcox, Elizabeth Clack and Cathrin Vaughan. I hope it exceeds your expectations and motivates you to continue working with us.

Thanks also to all those who have contributed chapters. I realise that I chased some of you and some of you chased me. I am grateful for your insight and learning. I think your work is rich with wisdom and will shine brightly in the field.

Thank you also to the people working in the field who inspire us to build our research, teaching and outreach programs. If our research can support your efforts we will have played a small part in your success.

Also, and on behalf of the contributors – thank you to all our colleagues, friends and family who continue to support and help us.

Finally, thanks to you the reader who will utilize and build upon this work in practice.

Introduction

Richard G. Seymour

Research, to abuse a popular saying, was not meant to be easy. Undertaking research is a complex task requiring skills and proficiency in data collection, management, analysis and reporting, not to mention the associated and supporting research fundraising and dissemination. Research projects can be further complicated by the complex nature of the phenomenon and activities studied, with messy and unorganised data requiring a kind of 'rummaging' process to complement these 'organising' processes mentioned above.

In the case of social entrepreneurship research, these compounding factors are significant. Furthermore, in practice the term 'social entrepreneurship' is being inconsistently (though increasingly) used. For example: the President of the United States of America (USA), Barack Obama, used the term to express how he hoped to support small non-profit organisations. The Director of Social Enterprise at the Centre for Social Impact, Cheryl Kernot, used the term to describe a recent acquisition of government-funded childcare centres by a syndicate of Australian charities. The leader of the (then) opposition British Conservative Party, David Cameron, used the term in a call to mainstream business to focus on quality and community. The recent announcement of the Australian of the Year highlights the morphing concepts:

> 2011 Australian of the Year, Simon McKeon. Described as a social entrepreneur and philanthropist, he has made a name for himself in helping community causes. The previous recipients of Australian of the Year have been philanthropists, sports champions, business figures and activists. The 2011 Australian of the Year has all of these traits rolled into one. (666 ABC Canberra, 26 January 2011)

The general confusion associated with the terms is shared by academics who debate the meanings of 'social' as well as 'entrepreneurship', with concepts such as creativity, innovation, passion and value further complicating and confusing their debates. Part II of this *Handbook* will attempt to resolve these confusions.

0.1 SOCIAL ENTREPRENEURSHIP AS RISING STAR

Despite these confusions and contradictions, the profile and popularity of social entrepreneurship are rapidly rising. This may be due to a number of factors, including: (1) the recent and seemingly rolling crises in the world economy; (2) the concern that capitalism lacks a moral heart; and (3) recognition that management education has lacked a framework or purpose that is 'good'. Perhaps because of these factors, but also in spite of these factors, we are witnessing the rise of social entrepreneurship.

Turning first to the recent crises in the world economy: these crises include the dot-com bubble, the housing crisis, the credit and financial crises, high-profile bank bailouts and bonuses, corporate greenwashing and high unemployment – particularly in the 'free-wheeling' USA and United Kingdom (UK) – prompting commentators to highlight the flaws in the capitalist system. As noted by Porter and Kramer (2011, p. 62):

> The capitalist system is under siege. In recent years business increasingly has been viewed as a major cause of social, environmental, and economic problems. Companies are widely perceived to be prospering at the expense of the broader community. Even worse, the more business has begun to embrace corporate responsibility, the more it has been blamed for society's failures. The legitimacy of business has fallen to levels not seen in recent history . . . A big part of the problem lies with companies themselves, which remain trapped in an outdated approach to value creation that has emerged over the past few decades. They continue to view value narrowly.

To address these behaviours, there have been many attempts to create philosophies and frameworks that will allow such a 'better place' to be created. These frameworks have included the triple-bottom-line concepts pushed by practitioners of corporate social responsibility and sustainable investment. The highest-profile recent work is the above-mentioned Michael Porter and Mark Kramer (2011) 'Creating shared value: how to reinvent capitalism and unleash a wave of innovation and growth', promisingly published in the *Harvard Business Review*. In this paper they note:

> The concept of shared value can be defined as policies and operating practices that enhance the competitiveness of a company while simultaneously advancing the economic and social conditions in the communities in which it operates. Shared value creation focuses on identifying and expanding the connections between societal and economic progress. (p. 66)

With an equally fluid attempt at definition – 'The concept of shared value blurs the line between for-profit and nonprofit organizations' (p. 68) – Porter and Kramer propose:

> not all profit is equal – an idea that has been lost in the narrow, short-term focus of financial markets and in much management thinking. Profits involving a social purpose represent a higher form of capitalism – one that will enable society to advance more rapidly while allowing companies to grow even more. (p. 75)

It may be that social entrepreneurship offers insight into the opportunities for 'mission-based' business activity, and indeed Porter and Kramer recognise that social entrepreneurs are not locked into traditional business thinking and are pioneering the creation of shared value. Nevertheless, outside the field of social entrepreneurship, it is difficult to imagine how these 'higher' forms of capitalism will arise in what is most frequently a short-term race to the bottom.

Finally, in the context of management education, there has been criticism that there is a lack of a 'good' in the frameworks utilised by students, researchers and practitioners. For example, frameworks typically used to understand an industry, such as Porter's Five Forces (Porter, 1998), review bargaining power, threats of entrants, intensity of rivalry and so on. Such perspectives are not unusual, with the overarching aim of strategy to 'outperform'. Proponents of such competitiveness will argue that this is the basis of capitalism, and will typically return to Adam Smith's (1776/1976) 'invisible hand' for shelter from the above criticisms. We should note, however, that Smith himself was not as 'conservative' as some modern-day leaders would like to believe, with other works equally as significant (see for example *The Theory of Moral Sentiments*, Smith, 1759/2000). Without resolving these questions, elements of society have long questioned the 'purity' of commercial profit (perhaps these elements now also include MBA students):

> Two-thirds of people believe companies should do more than just make profits. According to a recent poll, the public in 20 countries believes companies should contribute to broader social goals, including good labour practices, business ethics and environmental standards. But research by the Aspen Institute in the US suggests this view is shared by only 40 per cent of those enrolling on MBA programmes – and by only 30 per cent of graduates. (Duncan McLaren, *Telegraph*, 21 February 2003)

These three superficial examples of crises, concerns and recognitions highlight the need for alternative business practice, but also the anticipation of alternative practices by business leaders and academic researchers.

To temper the above enthusiasm, it should be noted that social entrepreneurship and social entrepreneurship research, though rising stars, are not magic cures for the above-mentioned malaise. Indeed, just as there is a 'dark side' to commercial entrepreneurship (Kets de Vries, 1985), so we can expect the same of social entrepreneurship. Criticisms of the former include: (1) commercial entrepreneurship encourages a 'transactional model of social relationships' such that entrepreneurship is about the creation and betrayal of trust (Collins et al., 1964); complicated by the fact that (2) most dishonesty by entrepreneurs is not found out, and if it is the entrepreneur is typically sufficiently powerful for it not to matter (Bhide and Stevenson, 1990); encouraged (perhaps) by (3) a society which emphasises achievement without a corresponding emphasis on the means to that achievement tends to produce high levels of innovation in the form of deviance (Merton, 1949); resulting in a kind of (4) tactical empathy (which has been argued to be crucial to the career of Sir Richard Branson and his retaining control of *Student* magazine and Virgin Music, which had little to do with creating those enterprises, but rather gaining or retaining control of them) (Armstrong, 2005).

It would be unusual if there is not also some mistaken and mismanaged activity by social entrepreneurs, especially given that they are 'active' in the challenging space traditionally occupied by not-for-profit organisations, government agencies and non-governmental organisations. Indeed, the recent criticisms of micro-credit and the organisations driving its growth may be the tip of the iceberg in the field. It is important, therefore, that researchers and practitioners alike do not actively (or passively) hide ignoble activities behind noble missions.

0.2 SOCIAL ENTREPRENEURSHIP RESEARCH IS INCREASINGLY VISIBLE AND SIGNIFICANT

Social entrepreneurship research is growing in profile and impact (for a review refer to the excellent Chapter 10 in this *Handbook* by Aaron McKenny, Jeremy Short and Tyge Payne). Its profile is rising in response to the discussions presented above, but also because of its peripheral and cross-disciplinary nature. As introduced by Dacin et al. (2010, p. 37):

> Social entrepreneurship continues to be a field of interest that crosses academic disciplines and challenges traditional assumptions of economic and business development . . . Some even suggest that the phenomenon transcends the individual domains of entrepreneurial studies, social movements, and nonprofit management.

The periphery has long been recognised as significant (see, for example, Day and Schoemaker, 2005; Cunha and Chia, 2007), and social entrepreneurship research promises insights into the periphery as well as the 'mainstream'. The stretch for researchers is to ensure that we are not blind to these alternative realities, or blinkered by our research methods developed in the context of a for-profit world of business.

This is not to imply that social entrepreneurship requires new theory, new methodologies or new methods. I agree with Dacin et al. (2010): social entrepreneurship should not be delineated as a theoretical domain in its own right. Instead, social entrepreneurship should be recognised as a setting for research that provides rich opportunity for researchers (whether we be primarily commercially or socially focussed) to advance our understandings of business activity (whether commercial or social).

0.3 THE FOCUS FOR THE *HANDBOOK*

With the above considerations and caveats noted, I turn to the focus for the *Handbook*: research methods that will have particular relevance for the context and phenomena of social entrepreneurship. It is written with early-career researchers in mind, with clear approaches to research documented by experienced and novice researchers alike. Unlike most handbooks focussed on research methods, this edited volume has organised itself around broad themes of research: curiosity, posture, gathering and voice (Figure 0.1). These themes develop the interactive model of data analysis proposed by Miles and Huberman (1994). Within each of these themes, chapters of this *Handbook* address specific approaches and methods. Note how the figure emphasises that the various themes are all interrelated and interactive.

0.3.1 Curiosity

All research begins (and perhaps also ends) with curiosity. That curiosity can be sparked from practical engagement with social enterprise, or inspired from theoretical pondering. Part I of the *Handbook* aims to spark and harness curiosity by reviewing both the social entrepreneurship phenomenon as well as the philosophies of science impacting upon its study.

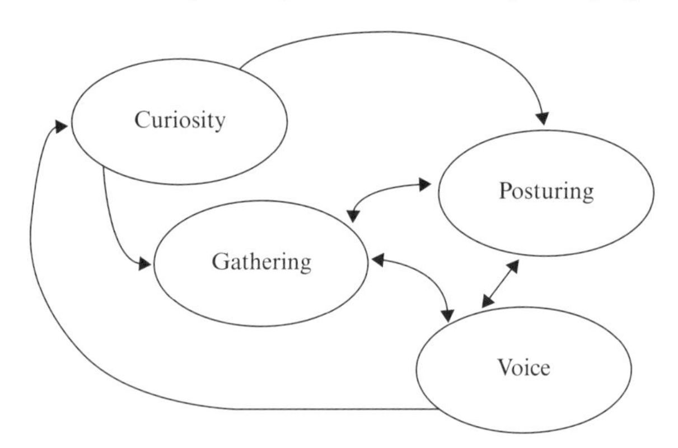

Figure 0.1 Themes of research activity: interactive model

To turn these sparks into a fire, attentive and fervent additional research is required.

0.3.2 Posture

The posture taken by a researcher will have an impact on the research project undertaken. By posture, I mean the research strategy or position that will determine the associated research methods. For example, how the researcher positions their research with regards to the sources of data (narratives and stories), participation or involvement in the project (action research) or how that research is bounded (multiple or single case studies). Part II also highlights how postures will impact upon the data gathered and the resulting insights.

0.3.3 Gathering

Gathering data and insight are the 'active' episodes of research, having a focus on the methods associated with research activity. Part III of the *Handbook* includes social network analysis, discourse analysis, and the quantitative methods associated with large data sets. These three key methods are each complemented by appropriate examples set in the context of social entrepreneurship.

0.3.4 Voice

The final (and perhaps greatest) challenge for a researcher is to find his or her voice. This voice is required to write up the research project and findings, as well as to find the audience that will appreciate that research. Part IV of the *Handbook* includes an overview of the challenge for researchers in the setting of social entrepreneurship.

0.4 AS INTRODUCTION

I would advise reading broadly within this *Handbook*; for example there are excellent insights for qualitative researchers in the quantitative chapters (and vice versa). As will be seen, social entrepreneurship research calls for some adventurous approaches to methods as well as requiring fundamental and core research skills. Finding the right balance between experience and enthusiasm is a challenge for us all, and it is hoped that the following chapters will support an adventurous engagement with social entrepreneurship research. The *Handbook* is not intended to be read in isolation: read widely and thoroughly within as well as outside it.

Finally, by way of introduction, a word about the writers of this *Handbook*. The contributors to this edited volume are all experienced researchers, some in the early stages of their career, some in an early phase of their research in the context of social entrepreneurship, and some are recognised leaders in the field. My thanks go to them for their efforts and for these chapters. What they share here is a passion for the context of social entrepreneurship, as well as their expertise in the practice of research. I hope that reading and developing their shared wisdom proves enjoyable, and that they will collectively inspire research activity. I remain grateful for their kind engagement with me as we developed this *Handbook*. I hope also that this short introduction to the *Handbook* has piqued the reader's curiosity; the real insights come from the following chapters, and of course from the reader's own research undertakings.

REFERENCES

Armstrong, P. (2005). *Critique of Entrepreneurship: People and Policy*. Basingstoke: Palgrave Macmillan.

Bhidé, A.V. and H.H. Stevenson (1990). Why be honest if honesty doesn't pay? *Harvard Business Review* **68**(5), 121–129.

Collins, O.F., D.G. Moore and D.B. Unwalla (1964). *The Enterprising Man*. East Lansing, MI: Bureau of Business and Economic Research, Michigan State University.

Cunha, M.P. and R. Chia (2007). Using teams to avoid peripheral blindness. *Long Range Planning* **40**, 559–573.

Dacin, P.A., M.T. Dacin and M. Matear (2010). Social entrepreneurship: why we don't need a new theory and how we move forward from here. *Academy of Management Perspectives* **24**(3), 37–57.

Day, G.S. and P.J.H. Schoemaker (2005). Scanning the periphery. *Harvard Business Review* November, 1–8.

Kets de Vries, M. (1985). The dark side of entrepreneurship. *Harvard Business Review* November–December, 160–167.

Merton, R.K. (1949). *Social Theory and Social Structure*. New York: Free Press.

Miles, M.B. and A.M. Huberman (1994). *Qualitative Data Analysis: An Expanded Sourcebook*. Thousand Oaks, CA: SAGE Publications.

Porter, M.E. (1998). *Competitive Strategy: Techniques for Analyzing Industries and Competitors*. New York: Free Press.

Porter, M.E. and M.R. Kramer (2011). Creating shared value: how to reinvent capitalism and unleash a wave of innovation and growth. *Harvard Business Review* January–February, 62–77.

Smith, A. (1759/2000). *The Theory of Moral Sentiments*. Amherst, MA: Prometheus Books.

Smith, A. (1776/1976). *An Inquiry into the Nature and Causes of the Wealth of Nations*. Oxford: Clarendon Press.

PART I

CURIOSITY

Our curiosity, inquisitiveness and desire to learn about things and people urge us to investigate the unknown. I am convinced that curiosity is the foundation of any research undertaking, and that social entrepreneurship provides a wonderful platform for those investigations.

Part I of this *Handbook* concentrates on marshalling that curiosity towards an initial research question in the context of social entrepreneurship. This marshalling typically starts with a 'big' research question of interest. 'Big' questions may be sparked from experience, thought and introspection as well as active discussion and engagement with people (whether they be experts, stakeholders or participants) and literature (whether that be academic, professional or documents). These sparks need to be fanned into a fire, and it is your formal research projects that will allow you to do so.

The first processes of research require (multiple) literature reviews. These literature reviews are different from a review of the web or other material publicly available: the term should imply that you will absorb existing theory and peer-reviewed material. Your curiosity will be a flowing cycle of learning between theory (and the ideas and what we think) and the data (and the reality of what is observed). The reviews should include literature specific to social and commercial entrepreneurship, but also incorporate literature from broader fields and settings.

One part of that literature review will be to understand the multiple conceptualisations of 'social entrepreneurship'. Chapter 1 introduces the field's extant literature (and seeks to frame some of the issues evident in the literature). It observes the buzz associated with the phenomena of entrepreneurial activity and the study of entrepreneurship, from the perspectives of both the practitioners (commercial entrepreneurs as well as not-for-profit activists) and academics alike. The context is shown to be rich, promising insights not readily apparent in other settings such as commercial entrepreneurship. The key aspects of entrepreneurial activity (human action, seeking to generate value, creating or expanding economic activity, identifying and exploiting new products, processes or markets) are then explored from the perspective of commercial and social entrepreneurship. To help prevent the field becoming hidden by perspectives and approaches, just as a dancer can be cloaked in fashionable clothing, Chapter 1 concludes with a working definition of social entrepreneurship, social entrepreneurial activity and the social entrepreneur.

At this stage it might also be appropriate to hop to Chapter 10 of this *Handbook* in which Aaron McKenny, Jeremy Short and Tyge Payne provide an excellent review of the extant social entrepreneurship literature.

Chapter 2 argues that your research project will not just be influenced by (for example) your focus of interest, the experts you consult, the literature you review, or even your chosen units of analysis, but also by your (whether proclaimed or unmentioned) philosophies of science. The chapter sets out the significance of the philosophies of science for the social entrepreneurship researcher, and explains the implications of various ontologies, epistemologies and methodologies on research activity. It gives examples of how two extreme (subjectivist and objectivist) perspectives can impact upon various research, and sets out the strengths and weaknesses associated with each. As can be expected, no philosophical perspective has a monopoly on truth or insight. Chapter 2 concludes with the implications of various perspectives in the context of social entrepreneurship, and clarifies why a researcher should make their assumptions explicit.

As you read through these first chapters, you should also be considering your theoretical perspectives of interest. Remember: theory does not suggest answers to your 'big' questions, instead it focusses your attention on the appropriate questions to pose in your primary research.

1 Understanding the social in social entrepreneurship

Richard G. Seymour

This chapter introduces the phenomenon of 'social entrepreneurship', highlighting that though not new in practice, it is certainly enjoying heightened attention in academic research. It then explores the meanings of the 'social' in social entrepreneurship, noting that 'social entrepreneurship' or 'social enterprise' are essentially umbrella terms for a considerable range of activities, some of which might be better considered as businesses, some of which might be better considered as charities. The chapter then proposes a working definition of social entrepreneurship to resolve the confusion over these activities.

1.1 AN OVERVIEW OF THE SOCIAL ENTREPRENEURSHIP PHENOMENON

There is a growing awareness, both within and outside the sector, of the significance and importance of social entrepreneurship. This awareness (some might refer to it as a buzz) has both positive and negative implications. Before entering the debate about what is and is not social entrepreneurship, some cursory conceptualisations of the different concepts are in order.

This chapter will work towards a definition of social entrepreneurship that is both pragmatic and meaningful. The first step towards that definition is a simple conceptualisation of the various business, activist and entrepreneurial activities, as shown in Figure 1.1.

Figure 1.1 is drawn to suggest two things: that social entrepreneurship can be differentiated from its cousins based on its means as well as its ends. First, it suggests that entrepreneurial activity, whether social or commercial, is associated with doing new things or doing those things 'differently' (means). This impression of 'difference' is sometimes referred to as creative destruction, change-makers or visionary activity. Though we are aware of the people who succeed in their 'newness', we often do not know of those who do not succeed. Whatever one's preferred terminology, it should reflect something that is rare and profound. The

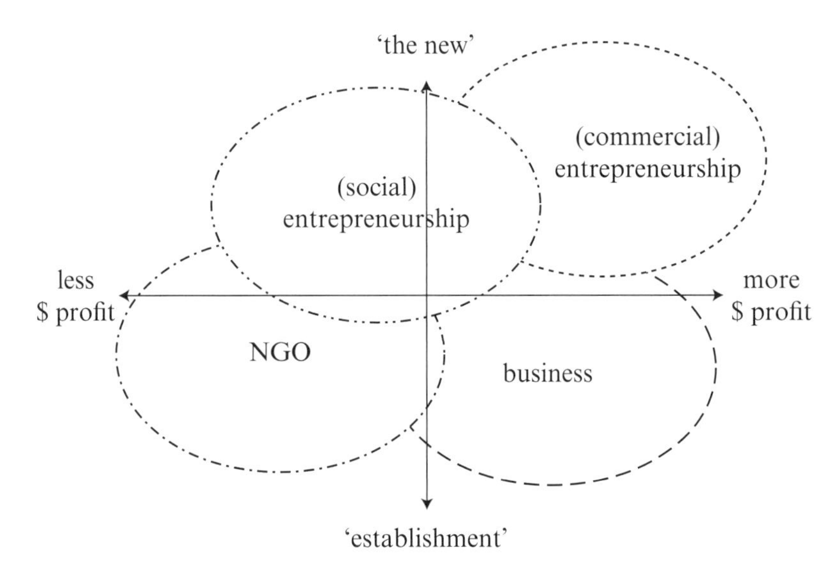

Figure 1.1 Conceptualizing entrepreneurship, business and NGO activities

implication is that the 'establishment' or 'status quo' of the NGO (non-governmental organisation), NFP (not-for-profit) or commercial business will be less likely than their entrepreneurial cousins to consider or incorporate new markets, new product offerings or new business models. This is not to devalue their operations or activities, just to differentiate them.

Second, the figure suggests that the outcomes of such activity can be differentiated along a pecuniary scale of more, of less, dollar profit (ends). The emphasis on 'more dollar profit' intentionally does not address the question of social value, cultural value or any other forms of value that may be created (such as ecological, spiritual or creative value). The axis is drawn to suggest that a social enterprise or NGO will most likely focus on seeking to generate other types of value (such as social or cultural value). It does not imply that a commercial entrepreneur will not create social or cultural value, nor does it imply that a social entrepreneur cannot make economic profit. It intends to highlight that the driving force behind commercial entrepreneurship and business activity will typically be higher financial profits. The significance of differentiating these means and ends will be revisited and explored in greater depth later in this chapter.

1.2 A 'SOCIAL' IN ENTREPRENEURSHIP RESEARCH?

Delving further into the issues of definition, there are multiple understandings of 'the social' in social entrepreneurship. Many researchers consider the creation of social value as core to the concept (see for example Austin et al., 2006; Austin, 2006; Nicholls, 2006; Weerawardena and Mort, 2006). Other scholars allude to 'the social' in social mission (Nicholls, 2006), social objectives or aims (Haugh, 2006; Henry, 2007; Tapsell and Woods, 2008), and social transformation (Alvord and Brown, 2002). The plastic nature of definitions has meant that the literature has failed to address the meaning of 'the social' (Cho, 2006; Marti, 2006). There have been attempts to rectify this shortfall (including Young, 2006), however the divisions remain: 'The social' is treated either as an obvious quality that does not require explanation, or as an exogenous factor (Cho, 2006).

Furthermore, wider debates consider whether the field is something 'special' and quite separate from commercial entrepreneurship. The practice of identifying new subfields of research attention can be appropriate in developing fields of researchers and research: for example, international, public, institutional and cultural entrepreneurship, as well as corporate venturing, intrapreneurship and academic venturing have all grown recently. It would appear that 'social' entrepreneurship has become its own field; the question remains whether it will develop its own frameworks and theories.

Dacin et al. (2010) give a detailed review of the history of attempts to define social entrepreneurship, and argue against new theories. They note that current attempts to define the phenomena, for example those

Table 1.1 Approaches in social entrepreneurship scholarship

Bias	Exemplary studies
Process demonstrated when government or NGO operate using business principles	Austin et al. (2006), Mort et al. (2002), Sharir and Lerner (2006)
Activities of commercial entrepreneurs focussed on corporate social responsibility	Baron (2005), Young (2001)
Outcomes of organised philanthropy and social innovation	Reis and Clohesy (1999), van Slyke and Newman (2006), Bornstein (2004)
Economically sustainable ventures that generate social value	Emerson and Twersky (1996), Robinson (2006)

Source: Dacin et al. (2010).

summarised in Table 1.1, have not achieved the balance between a broad definition (which risks being inclusive and devoid of meaning) and a tight definition (which risks being narrow and exclusive).

Such conflicts and divisions are present in many fields of literature; for example there are numerous conflicting understandings and applications of the terms 'entrepreneurship' and 'innovation' in the literature in academia as well as in practice. The implications of such divisions may not appear to be terribly important (a rose by any other name would smell as sweet). However, I would argue that the lack of a definition has important (negative) implications for the field. This chapter focusses our attention on a working definition and understanding of social entrepreneurship.

1.3 DEFINING (SOCIALLY) ENTREPRENEURIAL ACTIVITY

Returning to the paper of Dacin et al. (2010), I disagree with the outcomes (rather than the approach) of their attempt to delineate four types of entrepreneurial activity: conventional (or commercial), institutional, cultural and social. I take the finishing point of the paper as my starting point:

> Social Entrepreneur – An actor who applies business principles to solving social problems.
> Conventional entrepreneur – An agent who enables or enacts a vision based on new ideas in order to create successful innovations . . .
> Institutional Entrepreneur – An agent who can mobilize resources to influence or change institutional rules in order to support or destroy an existing institution, or to establish a new one . . .
> Cultural Entrepreneur – An individual who identifies an opportunity and acts upon it in order to create social, cultural or economic value. (Dacin et al., 2010, p. 44)

These definitions are interesting; however they fail to mention the aspect of business activity that differentiates entrepreneurial activity from leadership, innovation, activism or artistry. Some cheap shots at the above conceptualisations: (1) Would a social entrepreneur better apply entrepreneurial principles rather than business principles? (2) Would a social entrepreneur not also create cultural and economic value rather than just solve social problems? and (3) Why are social entrepreneurs 'actors' and yet conventional and institutional entrepreneurs are 'agents' and cultural entrepreneurs are 'individuals'?

I therefore turn attention away from these definitions, but not away from their (Dacin et al., 2010) excellent review. Specifically, I consider it

BOX 1.1 CREATIVITY

Both paradoxical and complex, 'creativity' is the ability to produce work that is both novel (i.e. original or unexpected), appropriate (i.e. useful, valuable or meeting the task constraints) (Amabile, 1983, 1996; Sternberg and Lubart, 1996). Creativity in a business context can be indicated by:

- research and development expenditures
- formal and informal intellectual property protection, including patents, copyright, trademarks or registered designs
- awards or recognition by industry organisations or panels of experts
- contracting or employment of high-cost professionals.

useful to focus on a small number of related concepts and terms: creativity, innovation and entrepreneurship.

1.3.1 Understanding Creativity and Innovation

'All innovation begins with creative ideas' (Amabile et al., 1996, p. 1154). Creativity occurs in the interactions between the individual, the field of experts and a public culture (Csikszentmihalyi, 1994; Feldman et al., 1994). Box 1.1 explores the nature of creativity. Note that the related term 'invention' is avoided: instead, 'creativity' is used. In business, 'invention' implies that there is something legally new. Creativity is the wellspring of activity for innovators and entrepreneurs alike.

Academics have typically focussed on creativity, even though creativity is a necessary, although not sufficient, condition for innovation and entrepreneurship. For social entrepreneurs, creativity is often associated with seeing the world differently, or with dreaming a better future. It is not, however, anything more than an inspiration for action and work.

As can be seen from Box 1.2, 'innovation' is a term that has very different meanings for practitioners and researchers. The innovator does not invent or create, but rather innovates (Schumpeter, 1934). Innovation can be based on creativity, invention, research and development (that is, something totally new); but it can also result from an extension, duplication or synthesis of existing knowledge. These innovations can be radical or incremental (see for example Stringer, 2000), disruptive or sustaining

BOX 1.2 INNOVATION

A generally accepted definition of innovation has been documented in the OECD-Eurostat Oslo Manual (OECD, 2005) and forms the basis for innovation surveys conducted in OECD member and non-member countries, including the ABS innovation survey:

'An innovation is the implementation of a new or significantly improved product (goods or services), or process, a new marketing method, or a new organisational method in business practices, workplace organisation or external relations' (OECD, 2005).

(refer for example to Christensen, 1997) and can be generated by a multitude of creative individuals, whether society, customers, research and development (R&D) departments, scientists, lead-users or employees.

Note in the definitions of 'innovation' the lack of reference to anything associated with the ultimate market acceptance (or rejection) of that new product/service/market/business approach. The 'newness' in the above innovation definitions must be newness to the business, not newness to the market or consumer. Thus, innovation research tends to focus on the processes and activities of the business, such as stocks and flows associated with human capital, information and data, facilities and institutions.

The third concept for examination is entrepreneurship. For this definition, I turn to the Organisation for Economic Co-operation and Development (OECD)-Eurostat Entrepreneurship Indicators Programme (OECD-Eurostat EIP) and its definitions.

1.3.2 Defining Entrepreneurship

Initiated in 2005, the OECD-Eurostat EIP is a coordinated effort to agree on a policy-relevant, analytical model, build a measurement infrastructure and gather comparable data. Given the diversity of outcomes and manifestations of entrepreneurship, the OECD-Eurostat EIP has recognised that no single indicator can paint the full picture for policymakers. The framework has focussed on three separate but interconnected flows that are important in the formulation, assessment and appraisal of entrepreneurship-friendly policy measures:

- determinants (a country's entrepreneurial performance depends on a myriad of underlying factors including market conditions, access

to finance and regulatory frameworks and so on, coupled with the personal attributes of entrepreneurs);
- performance (which considers the entrepreneurial actions that are instrumental in delivering the impacts such as business, employment and wealth growth, and so on); and
- impact (or the value resulting from entrepreneurial activity such as job creation and economic growth).

The research is focussed on understanding entrepreneurial activity at the national level, and so does not answer (directly) many of the questions confronting the study of social entrepreneurship. It does, however, provide a starting point for this *Handbook* with its definitions:

> Entrepreneurs are those persons (business owners) who seek to generate value, through the creation or expansion of economic activity, by identifying and exploiting new products, processes or markets.
>
> Entrepreneurial activity is the enterprising human action in pursuit of the generation of value, through the creation or expansion of economic activity, by identifying and exploiting new products, processes or markets.
>
> Entrepreneurship is the phenomena associated with entrepreneurial activity. (Ahmad and Seymour, 2008, p. 14)

These definitions have a number of important characteristics of note for research, as they:

- differentiate entrepreneurial activity from 'ordinary' business activity (note the emphasis on newness: new products, new processes or new markets);
- indicate corporations and other businesses can be entrepreneurial even though only the people in control and owners of organisations can be considered entrepreneurs (that is, only an entrepreneur is defined as a person (typically a business owner);
- emphasise that entrepreneurial action is manifested rather than planned or intended;
- do not equate activity with the formation of any particular corporate vehicle (it does not matter if these vehicles are companies limited by liability, sole traders, not-for-profit enterprises or partnerships); and
- incorporate economic, social and cultural value creation (even though they are defined in the context of business, these different indicators of value are extremely significant for the study of social entrepreneurship).

These definitions suggest that we may be missing the point by trying to define social entrepreneurship as a stand-alone field rather than a 'subset' of entrepreneurial activity.

1.4 SOCIAL ENTREPRENEURSHIP AND THE RESEARCHER

Entrepreneurial activity in the context of social enterprise can better be understood by examining the following aspects of the definitions: (1) enterprising human action; (2) the pursuit of the generation of value; (3) the creation or expansion of economic activity; and (4) identification and exploitation of new products, processes or markets. The following comparisons of commercial and social entrepreneurship are made (ignoring institutional and cultural entrepreneurship) for the sake of simplicity and the avoidance of secondary debates.

1.4.1 Enterprising Human Action

Enterprising human action has long been recognised as a key aspect of entrepreneurship. In the context of commercial entrepreneurship this has tended to be indicated by risk-taking (or coping with uncertainty), speculation and identification and exploitation of opportunity. However, there are other important (universal) aspects to enterprising human action:

> Acting man is eager to substitute a more satisfactory state of affairs for a less satisfactory. His mind imagines conditions which suit him better, and his action aims at bringing about this desired state. (von Mises, 1949/1996)

People can satisfy their needs by self-production (typical of primitive societies), by reducing needs and wants by allowing other values to override their inner desires (for example athletes practising forms of asceticism), and through exchange (Houston and Gassenheimer, 1987).

Enterprising (commercial) human action

The entrepreneur is often considered to be a heroic individual who possesses a number of skills and abilities to succeed where others fail. Stevenson and Jarillo (1990) proposed entrepreneurship to be the study of why, how and what happens when entrepreneurs act. The importance of this acting has long been recognised:

> Like every acting man, the entrepreneur is always a speculator. He deals with the uncertain conditions of the future. His success or failure depends on the correctness of his anticipation of uncertain events. If he fails in his understanding of things to come he is doomed . . . The specific entrepreneurial function consists in determining employment of the factors of production. The entrepreneur is the man who dedicates them to special purposes. In doing so he is driven solely by the selfish interest in making profits and in acquiring wealth. But he cannot evade the law of the market. He can succeed only by best serving the

> consumers. His profit depends on the approval of his conduct by the consumers. (von Mises, 1949/1996, pp. 290–291)

Understanding enterprising action has not, however, limited researchers to studying people. For example, Shane and Venkataraman (2000) recognise that as well as studying the set of individuals who discover, evaluate and exploit opportunities, the discipline of entrepreneurship includes the study of the discovery, evaluation and exploitation of opportunities. Understanding the organising process is one of the necessary conditions of entrepreneurship (Shane, 2003), with a focus on understanding how actors perceive of a previously unknown way to create a new means–ends framework (Eckhardt and Shane, 2003). This requires different people with different understandings, different intentions and different values:

> Entrepreneurship requires the preferential access to or ability to recognise information about opportunities, both of which vary across people . . . moreover entrepreneurship requires a decision by a person to act upon an opportunity because opportunities themselves lack agency. (Shane, 2003, p. 7)

Enterprising (social) human action

The literature would suggest that in the world of social entrepreneurship, appropriate research subjects would include the individual entrepreneur as well as the key stakeholders and community involved in the social enterprise. In spite of this, many studies focus on the significance of the individual heroic social entrepreneur (Drayton, 2002; Mair and Marti, 2006), defining and portraying their role as 'reformers and revolutionaries', who 'break new ground, develop new models, and pioneer new approaches' (Dees and Economy, 2001, p. 4). An alternative stream highlights that social entrepreneurship does not only emerge through individuals, but is an integration of the entrepreneur, entrepreneurial processes and the social (Anderson et al., 2006), such that groups of people are required (Nicholls and Cho, 2006; Peredo and McClean, 2006; Perrini and Vurro, 2006).

The social entrepreneurship phenomenon suggests we may need to move away from a rational, selfish conceptualisation of activity. For example: underlying motivation can be seen as being built into humans as the need to explore (Whitfield, 2005) or play (without belittling the importance or significance of the act) (Huizinga, 1955). If human action is also seen as exploration and 'play', there is a place for relational rather than (just) self-seeking behaviours and events (John Capper, in Rutledge, 2006).

Understand the 'social' of enterprising human action

In summary, the literature highlights that there are various and multiple parties involved in social enterprises, and suggests that these parties are not typically motivated by simple cause–effect activity and outcomes. This, in turn, suggests that the researcher consider research methodologies and strategies that will 'see' these multiple perspectives. Perspectives that will include multiple parties (perhaps network theory or action research), complexity (utilising case studies for example), and social understandings (for example, utilising discourse analysis).

1.4.2 Seeking to Generate Value

Management researchers are increasingly recognising the importance of value analysis (Lepak et al., 2007). The concept of value is implicitly considered in the fields of sociology, economics, ecology (studying social value creation), strategic management, organization theory (studying organizational value creation), psychology and human resources (studying individuals) (Lepak et al., 2007). To simplify the associated conflicts in research perspectives and definitions, I turn to the *Oxford English Dictionary* as my starting point. Value: 'That amount of some commodity, medium of exchange, etc., which is considered to be an equivalent for something else; a fair or adequate equivalent or return' (*OED*, 2006).

Value can be considered as a number of qualitatively different elements: (1) the value of an object in itself (artefact value); (2) the value associated with the person or society considering or utilising that object (social value); (3) the value associated with art, music or other creative pursuit (cultural value); (4) the value associated with the environment (natural value); and even (5) the value associated with life and the spiritual (sacred value).

Drilling into the question of the 'social value', what an entrepreneur often desires (in addition to, or in conflict to, the other forms of value) are the personal relationships that a transaction may initiate. This 'social value' is associated with attempts to move a relationship to a deeper level, or as a means of maintaining an existing relationship (Ruth et al., 1999). Aspects of social value include acquisitive value, which has the expectation of reciprocation, versus expressive value, which is not concerned with what can be gained from the other but with what can be conveyed to others (Miczo, 2002).

Value cannot be possessed by a thing, as it is only acquired the moment the thing appears in public (Arendt, 1958), as 'valued things have relative but not absolute value' (Emerson, 1982, p. 13). 'Value', therefore, must always mean 'value in exchange' as it is only in the marketplace that objects, labour and work become 'values' (refer, for example, to the social construction of value in auctions, Smith, 1989). Value arises from the possibility of exchange (Shackle, 1972). Value is, in fact, a trilateral relationship, with no common denominator. That is to say, the value of a good lies in its being preferred or not being preferred to other goods, subject to the same choice. I will further explore this concept of 'exchange' in relation to 'creation or expansion of economic activity' below.

Entrepreneurs prioritising (commercial) value

Entrepreneurs have long been considered to prioritise the commercial: 'Commercial: Interested in financial return rather than artistry; likely to make a profit; regarded as a mere matter of business' (*OED*, 2006).

This does not, however, suggest that a commercial entrepreneur can ignore social, cultural or natural value. Furthermore, and specifically, as reviewed in Walker and Brown (2004), entrepreneurs have also been shown to value a number of non-financial measures of success including autonomy, job satisfaction and the ability to balance work and family. These are all subjectively and personally defined, but can have a major impact on the decisions and exchanges involved in the creation and exploitation of opportunities.

The commercial entrepreneur exchanges value with a wide variety of actors in the entrepreneurial process, including customers, employees, society, financiers and alliance partners. Understanding the types of exchange, as well as the media and meaning of those exchanges, will provide a rich understanding of the behaviour of the entrepreneur and the entrepreneurial environments.

It could be argued that the majority of academic conceptualisations of value err in their research approach, attempting to consider value objectively. This has led to an overemphasis on pecuniary value, which is of less significance in the context of social entrepreneurship.

Social entrepreneurs prioritising (non-commercial) value

It is difficult to disaggregate values into their economic, social and cultural components, as they are often inextricably linked and dependent on each other (Young, 2006). Furthermore, it must be recognised that there are different types as well as different layers of value; hence social entrepreneurship can entail the creation of social value which ranges from social added value, to empowerment, to systemic change (Young, 2006). This contrasts with the view that social entrepreneurship only includes those activities which generate overarching systemic change (Martin and Osberg, 2007).

Seen as a process, social entrepreneurship is a collection of innovation and strategic actions aimed to create social value (Dees and Elias, 1998; Alter, 2006; Dees and Economy, 2001; Dees and Emerson, 2002). The objective and process, rather than the organisational structure or outcomes, become critical units of analysis.

Focussing on this process requires understanding of the social sphere, which is heterogeneous rather than homogeneous, with multiple participants having competing and conflicting interests (Cho, 2006). Nicholls and Cho (2006, p. 106) highlight that visions and interpretations of the social are 'inextricably linked to varying sets of potentially incompatible values and normative commitments'. It would be a naive and superficial understanding of the social if we failed to examine multiple perspectives of value.

Understanding the social in value generation

Note that atomising or quantifying 'value' into its constituent elemental constructs (for example, whether value is 20 per cent pecuniary and 80 per cent social in a particular transaction or business activity) is not sensible. Measuring value exchanges objectively cannot be the (sole) appropriate concept for value enquiry (Marietta, 1984): 'By its insistence on measuring the unmeasurable [*sic*], economics bludgeons the face of reality, the detail and vitality of human concerns are flattened to an unrecognizable tedium' (Shackle, 1972, p. 111).

However, it could be argued that commercial literature prioritises the economic aspects of value, typically concentrating on the output of activity, and studies focussing on social entrepreneurship typically including value associated with processes of activity. The reality for researchers is that there are many alternative perspectives of value (see for example Figure 1.2), which typically should be considered by those focussed on social entrepreneurship.

Semantics would suggest that there is a difference between seeking to generate value (whatever kind of value that may be) and seeking to generate change (that in turn generates some kind of value). However, in practice there may be quite a difference in the implications of differences between the expectations and intentions.

1.4.3 The Creation or Expansion of Economic Activity

The reference to economic activity is not intending to suggest that the activity must be generating pecuniary profits (alone). It does, however, suggest that the activity must 'look like' business activity (that is, not be activities that look like, for example, activism or lobbyism, projects or events). The creation or expansion of economic activity should suggest that a business venture is intended, with its associated considerations of revenues, expenses and sustainable activity.

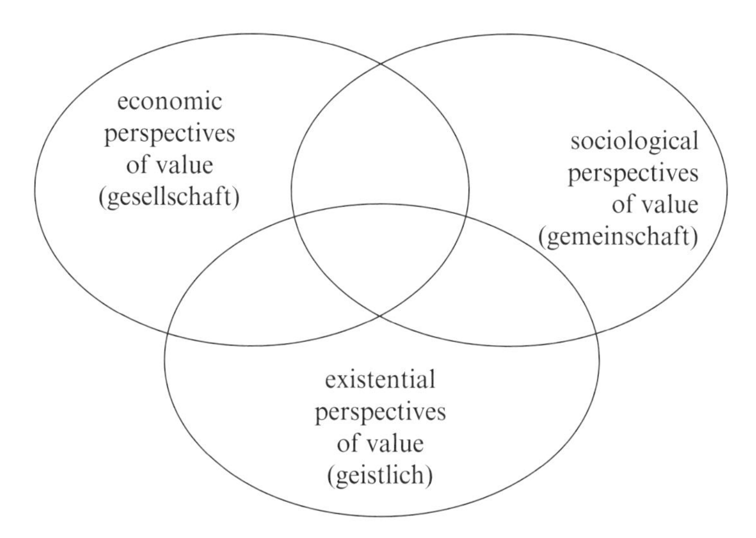

Figure 1.2 Alternative perspectives of value

For insights into to the creation or expansion of economic activity, I turn to the significance of 'exchange'. Exchange theory has become a conceptual foundation for the marketing discipline (Bagozzi, 1974, 1975; Houston and Gassenheimer, 1987; Kotler, 1972; Kotler and Levy, 1969; Pandya and Dholakia, 1992). Recognising exchange can involve the transfer of psychological, social or other intangibles (Bagozzi, 1975; Levy, 1977) involving often inseparable utilitarian and symbolic aspects (mixed exchanges) (Bagozzi, 1975). I propose that exchange theory should also be a central concept for the study of entrepreneurship (Styles and Seymour, 2006) and in particular for social entrepreneurship.

Exchange relationships are considered to relate to three broad determinants: (1) the characteristics of the social actors; (2) the social influence exercised by the actors; and (3) the situation constraining the exchange (Bagozzi, 1978). Behaviour is theorised to relate to the decision rules that actors use in their transactions (whether they be based on maximising utility, altruistic or based on group-gain, competition, status contingency or reciprocity), and the structures of exchange and exchange behaviours over time (Bagozzi, 1978).

Creation or expansion of (commercial) economic activity

Eckhardt and Shane (2003, p. 339) refer to individuals acquiring resources and engaging in activities that change prices and provide information to others, arguing that in the process of exploiting opportunities:

> the process of exchange and interaction provides information that increases the mutual awareness among market participants about the characteristics of the opportunity . . . This information may either encourage or discourage the individual pursuing the opportunity from continuing.

Exchange involves a transfer of value (tangible or intangible, actual or symbolic) between two or more parties, with the implication that all parties to the exchange both give and receive value (Houston and Gassenheimer, 1987). It is a fundamental consideration in the commercial activities of enterprises, framing both the activity within a firm as well as outside the firm.

Creation or expansion of (social) economic activity

The narrow conceptualisation of social entrepreneurship equates social entrepreneurship with social enterprise, and focuses on income generation and capture (Boschee, 2006; Brinckerhoff, 2000; Haugh, 2006; Reis, 1999; Fowler, 2000; Robinson, 2006; Cho, 2006; Alter, 2006). Such conceptualisations would require a social undertaking to generate and capture a sustained and ongoing economic surplus. Social value such as education, experience and relationships are excluded from such analysis (that is, what this would mean for the corporate examples mentioned above). Similarly, cultural or creative value such as cultural artefacts would be excluded from such analysis (that is, what this would mean from the corporate examples mentioned above). Broader conceptualisations of the social argue that, though beneficial, economic profit is not a necessary component of social entrepreneurship (see for example Peredo and McLean, 2006; Seelos and Mair, 2005; Mair and Marti, 2006; Perrini and Vurro, 2006; Nicholls, 2006; Young, 2006).

Social entrepreneurship initiatives can take various organisational forms and structures, and should not be conflated with the more narrow term of social enterprise, in which a sustained income is often deemed a necessity. As Nicholls (2006, p. 11) highlights, 'many social ventures can be highly entrepreneurial without generating independent profit streams'. This is in line with the view that successful outcomes are not a necessary condition of entrepreneurship (Shane, 2003; Ahmad and Seymour, 2008), and nor should it be of social entrepreneurship.

Understanding the social in creating or expanding economic activity

The 'social' in economic activity is a complex consideration, requiring examination of the nature of transactions, as well as the nature of the broader economy. Although some business activity could be explained by the model 'economic person', for example bond traders on Wall Street classified as *Homo economicus unbound* (Abolafia, 1996) or entrepreneurs relying on a 'transactional' attitude to relationships or contracts

(Armstrong, 2005; Collins et al., 1964), if everyone is assumed to be an 'evaluator' constantly making trade-offs and substitutions amongst wants (refer for example to Jensen and Meckling, 1994), the gift (similarly, the mission of social entrepreneurship) is an impossibility (Callari, 2002):

> Obviously there is no place in such theories for gifts, which are represented as commodities in sheep's clothing; gift exchange, likewise, is just an alias for self-interest. But this conceptual scheme is powerful because it can translate virtually human interaction into its own terms (Osteen, 2002, p. 231).

Without the possibility of the gift and play, social entrepreneurship may also be an impossibility. Social entrepreneurship, I would argue, provides business researchers with the context that allows us to re-evaluate the following proposition, one which has been largely unchallenged over the last 40 years: 'Whenever two people A and B engage in a voluntary exchange, they must both expect to profit from it . . . Whenever exchange is not voluntary but coerced, one party profits at the expense of the other' (Hoppe, 1995, p. 15). Social entrepreneurship need not be seen through the lens of behaviours originating from Bentham's[1] objective, rational and utility-maximising 'machines'. It allows us to revisit the (largely unstated) utility-maximising views of human behaviours that have been challenged within many fields of research (see for example Tönnies, 1887/2001; McGregor, 1960/2006; Belk, 1988; Galbraith, 1958/1998; Mintzberg et al., 2002), and contexts (for example by Curasi et al., 2004; Weiner, 1980; Caves, 2003; Hirschman, 1983).

The exciting challenge for researchers is to explore some of these issues in the context of enterprise. As with the other differentiating aspects of social entrepreneurship, the challenge will require a researcher to be open to alternative ontologies and epistemologies, as well as methodologies and methods (explored in Chapter 2 of this volume).

1.4.4 Identifying and Exploiting New Products, Processes or Markets

The concept of doing things differently (or of identifying and exploiting new products, markets or business processes) is perhaps one of the most clearly established indicators of entrepreneurial activity. Unfortunately, the study of this identification and exploitation is extremely complex and difficult to research.

Identifying and exploiting new (commercial) products, processes or markets
Identifying new products, processes or markets has been associated with entrepreneurial activity for almost a century. As noted in the OECD-Eurostat EIP:

> it was not until Joseph Schumpeter's definition of an entrepreneur in 1934 that the more modern interpretation [of entrepreneurial activity] entered the mainstream. Schumpeter defined entrepreneurs as innovators who take advantage of change, including: (i) the introduction of a new (or improved) good; (ii) the introduction of a new method of production; (iii) the opening of a new market; (iv) the exploitation of a new source of supply; and (v) the re-engineering/organization of business management processes. Schumpeter's definition therefore equates entrepreneurship with innovation in the business sense; that is identifying market opportunities and using innovative approaches to exploit them. (Ahmad and Seymour, 2008, p. 8)

Entrepreneurship literature has further developed this focus with multiple definitions focussing on aspects of the 'new', whether that be involving identifying new opportunities within the economic system (Penrose, 1959/1980), or new entry accomplished by entering new or established markets with new or existing goods or services (Lumpkin and Dess, 1996).

Identifying and exploiting new (social) products, processes or markets

Similarly, in the context of social entrepreneurship, the concepts of dynamism and change have been central to extant research. For example: Voelker (2006) reviews ten social enterprises that received awards for 'technology benefitting humanity' from the Tech Museum of Innovation in San Jose, California; and Drayton (2002) considers how the 'citizen sector' is becoming as entrepreneurial and competitive as business. Note that this focus on social value and change means that the 'newness' requires a purpose (rather than a vehicle):

> The central driver for social entrepreneurship is the social problem being addressed, and the particular organizational form a social enterprise takes should be a decision based on which format would most effectively mobilize the resources needed to address that problem. Thus, social entrepreneurship is not defined by legal form, as it can be pursued through various vehicles. Indeed, examples of social entrepreneurship can be found within or can span the nonprofit, business, or governmental sectors. (Austin et al., 2006, p. 2)

Understanding the social in the identification and exploitation of the 'new'

This focus on the 'new', whether commercial or social enterprise, means that researchers are not always dealing with the predictable and repeatable (the core of normal science), but rather with the unique and unrepeatable (Rothenberg and Hausman, 1976) which require integrative perspectives and methods from a range of fields (Amit et al., 1993; Bruyat and Julien, 2000; Crawford, 1977; Gardner, 1988; Swedberg, 2000). There will be no 'causal' explanation for creativity or 'newness':

> the classical positivist paradigm[2] will only be useful for the portion of the field concerned with small changes. Issues of complexity raise significant methodological problems, in particular because they necessarily require that the dynamic of the systems studies (individual, new value creation, environment) be taken into consideration. (Bruyat and Julien, 2000, p. 177)

Analysis, and interpretation and insight, have been shown to be necessary for successful innovation (Lester and Piore, 2004; Lester et al., 1998) even though they are distinct and can be regarded as contradictory and antagonistic to each other. In the context of innovation, 'success actually seems dependent upon the ability to move away from rational decisionmaking to a more hermeneutic process' (Piore, 1995, pp. 133–134). This contradictory aspect of innovation is also reflected in the uneasy relationship between economic theory and the entrepreneur, with entrepreneurship being about creating new knowledge and ushering in change, activities beyond the scope of rational choice theory (Metcalf, 2004).

1.5 WORKING DEFINITIONS ASSOCIATED WITH SOCIAL ENTREPRENEURSHIP

The review adds further weight to the suggestion that any research project in the context of social entrepreneurship will need to consider carefully research methodologies as well as settings if insight and understanding are to be developed. The review also highlights the various definitions and alternative foci of the extant research. Taking very broad summary concepts from the above review, Table 1.2 sets out the key differences between social and commercial entrepreneurship.

We can imagine some things unique to social entrepreneurship, and other things consistent with commercial entrepreneurship. A working definition, nevertheless, would be beneficial for research projects. The following definitions, drawn from the above literature and the OECD-Eurostat EIP work, can be used to explore social entrepreneurship.

Note the commonalities of the entrepreneur and the social entrepreneur: as noted by Austin (2006, p. 22) social entrepreneurship is 'innovative, social value creating activity that can occur within or across the non profit, business and public sectors'. We should not get caught up in isolating the practice by corporate vehicle, mission or any other bounding premise unrelated to the above. Referring to, and building upon, the OECD-Eurostat EIP definitions:

> Social Entrepreneurs are those persons (key stakeholders) who seek to generate change (creating social, cultural or natural value), through the creation or

Table 1.2 Summary of key differences between social and commercial entrepreneurship

Concept	Commercial entrepreneurship	Social entrepreneurship
Enterprising human action	Implied lone heroic *homo economicus*	Implied community of key stakeholders (perhaps led by an individual) *Homo ludens*
Seeking to generate value	Seeking to create and capture value (in doing so, creating change)	Seeking to create and establish change (in doing so, creating value)
Creation or expansion of economic activity	Implied prioritisation of pecuniary value and exchanges, with focus on outcomes rather than process	Implied subordination of pecuniary value and exchanges, and focus on the process rather than outcomes
Identifying and exploiting new products, processes or markets	Doing things differently	Doing things differently

expansion of economic activity, by identifying and exploiting new products, processes or markets.

Socially Entrepreneurial Activity is the enterprising human action in pursuit of the generation of change (creating social, cultural or natural value), through the creation or expansion of economic activity, by identifying and exploiting new products, processes or markets.

Social Entrepreneurship is the phenomena associated with socially entrepreneurial activity.

1.6 CONCLUSION

This chapter has, I hope, highlighted the need for researchers to shift their research perspectives and focus. The vast majority of extant research exploring the process of innovation, entrepreneurship and social change is anchored in the individualistic perspective and the *Homo economicus* (or economic person) paradigm. Researchers can address that bias.

These definitions may be used as a starting point for investigation, building on them and adapting them with flexibility to suit the context and phenomena of interest. I would advise not to stray far from them, however, as without a clear conceptualisation of social entrepreneurship and how it differs from other forms of entrepreneurship, we will dilute our understanding and insights.

The challenge for social entrepreneurship researchers is to reconceptualise our curiosity: to include the behaviours of teams of social entrepreneurs and (more broadly) key stakeholders; to understand the multiple exchanges of value amongst participants; to focus on processes rather than just outcomes of activity; and to understand how participants see the possibility for change, as well as bring that change about.

NOTES

1. 'Nature has placed mankind under the governance of two sovereign masters, pain and pleasure. It is for them alone to point out what we ought to do, as well as to determine what we shall do' (Bentham, 1789/1962, p. 33).
2. These concepts will be explored in Chapter 2 of this volume.

REFERENCES

Abolafia, M.Y. (1996). *Making Markets: Opportunism and Restraint on Wall Street*. Cambridge, MA: Harvard University Press.

Ahmad, N. and R.G. Seymour (2008). Defining entrepreneurial activity: definitions supporting frameworks for data collection. OECD Statistics Working Papers Series. Paris: OECD Publications.

Alter, S.K. (2006). Social enterprise models and their mission and money relationships. In A. Nicholls (ed.), *Social Entrepreneurship: New Models of Sustainable Social Change*. Oxford: Oxford University Press, pp. 205–232.

Amabile, T.M. (1983). *The Social Psychology of Creativity*. New York, USA: Springer Verlag.

Amabile, T.M., R. Conti, H. Coon, J. Lazenby and M. Herron (1996). Assessing the work environment for creativity. *Academy of Management Journal* **39**(5), 1154–1184.

Amabile, T.M. (1996). Creativity in Context. Boulder, USA: Westview Press.

Amit, R., L. Glosten and E. Muller (1993). Challenges to theory development in entrepreneurship research. *Journal of Management Studies* **30**(5), 815–834.

Anderson, R.B., L.P. Dana and T. Dana (2006). Aboriginal land rights, social entrepreneurship and economic development in Canada: 'opting-in' to the global economy. *Journal of World Business* **41**(1), 45–55.

Arendt, H. (1958). *The Human Condition*. Chicago, IL, USA and London, UK: University of Chicago Press.

Armstrong, P. (2005). *Critique of Entrepreneurship: People and Policy*. Basingstoke: Palgrave Macmillan.

Austin, J.E. (2006). Three avenues for social entrepreneurship research. In J. Mair, J. Robinson and K. Hockerts (eds), *Social Entrepreneurship*. New York: Palgrave Macmillan, pp. 22–33.

Austin, J., H. Stevenson and J. Wei-Skillern (2006). Social and commercial entrepreneurship: same, different, or both? *Entrepreneurship Theory and Practice* **30**(1), 1–22.

Bagozzi, R.P. (1974). Marketing as an organized behavioral system of exchange. *Journal of Marketing* **38**(4), 77–81.

Bagozzi, R.P. (1975). Social exchange in marketing. *Journal of the Academy of Marketing Science* **3**(4), 314–327.
Bagozzi, R.P. (1978). Marketing as exchange: a theory of transactions in the marketplace. *American Behavioral Scientist* **21**(4), 535−556.
Baron, D.P. (2005). Corporate social responsibility and social entrepreneurship. Working Paper, Stanford University. http://papers.ssrn.com/sol3/papers.cfm?abstract_id=861145, (accessed 10 December 2011).
Belk, R.W. (1988). Possessions and the extended self. *Journal of Consumer Research* **15**, 139–168.
Bentham, J. (1789/1962). Introduction to the Principles of Morals and Legislation (Chapters I−V). In M. Warnock (ed.), *Utilitarianism*. Glasgow: William Collins Sons & Co., pp. 33−77.
Bornstein, D. (2004). *How to Change the World: Social Entrepreneurs and the Power of New Ideas*. Oxford: Oxford University Press.
Boschee, J. (2006). Social entrepreneurship: the promise and the perils. In A. Nicholls (ed.), *Social Entrepreneurship: New Models of Sustainable Social Change*. Oxford: Oxford University Press, pp. 356–390.
Brinckerhoff, P.C. (2000). *Social Entrepreneurship: The Art of Mission-Based Venture Development*. New York: John Wiley & Sons.
Bruyat, C. and P.-A. Julien (2000). Defining the field of research in entrepreneurship. *Journal of Business Venturing* **16**, 165–180.
Callari, A. (2002). The ghost of the gift: the unlikelihood of economics. In M. Osteen (ed.), *The Question of the Gift: Essays across Disciplines*. London, UK and New York, USA: Routledge, pp. 248–265.
Caves, R.E. (2003). Contracts between art and commerce. *Journal of Economic Perspectives* **17**(2), 73−83.
Cho, A.H. (2006). Politics, values and social entrepreneurship: a critical appraisal. In J. Mair, J. Robinson and K. Hockerts (eds), *Social Entrepreneurship*. New York: Palgrave Macmillan, pp. 34–56.
Christensen, C.M. (1997). *The Innovator's Dilemma: When New Technologies Cause Great Firms to Fail*. Boston, MA: Harvard Business School Press.
Collins, O.F., D.G. Moore and D.B. Unwalla (1964). *The Enterprising Man*. East Lansing, MI: Bureau of Business and Economic Research, Michigan State University.
Crawford, C.M. (1977). Marketing research and the new product failure rate. *Journal of Marketing*, 51–61.
Csikszentmihalyi, M. (1994). The domain of creativity. In D.H. Feldman, M. Csikszentmihalyi and H. Gardner (eds), *Changing the World: A Framework for the Study of Creativity*. Westport, CT: Praeger Publishers.
Curasi, C.F., L.L. Price and E.J. Arnould (2004). How individuals' cherished possessions become families' inalienable wealth. *Journal of Consumer Research* **31**(December), 609–622.
Dacin, P.A., M.T. Dacin and M. Matear (2010). Social entrepreneurship: why we don't need a new theory and how we move forward from here. *Academy of Management Perspectives* **24**(3), 37–57.
Dees, G.J. and P. Economy (2001). Social entrepreneurship. In G.J. Dees, J. Emerson and P. Economy (eds), *Enterprising Nonprofits: A Toolkit for Social Entrepreneurs*. New York: John Wiley & Sons, pp. 1–18.
Dees, G.J. and J. Elias (1998). The challengers of combining social and commercial enterprise. *Business Ethics Quarterly* **8**(1), 165–178.
Dees, G.J. and J. Emerson (2002). *Strategic Tools for Social Entrepreneurs: Enhancing the Performance of Your Enterprising Nonprofit*. New York: Wiley.
Drayton, B. (2002). The citizen sector: becoming as entrepreneurial and competitive as business. *California Management Review* **44**(3), 120–132.
Eckhardt, J.T. and S.A. Shane (2003). Opportunities and entrepreneurship. *Journal of Management* **29**(3), 333–349.

Emerson, R.M. (1982). Toward a theory of value in social exchange. In K.S. Cook (ed.), *Social Exchange Theory*. Newbury Park, CA: SAGE Publications, pp. 11–46.
Emerson, J. and F. Twersky (1996). *New Social Entrepreneurs: The Success, Challenge and Lessons of Nonprofit Enterprise Creation*. San Francisco, CA: Roberts Foundation.
Feldman, D.H., M. Csikszentmihalyi and H. Gardner (1994). *Changing the World: A Framework for the Study of Creativity*. Westport, CT, Greenwood Publishing Group.
Fowler, A. (2000). NGOs as a moment in history: beyond aid to social entrepreneurship or civic innovation? *Third World Quarterly* **21**(4), 637–654.
Galbraith, J.K. (1958/1998). *The Affluent Society*. Boston, MA: Mariner.
Gardner, H. (1988). Creative lives and creative works. In R.J. Sternberg (ed.), *The Nature of Creativity: Contemporary Psychological Perspectives*. Cambridge: Cambridge University Press, pp. 298–324.
Haugh, H. (2006). Social enterprise: beyond economic outcomes and individual returns. In J. Mair, J. Robinson and K. Hockerts (eds), *Social Entrepreneurship*. New York: Palgrave Macmillan, pp. 180–206.
Henry, E. (2007). Kaupapa Maori entrepreneurship. In D. Leo Paul and R.B. Anderson (eds), *International Handbook of Research on Indigenous Entrepreneurship*. Cheltenham, UK and Northampton, MA, USA: Edward Elgar, pp. 536–548.
Hirschman, E.C. (1983). Aesthetics, ideologies and the limits of the marketing concept. *Journal of Marketing* **47**(Summer), 45–55.
Hoppe, H.-H. (1995). *Economic Science and the Austrian Method*. Auburn, AL: Ludwig von Mises Institute.
Houston, F.S. and J.B. Gassenheimer (1987). Marketing and exchange. *Journal of Marketing* **51**, 3–18.
Huizinga, J. (1955). *Homo Ludens: A Study of the Play-Element in Culture*. Boston, MA: Beacon Press.
Jensen, M.C. and W.H. Meckling (1994). The nature of man. *Journal of Applied Finance* **7**(2), 4–19.
Kotler, P. (1972). A generic concept of marketing. *Journal of Marketing* **36**(April), 46–54.
Kotler, P. and S.J. Levy (1969). Broadening the concept of marketing. *Journal of Marketing* **33**(January), 10–15.
Lepak, D.P., K.G. Smith and M.S. Taylor (2007). Value creation and value capture: a multilevel perspective. *Academy of Management Review* **32**(1), 180–194.
Lester, R.K. and M.J. Piore (2004). *Innovation: The Missing Dimension*. Cambridge, MA, USA and London, UK: Harvard University Press.
Lester, R.K., M.J. Piore and K.M. Malek (1998). Interpretive management: what general managers can learn from design. *Harvard Business Review* **76**(2), 86–96.
Levy, S. (1977). Symbols for sale. *Harvard Business Review* **37**, 117–119.
Lumpkin, G.T. and G.G. Dess (1996). Clarifying the entrepreneurial orientation construct and linking it to performance. *Academy of Management Review* **21**(1), 135–172.
Mair, J. and I. Marti (2006). Social entrepreneurship research: a source of explanation, prediction and delight. *Journal of World Business* **41**(1), 36–44.
Marietta, D.E. (1984). Objectivity: wrong concept for value inquiry. In T. Magnell (ed.), *Explorations of Value*. Vol. 55, Amsterdam, Netherlands and Atlanta, GA: Rodopi, pp. 47–59.
Marti, I. (2006). Introduction to Part I – Setting a research agenda for an emerging field. In J. Mair, J. Robinson and K. Hockerts (eds), *Social Entrepreneurship*. New York: Palgrave Macmillan, pp. 17–21.
Martin, R.L. and S. Osberg (2007). Social entrepreneurship: the case for definition. *Stanford Social Innovation Review* Spring, 29–39.
McGregor, D. (1960/2006). *The Human Side of Enterprise*. New York: McGraw-Hill.
Metcalf, J.S. (2004). The entrepreneur and the style of modern economics. *Journal of Evolutionary Economics* **14**, 157–175.
Miczo, N. (2002). Hobbes, Rousseau, and the 'Gift' in interpersonal relationships. *Human Studies* **25**, 207–231.

Mintzberg, H., R. Simons and K. Basu (2002). Beyond selfishness. *MIT Sloan Management Review* **44**(1), 67–74.
Mort, G., J. Weerawardena and K. Carnegie (2002). Social entrepreneurship: towards conceptualization and measurement. *American Marketing Association Conference Proceedings* **13**, 5.
Nicholls, A. (2006). *Social Entrepreneurship: New Models of Sustainable Social Change*. Oxford: Oxford University Press.
Nicholls, A. and A.H. Cho (2006). Social entrepreneurship: the structuration of a field. In A. Nicholls (ed.), *Social Entrepreneurship: New Models of Sustainable Change*. Oxford: Oxford University Press, pp. 99−118.
OECD, 2005 Oslo Manual: Guidelines for Collecting and Interpreting Innovation Data, 3rd ed. Statistical Office of the European Communities, Luxembourg.
OED (2006). *Oxford English Dictionary Online*.
Osteen, M. (ed.) (2002). *The Question of the Gift: Essays across Disciplines*. London, UK and New York, USA: Routledge.
Pandya, A. and N. Dholakia (1992). An institutional theory of exchange in marketing. *European Journal of Marketing* **26**(12), 19–41.
Penrose, E.T. (1959/1980). *The Theory of the Growth of the Firm*. Oxford: Basil Blackwell.
Peredo, A.M. and M. McLean (2006). Social entrepreneurship: a critical review of the concept. *Journal of World Business* **41**, 56–65.
Perrini, F. and C. Vurro (2006). Social entrepreneurship: innovation and social change across theory and practice. In J. Mair, J. Robinson and K. Hockerts (eds), *Social Entrepreneurship*. New York: Palgrave Macmillan, pp. 57–86.
Piore, M.J. (1995). *Beyond Individualism: How Social Demands of the New Identity Groups Challenge American Political and Economic Life*. Cambridge, MA, USA and London, UK: Harvard University Press.
Reis, T. (1999). *Unleashing the New Resources and Entrepreneurship for the Common Good: A Scan, Synthesis and Scenario for Action*. Battle Creek, MI: W.K. Kellogg Foundation.
Reis, T. and S. Clohesy (1999). Unleashing new resources and entrepreneurship for the common good: a scan, synthesis, and scenario for action. Working Paper. Battle Creek, MI: W.K. Kellogg Foundation. http://www.wkkf.org/knowledge-center/resources/2001/12/Unleashing-New-Resources-And-Entrepreneurship-For-The-Common-Good-A-Scan-Synthesis-And-Scenario-For.aspx (accessed 10 December 2010).
Robinson, J. (2006). Navigating social and institutional barriers to markets: how social entrepreneurs identify and evaluate opportunities. In J. Mair, J. Robinson and K. Hockerts (eds), *Social Entrepreneurship*. Basingstoke: Palgrave Macmillan.
Rothenberg, A. and C.R. Hausman (1976). Introduction: the creativity question. In A. Rothenberg and C.R. Hausman (eds), *The Creativity Question*. Durham, NC: Duke University Press, pp. 3–26.
Ruth, J.A., C.C. Otnes and F.F. Brunel (1999). Gift receipt and the reformulation of interpersonal relationships. *Journal of Consumer Research* **25**, 385–402.
Rutledge, D. (2006). Happiness. *Encounter*. http://www.abc.net.au/rn/encounter/stories/2006/1814028.htm#transcript.
Schumpeter, J.A. (1934). *The Theory of Economic Development: An Enquiry into Profits, Capital, Credit, Interest and the Business Cycle*. Cambridge, MA: Harvard University Press.
Seelos, C. and J. Mair (2005). Social entrepreneurship: creating new business models to serve the poor. *Business Horizons* **48**, 241–246.
Shackle, G.L.S. (1972). *Epistemics and Economics: A Critique of Economic Doctrines*. Cambridge: Cambridge University Press.
Shane, S. (2003). *A General Theory of Entrepreneurship: The Individual-Opportunity Nexus*. Cheltenham, UK and Northampton, MA, USA: Edward Elgar.
Shane, S. and S. Venkataraman (2000). The promise of entrepreneurship as a field of research. *Academy of Management Review* **25**(1), 217–226.
Sharir, M. and M. Lerner (2006). Gauging the success of social ventures initiated by individual social entrepreneurs. *Journal of World Business* **41**, 6–20.

Smith, C. (1989). *Auctions: The Social Construction of Value*. New York: Free Press.
Sternberg, R.J. and T.I. Lubart (1996). Investing in Creativity. *American Psychologist* **51**(7): 677–688.
Stevenson, H.H. and J.C. Jarillo (1990). A paradigm of entrepreneurship: entrepreneurial management. *Strategic Management Journal* **11**(5), 17–27.
Stringer, R. (2000). How to manage radical innovation. *California Management Review* **42**(4), 70–88.
Styles, C. and R.G. Seymour (2006). Opportunities for marketing researchers in international entrepreneurship. *International Marketing Review* **23**(2), 126–145.
Swedberg, R. (ed.) (2000). *Entrepreneurship: The Social Science View*. Oxford Management Readers. Oxford: Oxford University Press.
Tapsell, P. and C. Woods (2008). A spiral of innovation framework for social entrepreneurship: social innovation at the generational divide in an indigenous context. *Emergence: Complexity and Organisation* **10**(3), 25.
Tönnies, F. (1887/2001). *Community and Civil Society (Gemeinschaft Und Gesellschaft)*. Cambridge: Cambridge University Press.
Van Slyke, D.M. and H.K. Newman (2006). Venture philanthropy and social entrepreneurship in community redevelopment. *Nonprofit Management and Leadership* **16**(3), 345–368.
Voelcker, J. (2006). Creating social change. *Stanford Social Innovation Review* **4**(2), 44–53.
von Mises, L. (1949/1996). *Human Action: A Treatise on Economics*. San Francisco, CA: Fox & Wilkes.
Walker, E. and A. Brown (2004). What success factors are important to small business owners? *International Small Business Journal* **22**(6), 577–594.
Weerawardena, J. and G.S. Mort (2006). Investigating social entrepreneurship: a multidimensional model. *Journal of World Business* **41**, 21–35.
Weiner, A. (1980). Reproduction: a replacement for reciprocity. *American Ethnologist* **7**, 71–85.
Whitfield, T.W.A. (2005). Aesthetics as pre-linguistic knowledge: a psychological perspective. *Design Issues* **21**(1), 3–17.
Young, D. (2001). Social enterprise in the United States: alternate identities and forms. Paper presented at the 1st International EMES Conference: The Social Enterprise: A Comparative Perspective. Trento, Italy.
Young, R. (2006). For what it is worth: social value and the future of social entrepreneurship. In A. Nicholls (ed.), *Social Entrepreneurship: New Models of Sustainable Change*. Oxford: Oxford University Press, pp. 56–73.

2 Researching social entrepreneurship

Richard G. Seymour

Chapter 1 of the *Handbook* has introduced this thing that we call 'social entrepreneurship'. This second chapter develops the research journey by focussing on a researcher's ways of thinking. The chapter emphasises the significance and importance of philosophies of science for social entrepreneurship researchers. Though occasionally referring to social entrepreneurship research, this chapter is anchored in examples from entrepreneurship research in general (whether commercial or social).

This chapter is organised as follows. It first introduces how philosophies of science can impact upon researchers. This opening is followed by a review of the impact of these alternative perspectives, with the review organised into four broad areas: opportunity, management, markets and the entrepreneur. The chapter then reviews how each of these 'extreme' perspectives alone cannot be entirely appropriate, and why a researcher should be aware of their prioritisation. The chapter concludes that alternative research methodologies may benefit the social entrepreneurship researcher.

2.1 PHILOSOPHIES OF SCIENCE DO IMPACT UPON RESEARCHERS

A researcher is required (implicitly or explicitly) to understand examined reality and being (ontology), the relationship between that reality and the researcher (epistemology) and the theoretical analysis of the techniques used by a researcher to understand that reality (methodology) (Perry et al., 1999; Denzin and Lincoln, 2003; Lincoln and Guba, 2003). Methods (those techniques used by researchers) result from that earlier analysis, and are mere tactics or strategies to support a research project (Noorderhaven, 2004; Prasad, 2005). For a social entrepreneurship researcher, then, methodology is an important place to start, as our research is inevitably value-laden, influencing choices of phenomenon and context, method, data and findings as well as the form of expression (Hirschman, 1986; Arnold and Fischer, 1994; Carson et al., 2001): 'For methods to prove insightful . . . more than knowledge of technique is required. Methods themselves are linked to larger paradigmatic issues and are often appropriated in diverse ways within the same and different paradigms' (Prasad, 2005, p. 8).

A Cartesian subject–object split continues to impact upon social researchers. A review of extant research explores that impact in the context of entrepreneurship research in general. Researchers have repeatedly called on alternative conceptualisations for research investigations of the creative and innovative (Rothenberg and Hausman, 1976; Gruber and Davis, 1988; Coyne and Snodgrass, 1991; Beckert, 1997; Lester and Piore, 2004), requiring integrative perspectives and methods from a range of fields (Crawford, 1977; Amit et al., 1993; Bruyat and Julien, 2000; Swedberg, 2000). Although developing rapidly, philosophies of science evident in the current literature are limited in their variety and frequency.

2.1.1 The Significance of Philosophy of Science for the Social Entrepreneurship Researcher

The ontological roots of the vast majority of modern philosophies of science are based around a Cartesian subject–object cleavage (Jaspers, 1956). This modern cleavage commenced with Descartes (1637/1960, 1641/1960), who based his view of the world on the fundamental division between two independent and separate realms – that of mind, the 'thinking thing' (*res cognitans*); and that of matter, the 'extended thing' (*res extensa*). Mind was seen as a thing – a thing without extension, with no parts, unable to decay, immortal and enduring (Lyons, 1995).

The 'Cartesian Moment' saw mechanism enshrined by Enlightenment scholars 'as the model to explain all phenomena of matter, life, and mind' (Richards, 2002, p. 308). This is evidenced in Hume's (1739/1969) mechanical model of mind and John Locke's (1700/1975) conceptualisation of the mind as a *tabula rasa* (an empty slate upon which external reality is mapped through experience). As a consequence, intelligibility became rooted in rationality (Guignon, 1983), with most Western individuals aware of themselves as isolated egos existing 'inside' their bodies (Capra, 1997, 2002).

It was not until the eighteenth and nineteenth centuries that Cartesian ontology was re-examined, with critics including Kant, Fichte, Schelling, Hegel, Dilthey, Brentano and Husserl. Disputes over method (*Methodenstreit*) also embroiled sociologists and scientists.

The network of basic assumptions characterising the subjective-objective debate within social science are summarised in Table 2.1.[1] Note that the vast majority of research has prioritised the objectivist approach, considering reality to be a concrete structure or process, with humans as responders or adapters. Refer also to Chapter 10 in this *Handbook*, in

Table 2.1 Network of basic assumptions characterizing the subjective–objective debate within social science

	Objectivist approaches to social science					Subjectivist approaches to social science
Core ontological assumptions	Reality as a concrete structure	Reality as a concrete process	Reality as a contextual field of information	Reality as a realm of symbolic discourse	Reality as a social construction	Reality as a projection of human imagination
Assumptions about human nature	Man as a responder	Man as an adaptor	Man as an information processor	Man as an actor, the symbol user	Man as a social constructor, the symbol creator	Man as pure spirit, consciousness, being
Basic epistemological stance	To construct a positivist science	To study systems, process, change	To map contexts	To understand patterns of symbolic discourse	To understand how social reality is created	To obtain phenomenological insight, revelation
Some favoured metaphors	Machine	Organism	Cybernetic	Theatre, culture	Language game, accomplishment, text	Transcendental

Source: Morgan and Smircich (1980, pp. 492, 494, 495).

which Aaron McKenny, Jeremy Short and Tyge Payne review some of the key social entrepreneurship literature.

The essence of the debates were over whether truth resided in the object or the subject, in the relationships between them, or elsewhere. For example, objectivists (or defenders of positivism[2]) and proponents of the unity of the sciences continue to hold the view that the purpose of any science (natural or social) is to offer causal explanations of social, behavioural and physical phenomena. In contrast, many sociologists sought to differentiate the social sciences from the natural sciences, arguing that the behaviour of human beings is not 'caused' by uniform laws: that we are sentient, creative and imbued with an understanding of the worlds in which we live and act (unlike the behaviour of inanimate objects or lower life forms) (Weinberg, 2002). The debates continue to rage. From these basic assumptions, research 'schools' have developed a number of approaches to explore these alternative realities, summarised in Table 2.2.

There is little consensus as regards the focus or even the boundaries of these alternative beliefs: for example, there are a number of alternative perspectives (such as phenomenology) or alternative terminologies (such as constructivism with a small 'c') which are not included in multiple reviews. What is more, in the context of social entrepreneurship these debates and issues have largely been ignored. This introduction is intended as a start- rather than an end-point. The researcher should read broadly, and seek to understand how these alternative prioritisations and methodologies can appropriately be applied for particular research questions of interest.

2.2 THE IMPACT OF ALTERNATIVE PRIORITISATIONS

The meaning and implications of alternative prioritisations in the context of business research are introduced in Table 2.3. For ease of discussion, the two extreme perspectives are discussed. These alternative approaches impact upon a researcher's view of reality, with the two 'extreme' positions resulting in either a researcher focussing: (1) on what lies beyond the realm of appearances, with a detached attitude of contemplation prioritised; or alternatively (2) on individual's 'internal' data or processing given to a subject.

A researcher interested in the context of social entrepreneurship should pay particular attention to these impacts, as they potentially are confronted with the challenges of opportunity, insight and human activity.

Table 2.2 Basic beliefs of alternative enquiry paradigms

Issue	Positivism	Postpositivism	Interpretive phenomenology	Critical theory	Constructivism
Ontology	Naive realism – 'real' reality but apprehendable	Critical realism – 'real' reality but only imperfectly and probabilistically apprehendable	Our activities are primordial, familiar and not grasped theoretically. Our worldliness is ontologically central to any human activity	Historical realism – virtual reality shaped by social, political, cultural, economic, ethnic and gender values crystallised over time	Relativism – local and specific constructed realities
Epistemology	Dualist/objectivist; findings true	Modified dualist/ objectivist; critical tradition/community; findings probably true	Care and solicitude	Transactional/ subjectivist; value-mediated findings	Transactional/ subjectivist; created findings
Axiology	Propositional knowing about the world is an end in itself, is intrinsically valuable		Propositional, transactional knowing is instrumentally valuable as a means to social emancipation, which as an end in itself, is intrinsically valuable		
Methodology	Experimental/ manipulative; verification of hypotheses; chiefly quantitative methods	Modified experimental/ manipulative; falsification of hypotheses; may include qualitative methods	Hermeneutic phenomenology (based on the writings of Heidegger)	Dialogic/dialectic	Hermeneutic/ dialectic

Source: Based on Lincoln and Guba (2003).

Table 2.3 Alternative philosophical priorities of research

	Objectivist approaches	Subjectivist approaches
Researcher's view of reality	Objectivists: 'treat everything as an object in the world, or as relations between such objects, exclusively' (Skjervheim, 1974, p. 216). Reality is a concrete structure or process, with humans responding (or at least adapting) to that reality in a machine-like manner (Morgan and Smircich, 1980). The object is perceived as having an 'intrinsic' or 'inherent' character that can be studied independently of any perceiving subject (noumena). Researchers focus on what lies beyond the realm of appearances, with a detached attitude of contemplation prioritised.	Reality is a projection of human imagination (or a social construction) and that humans are pure spirit constructing reality (Morgan and Smircich, 1980). We cannot know the noumena (the things as they really are in themselves) but only the phenomena (what our synthesising cognition makes of the things). Researchers focus on an individual's 'internal' data or processing given to a subject.
Business researchers	Structures are seen to be independent of any one agent, such as governance structures, labour and product markets, frameworks of regulations, and firm resources (to name but a few).	Rules and principles cannot exist independently of the people they constrain. Researchers explore consciousness, experience, ego, self and psyche. Data consists of organisational stories, legitimating constructions and identity constructions.
Classic studies	The vast majority of business research has taken such objectivist priorities (Grant and Perren, 2002), for example Porter's (1980) Five Forces Framework, Penrose's (1959/1980) resource-based view of the firm.	Pettigrew's (1973) processual approach to information management and the Austrian School of Economics (for example von Hayek, 1945; von Mises, 1949/1996).

I will now seek to address Shapiro's (2005, p. 19) questions: 'Should explanations of social life be deduced from observable facts? Should they be grounded on people's self-understandings? Should they be based on whatever enables us to intervene with effect in the world?'

2.2.1 Objectivist Approaches

Objectivist approaches to social science tend to view reality as a concrete structure or process, with humans responding (or at least adapting) to that reality in a machine-like or organic manner (Morgan and Smircich, 1980). The attributes of the object studied are prioritised, and things are perceived as having an intrinsic or inherent character that can be studied independently of any perceiving subject. The ontological claim is that the ultimate reality is made up of context-free, independent substances that privilege a detached attitude of contemplation. For a history of objectivity and subjectivity and science practice, see the excellent review by Daston and Galison (2010).

The realm of the objective in business research consists of structures that are seen to be independent of any one agent, such as governance structures, labour and product markets, frameworks of regulations, and firm resources (to name but a few). Reality is seen to be something that lies beyond the realm of appearances and perceptions, beyond the world of lived-experience. Classic approaches that have utilised such objectivist perspectives include Porter's (1980) 'Five Forces Frameworks', Penrose's (1959/1980) resource-based view of the firm, and McClelland's (1961) (less enduring) concept of the heroic entrepreneur. The vast majority of research in entrepreneurship and business has taken such objectivist priorities (Grant and Perren, 2002).

2.2.2 Subjectivist Approaches

At the other extreme is the subjectivist approach, which prioritises the subject over the object, exploring, for example, consciousness, experience, ego, self and psyche. The subjectivist perspective has the core ontological assumptions that reality is a projection of human imagination (or a social construction) and that humans are pure spirit, constructing reality (Morgan and Smircich, 1980). This approach argues that we cannot know the things as they really are in themselves, but only the phenomena (what our synthesizing cognition makes of the things); and the approach focuses on the individual 'internal' data or processing given to a subject.

The realm of the 'subjective' in business research consists of organizational stories, legitimating constructions, identity constructions and processual approaches to decision-making. The subjectivist perspective argues that rules and principles cannot exist independently of the business people, or social entrepreneurs, they constrain. Classic studies that have utilised the subjectivist perspective include Pettigrew's (1973) processual approach to information management and the Austrian School of Economics (for example von Hayek, 1945; von Mises, 1949/1996).

2.3 IMPACTS ON VARIOUS PHENOMENA AND UNITS OF ANALYSIS

These prioritisations have substantial implications for an entrepreneurship researcher. The following section summarises some of the impacts of different philosophies of science on our understanding of opportunity, management, markets and entrepreneurs. The section concludes with a discussion of the implications of making these (often) implicit prioritisations explicit.

2.3.1 Obvious versus Perceived Opportunity

Opportunity refers to the time or set of circumstances that makes it possible to do something (*Oxford English Dictionary*, 1992). It can describe a range of phenomena that can be seen by an entrepreneur to develop over time. In the context of business, opportunity is considered in terms of a chance or occasion of arbitrage (Kirzner, 1997) leading to supernormal profits (Shane and Venkataraman, 2000). The opportunity can therefore refer to the entrepreneur recognising the opportunity to start a business or exploit a gap in the marketplace, or a social entrepreneur seeing a situation that needs to change.

Strange though it may seem, the researcher's philosophical prioritisation will result in different perspectives of creativity and opportunity. These conceptualisations can be conceived as obvious versus perceived opportunities.

Obvious opportunity awaiting discovery

Objectivist perspectives will consider opportunities to exist independently of the entrepreneur (with discovery inevitable). Entrepreneurs will recognise the same opportunities in a given technological change (Kihlstrom and Laffont, 1979), or recognise opportunities that are uncorrelated with the attributes of the discoverer (Evans and Jovanovic, 1989). Information and knowledge (as resources) are tradable.

Practical implications of these assumptions are that human creativity does not play a fundamental role in opportunity recognition (creativity is comprehendible causally, with discovery possible *ex ante*). Entrepreneurs will be able to research actively (utilising analysis and objective research) to recognise opportunity (that is, gaps) in the marketplace. Unsurprisingly, researchers with this prioritisation tend to investigate the entrepreneurial process after opportunities have been discovered (Shane, 2000), with the focus on known (or given) conditions (of resource availability, technology and preferences) and individual action resulting from rational choices (Rosen, 1997). The critical question becomes: 'How can entrepreneurs discover opportunity?' The systematic sorting and winnowing of existing opportunities is thus considered to be a critical entrepreneurial skill (with key activities being goal setting, environmental scanning, competitive analysis and strategic planning).

Opportunity hidden but perceivable

In contrast, subjectivist approaches explore the subjective nature of knowledge and understanding. Informational distortions exist because knowledge is difficult to pass on to others: it is localised (in terms of time and place) and tacit (that is, knowledge 'how' rather than knowledge 'what') (von Hayek, 1945; Caldwell, 1997). Entrepreneurs are considered as those who act on informational distortions (Burt, 1993), and interaction and exchange between actors either encourages or discourages pursuit of opportunity (Eckhardt and Shane, 2003). Opportunity cannot be understood or defined without the entrepreneur's participation:

> Without knowing what to look for, without deploying any deliberate search technique, the entrepreneur is at all times scanning the horizon, as it were, ready to make discoveries. Each such discovery will be accompanied by a sense of surprise (at one's earlier unaccountable ignorance). (Kirzner, 1997, p. 70)

Researchers therefore seek to understand opportunities from a passive search perspective (Kirzner, 1973), exploring their prepared minds (Smilor, 1997) or 'alertness' to opportunity (Kirzner, 1973, 1999). The critical question becomes: 'How can an entrepreneur be "alert" to opportunity?' For example, Shane (2003) proposes 'prior knowledge' as a means of 'solidifying' this concept of alertness. This concept of prior knowledge is also proposed as moderating the relationship between the attributes of the technological invention and how the entrepreneur chooses to exploit the opportunity (Shane, 2000, 2003).

Implications for the social entrepreneurship researcher

How can a social entrepreneur discover (or is it 'be alert to'?) a social problem of significance? Should we focus on informational distortions or activity to discover insight? How does that understanding of opportunity differ over time and between actors? Take care in your research and seek to understand your philosophical posture and what happens once your assumptions are made explicit. Also, ensure that your approach is consistent between your 'big' research question, the perspectives evident in your literature review, and your research design.

2.3.2 Knowledge-Based versus Non-Analytic Approaches to Management Activity

Research perspectives will also influence a researcher's understanding of any approach to the management of any enterprise. By 'management' I mean how an entrepreneurial organisation organises its resources and capabilities. Depending on the philosophical prioritisation of the researcher, perspectives of management could be conceived as knowledge-based versus non-analytic perspectives.

Knowledge-based approaches to management activity

With an objectivist prioritisation, the entrepreneur becomes someone who 'specialises in taking judgemental decisions about the coordination of scarce resources' (Casson, 2003, p. 20). As a coordinator of scarce resources (Casson, 2003), the economic function of the entrepreneur is explored (something that is not explored in standard neoclassical economic theory), with the entrepreneur theorised to shift the economy 'away' from its equilibrium point (Schumpeter, 1934). Technology is seen as 'useful knowledge' with the causal relationships between resources as means and goods as ends (Piore, 1995).

Objectivist perspectives typically focus on analytical tools and frameworks (Poolton and Barclay, 1998). These are extremely appropriate for 'me-too' and incremental innovation (Bennett and Cooper, 1982; Crawford, 1991; Wind and Mahajan, 1997) as these are often situations in which rational analysis is possible. Actors are seen as screening based on 'must-meet' and 'should-meet' criteria including strategic alignment, feasibility, attractiveness and advantages (Cooper, 2001; Hart et al., 2003), and utilising a number of models including: ranking models (comparing products and selecting the best), scoring models (using critical criteria and selecting those products satisfying the hurdles), economic models (based on deterministic or probabilistic pay-offs, profits, return on investment – ROI and so on); and optimisation models (based on selecting products which maximise some identified mathematical function) (Baker and Albaum, 1986).

Non-analytic approaches to management activity

Subjectivist prioritisations recognise that problems arise at the marketing interface of creative new products, particularly in relation to perceiving customers' understandings of aesthetics, emotional appeal, ergonomics, and usability and quality (see for example Gupta et al., 1986; Johansson and Nonaka, 2001; Lauglaug, 1995; Leinbach, 2002; Leonard and Straus, 1999; Srinivasan et al., 1997). These difficulties arise because aesthetics and culture cannot be measured as such (their expressions and manifestations can; however the aesthetics of culture must be interpreted) (Hirschman, 1983; McCracken, 1988).

Subjectivists recognise that judgements include many non-rational and non-objective measures, including perceptions of creative potential (Kelley, 2001) and reputational information (Elsbach and Kramer, 2003). They focus on the subjective insights (that may not necessarily be generalizable) seeking to understand the unlikely and peculiar social entrepreneur.

Implications for the social entrepreneurship researcher

The implication of such perspectives is that a researcher must be aware that there will be clear objectively measurable and identifiable practices undertaken by a social entrepreneur. There will also be a host of issues that are very much perceptions of the social entrepreneur. If a researcher is blind to either, he or she will only be understanding part of the story. Again, aligning the phenomena of interest with the research philosophy, theoretical lens and units of analysis is the challenge facing the researcher.

2.3.3 Market as 'Thing' versus 'Process'

Research perspectives will also influence a researcher's understanding of any social entrepreneurs' market or society. Markets are considered as structured 'things' that exist, or alternatively as activity that has meaning only in the process.

Market as 'thing'

Objectivist prioritisations conceive of the market as a 'thing' rather than a process. The implications of such a perspective include: (1) researchers focus on marketing to different audiences, and how they should be segmented, targeted and so on (refer, for example, to Colbert, 2003a, 2003b); and (2) researchers utilise the technique of social network analysis, strong and weak ties of agents and so on (Narotzky, 1997; Rogers, 2003).

Thus, the entrepreneur becomes someone who 'specialises in taking judgmental decisions about the coordination of scarce resources' (Casson, 2003, p. 20). As a coordinator of scarce resources (Casson, 2003), the economic function of the entrepreneur is explored (something that is not explored in standard neoclassical economic theory), with the entrepreneur theorised to shift the economy 'away' from its equilibrium point (Schumpeter, 1934).

Market as 'process'

Subjectivist prioritisations tend to consider markets as processes that discover, mobilise and coordinate dispersed information (von Hayek, 1945; Jacobson, 1992). For example, a creative artist cannot deal directly with a consumer as there are often experts (whether they be scouts, curators, critics or judges) whose judgements stand between an artist and the mass audience (Hirsch, 1972, 2000). Furthermore, these experts also partially create the value of literary, artistic or scientific work by participating in the complex social processes within the communities that accept that work (Baumann, 2002; Harrington, 1990; Janssen, 1999; Meyer and Even, 1998). There are a number of implications of this: (1) herd behaviour can be initiated by experts or buffs (Gans, 1974); (2) the demand for different goods will differ based on the 'buffness' distribution of the audience; and (3) buffs may support would-be cutting-edge performers or activity (Caves, 2003; Gans, 1974).

Equilibrium is never reached, nor automatic; however it is the entrepreneur who acts as an equilibrating agent, agitating towards market equilibrium by doing something a little differently (Kirzner, 1973).

Implications for the social entrepreneurship researcher

Markets are incredibly complex, and any attempt to understand them should recognise the implications of any particular philosophy of science prioritisation. The issues above relate to markets, but can also relate to the society that harbours the need for a social enterprise. The researcher must be careful to articulate their paradigms, and align their activities to address the 'big' research question driving the primary research.

2.3.4 The Entrepreneur as Object or Subject

The fourth example of how these different philosophical prioritisations can impact upon a research project is when a researcher focuses their study on the entrepreneur.

The entrepreneur as object

Objectivist researchers have sought to reify the subject (that is, the entrepreneur), with humans interpreted as another 'object' to be investigated (Stewart and Mickunas, 1974), with their nature discoverable and describable (Barron, 1955). These trait research studies focus on the variables associated with the subject, including: (1) aspects of human capital – for example, age, experience or education; (2) personal characteristics and traits – for example, personality and marital status; and (3) psychological factors – for example, risk-taking propensity, tolerance of ambiguity, independence or overoptimism. A long list of factors has also been developed to identify situational characteristics that influence an entrepreneur, including: societal attitudes towards a business and towards starting a business; availability of funds (Shapero, 1984); and supporting role models (Brockhaus and Horowitz, 1986), to name but a few.

The entrepreneur as subject

In contrast, subjectivist prioritisations emphasise that entrepreneurs act because they have purposes which they think can be accomplished if they act (von Mises, 1949/1996), involving conscious decisions, intentions and actions (Madison, 1990). Alternative streams of research, such as Collins et al. (1964), recognise this philosophical issue, and revive the conceptualisation first utilised by Defoe (1887/2001):

> The act of entrepreneurship – that is, of going into business for one's self, begins with the conception or the idea of going into business . . . we will refer to this as *projecting the business*. During this phase, the men [and women] we are talking about play the *social role of projectors*. (Collins et al., 1964, p. 124)

This concept of 'projecting' can be differentiated from predicting the future of the business as it involves the human actions that also create that future. The entrepreneurial steps taken 'represent the imagination and vision of the entrepreneurs peering into the unknown' (Kirzner, 1992, p. 76). In time the market may ultimately clarify whether these steps were foolish or insightful.

Understanding the social entrepreneur's world view becomes the key objective. The challenge then becomes how to determine how this world view relates to the objective.

Implications for the social entrepreneurship researcher

The social entrepreneur can be understood as a bundle of attributes or traits, or as a complex subject who has unique understandings of the world. As mentioned above, the implications of such prioritisations for any researcher are significant.

2.4 WEAKNESSES OF OBJECTIVE SUBJECTIVE DICHOTOMY AND ENTREPRENEURSHIP RESEARCH

As can be inferred from the above review, weaknesses exist with both the objectivist and subjectivist perspectives of entrepreneurship and innovation, as summarised in Table 2.4. Neither perspective is appropriate in

Table 2.4 Weaknesses of objectivist and subjectivist perspectives in the context of innovation

Weaknesses of objectivist perspectives	Weaknesses of subjectivist perspectives
We are studying phenomena (things as perceived or experienced) not the things as they are in themselves, independent of human perception	The issue of relativism means that it is difficult to determine the relationship between multiple subjective experiences
We cannot assume away the essential aspects of the phenomena with which we deal	It is difficult to understand the barriers between the individual and society, leading to the problem of research solipsism
Novelty cannot be understood within a lawful, causal, framework	'Subjective' meaning can be equated with 'private' understanding which can exclude the social scientist
The trait approach has not led to any significant insights into innovation and creativity	

the context of radical innovation, creativity or entrepreneurial activity (Seymour, 2006), and this is especially the case in the context of social entrepreneurship.

2.4.1 Weaknesses of the Objectivist Perspectives

The first weakness lies in the assumption that things exist independently of the social entrepreneur or artist; the objectivist perspective prioritises 'the things as they are in themselves', independent of human perception. However, an opportunity (or creativity) is anchored in time, in the social market and in the recognising eye of the entrepreneur (Penrose, 1959/1980). Our human environment is not given by the physical universe but rather by the social environment in which even physical objects derive their meaning from the social context in which they appear (Dilthey, 1939/1989; Piore, 1995). Any thing, any human act, looked at in isolation from its situation, 'is likely to be ambiguous to the point of opacity or obscurity' (Packer, 1985, p. 1081). The opportunity itself should not be confused with the presence of its phenomenon: 'Objectivism is a false ideal because its very stance is not faithfully descriptive of the state of affairs required to bring it about' (Giorgi, 2004, p. 4).

Secondly, the 'unavoidable imperfection of man's knowledge' (von Hayek, 1945, p. 530) and information asymmetry (Caldwell, 1997) cannot be assumed away (as Schumpeter's, 1942 concept of equilibrium analysis implies). Information does not spread evenly through the competitive arena (Burt, 1992, 1993; Granovetter, 1973, 1985; von Hayek, 1945), and faceless automata do not people markets. As von Hayek (1945, p. 530) notes, 'there is something fundamentally wrong with an approach which habitually disregards an essential part of the phenomena with which we have to deal'.

Thirdly, it is difficult to conceive 'how novelty could be subjected to the positivistic program for rational understanding' of repeated and repeatable patterns of observations and classifications of kinds and classes of previously known observable events (Hausman, 1964, p. 38). Creations and opportunities, when they appear, must be in some way recognisable and familiar to us and yet must be radically new and unfamiliar or else they would not be novel and unexpected (Amabile, 1996). Furthermore, they cannot be explained according to any traditional model or cause or prediction, as their specific nature cannot be predicted by a knowledge of their antecedents (Rothenberg and Hausman, 1976). Whatever cannot be understood (in an objectivist sense) as occurring within a lawful framework must be interpreted as the following: (1) as an illusion (appearing as unlawful because of our ignorance to technology or theory); (2) as unintelligible (as arbitrary and not amenable to scientific knowledge); and/or (3) as meaningless (and an improper phenomenon for science) (Rothenberg and Hausman, 1976): 'Predictability may be a false god. Nontrivial novelty cannot be predicted' (Gruber and Wallace, 1999, p. 93). The non-analytic nature of creativity and innovation (Coyne and Snodgrass, 1991; Lester and Piore, 2004; Rothenberg and Hausman, 1976) means that any reductionist approach will fail; for example, considering a melody as a collection of isolated notes will be destined for failure, as 'a whole is different to the sum of its parts . . . [and] cannot be elucidated by examining its individual elements' (Elias, 1991, p. 7). Researchers require integrative perspectives and methods from a range of fields (Amit et al., 1993; Bruyat and Julien, 2000; Crawford, 1977; Gardner, 1988; Swedberg, 2000).

Finally, on a more pragmatic level, the trait-approach perspectives often erroneously conceive of the subject as that of a substance (Heidegger, 1927/1962). Not unsurprisingly, researchers have met with little success in their attempts to objectify the creative and innovative entrepreneur (Goodman, 1994). Dilthey's (1939/1989) 'double focus principle' (Rickman, 1979) reminds us that we must be considered both as an object and as a subject: (1) as an object we humans are a creature to be explained (causally) in terms of the circumstances which made us what we are; and

(2) as a subject we are conscious to be understood (interpretively) as a being who knows their self, creates their environment and controls their actions.

These criticisms should not imply that the objectivist perspective has been without value for researchers; on the contrary. However, as the vast majority of extant research prioritises the objective, there may be some valuable insights through a different approach. Researchers into social entrepreneurship must understand these issues. They should not become ideologues for any perspective, but rather wise practitioners of alternative prioritisations as required by alternative research projects.

2.4.2 Weaknesses of the Subjectivist Perspectives

The first weakness is that subjectivist approaches are forced to explore the multiple alternative ways of constructing the world, emphasising the roles of language or gender, rather than the concepts of truth, control or explanation. Just as the object is constituted by the subject, so the subject is oriented toward the object. It is ultimately the market (not the social entrepreneur) that determines whether an opportunity is indeed such a thing, not a relativist or social construction of veracity. Reality is not as malleable as the subjectivist's approach would suggest; for example, 'whether penicillin cures bacterial infections is a matter of fact, regardless of how related events are embedded in social practices' (Fletcher, 1996, p. 416). As argued by Giorgi (2004, p. 12): 'it would be far more prudent to say that social consensus constitutes the *meaning* of reality for us [rather] than reality itself'.

Secondly, it is difficult to know where the borders exist between the individual subject and the world, both in terms of networks of individuals, information and contexts, and in terms of searching and planning (Granovetter, 1973, 1985, 1993). The subjectivist conceptualisation does little to explore the critical social aspects of knowledge and understanding in entrepreneurship (Carsrud and Krueger, 1995). For example, Shane's (2003) concept of prior knowledge attempts to solidify the concept of 'alertness', yet does not explain why some people possessing what could be identified as 'prior knowledge' fail to see an opportunity, or why, if there are a number of opportunities, entrepreneurs are likely to select the one with the clearer path to success (Burt, 1993). 'Prior knowledge' also ignores the learning and temporal aspects of activity, motivations and abilities, competencies (Bird, 1995), power bases and dominant market-driven values (Caust, 2003).

Finally, it could be argued that 'subjective' meaning can be equated with 'private' understanding of the individual social actor, with the resulting 'privacy' excluding the social scientist (Hekman, 1980). Giorgi (2004) notes that researchers have attempted to answer the question, 'How can the researcher know a subjective position unbiasedly?' by: (1) removing the subjectivity and making it irrelevant – for example the behaviourist approaches of Skinner (1953/1965) and deconstructionist dismantlings of the postmodernists; (2) acknowledging the subjective as an inference (Kimble, 1996); and/or (3) reifying the subject (as discussed above).

The majority of subjectivist research is published as biography or autobiography, with such publications keenly sought in the market. There remains much work to be done in the context of social entrepreneurship. As mentioned above, researchers should not become ideologues for the alternative perspectives, but rather wise practitioners of alternative prioritisations as required by alternative research projects.

2.5 IMPLICATIONS OF PRIORITISATION IN THE CONTEXT OF SOCIAL ENTREPRENEURSHIP

In conclusion, the literature would suggest that the assumptions underlying the Cartesian framework itself (the subject–object model of our everyday epistemic predicament) could be re-evaluated and provide rich opportunities for researchers to advance knowledge. In the context of innovation and creativity research, the researcher's challenge is to develop new research and modelling approaches (Biemans, 2003; Wind and Mahajan, 1997). As recognised by Cooper (1999a, p. 16):

> the question of whether descriptions of the world are objective or subjective is a bad one. They are not objective, if this means being of a kind which a scrupulously detached spectator would provide, for a spectator completely disengaged from the world could have no conception of it at all. But nor are they subjective.

In the context of social entrepreneurship the researcher might be limited by unintentionally prioritising one of these extreme perspectives. Similarly, a researcher could be limited by seeking to cover all perspectives, or by inconsistently utilising them across a research project (for example, across the literature review, research questions and research design).

The following chapters provide appropriate research strategies and methods that will allow you to develop valuable and insightful research projects. Consider your research question with relation to ontology, epistemology and methodology, not just with relation to method. The appropriate prioritisation will provide the foundation of any research project.

NOTES

1. Note that the table is presented with the objective–subjective characteristics in reverse to the original Morgan and Smircich table to maintain the coherence with the presentation of Table 2.4.
2. This term 'positivism' is a narrower designation of the views about the goals and nature of scientific knowledge encompassed by the term 'objectivism' (Harrington, 2001).

REFERENCES

Amabile, T.M. (1996). *Creativity in Context*. Boulder, CO: Westview Press.

Amabile, T.M., R. Conti, et al. (1996). Assessing the work environment for creativity. *Academy of Management Journal* **39**(5), 1154–1184.

Amit, R., L. Glosten and E. Muller (1993). Challenges to theory development in entrepreneurship research. *Journal of Management Studies* **30**(5), 815–834.

Arnold, S.J. and E. Fischer (1994). Hermeneutics and consumer research. *Journal of Consumer Research* **21**(1), 55–70.

Baker, K.G. and G.S. Albaum (1986). Modeling new product screening decisions. *Journal of Product Innovation Management* **1**, 32–39.

Barron, F. (1955). The disposition toward originality. *Journal of Abnormal and Social Psychology* **51**, 478–485.

Baumann, S. (2002). Marketing, cultural hierarchy, and the relevance of critics: film in the United States, 1935–1980. *Poetics* **30**, 243–262.

Beckert, J. (1997). *Beyond the Market: The Social Foundations of Economic Efficiency*. Princeton, NJ, USA and Oxford, UK: Princeton University Press.

Bennett, R.C. and R.G. Cooper (1982). The misuse of marketing. *McKinsey Quarterly* **3**, 52–70.

Brockhaus, R. and P. Horowitz (1986). The psychology of the entrepreneur. In D. Sexton and R. Smilor (eds), *The Art and Science of Entrepreneurship*. Cambridge, MA: Ballinger.

Bruyat, C. and P.-A. Julien (2000). Defining the field of research in entrepreneurship. *Journal of Business Venturing* **16**, 165–180.

Burt, R.S. (1992). *Structural Holes: The Social Structure of Competition*. Cambridge, MA: Harvard University Press.

Burt, R.S. (1993). The social structure of competition. In R. Swedberg (ed.), *Explorations in Economic Sociology*. New York: Russell Sage Foundation, pp. 65–102.

Caldwell, B. (1997). Hayek and socialism. *Journal of Economic Literature* **35**(4), 1856–1890.

Capra, F. (1997). *The Web of Life: A New Scientific Understanding of Living Systems*. New York: Anchor Books (Random House).

Capra, F. (2002). *The Hidden Connections*. London: Harper Collins.

Carson, D., A. Gilmore, C. Perry and K. Gronhaug (2001). *Qualitative Marketing Research*. London: SAGE Publications.

Carsrud, A.L. and N.F. Krueger (1995). Entrepreneurship and social psychology: behavioral technology for understanding the new venture initiation process. In J.A. Katz and R.H. Brokhaus (eds), *Advances in Entrepreneurship, Firm Emergence and Growth*, Vol. 2. Greenwich, CT: JAI Press, pp. 73–96.

Casson, M. (2003). *The Entrepreneur: An Economic Theory*, second edn. Cheltenham, UK and Northampton, MA, USA: Edward Elgar.

Caust, J. (2003). Putting the 'Art' back into arts policy making: how arts policy has been captured by the economists and the marketers. *International Journal of Cultural Policy* **9**(1), 51–63.

Caves, R.E. (2003). Contracts between art and commerce. *Journal of Economic Perspectives* **17**(2), 73–83.

Colbert, F. (2003a). Entrepreneurship and leadership in marketing the arts. *International Journal of Arts Management* **6**(1), 30–39.
Colbert, F. (2003b). Marketing the arts. In R. Towse (ed.), *A Handbook of Cultural Economics*. Cheltenham, UK and Northampton, MA, USA: Edward Elgar, pp. 293–300.
Collins, O.F., D.G. Moore and D.B. Unwalla (1964). *The Enterprising Man*. East Lansing, MI: Bureau of Business and Economic Research, Michigan State University.
Cooper, R.G. (2001). *Winning at New Products: Accelerating the Process from Idea to Launch*. New York: Basic Books.
Coyne, R. and A. Snodgrass (1991). Is designing mysterious? Challenging the dual knowledge thesis. *Design Studies* **12**(3), 124–131.
Crawford, C.M. (1977). Marketing research and the new product failure rate. *Journal of Marketing* **41**(2), 51–61.
Crawford, C.M. (1991). The dual-drive concept of product innovation. *Business Horizons* **34**(3), 32–38.
Daston, L. and P. Galison (2010). *Ojectivity*. New York: Zone Books.
Defoe, D. (1887/2001). *An Essay on Projects*. Project Gutenberg eTexts.
Denzin, N.K. and Y.S. Lincoln (2003). Introduction: the discipline and practice of qualitative research. In N.K. Denzin and Y.S. Lincoln (eds), *The Landscape of Qualitative Research: Theories and Issues*, Vol. 1. Thousand Oaks, CA: SAGE Publications, pp. 1–46.
Descartes, R. (1637/1960). *Discourse on Method*. In *Discourse on Method and Other Writings*. Harmondsworth: Penguin Books, pp. 35–100.
Descartes, R. (1641/1960). *Meditations*. In *Discourse on Method and Other Writings*. Harmondsworth: Penguin Books, pp. 101–172.
Dilthey, W. (1939/1989). *Selected Works, Volume 1: Introduction to the Human Sciences*. Princeton, NJ: Princeton University Press.
Eckhardt, J.T. and S.A. Shane (2003). Opportunities and entrepreneurship. *Journal of Management* **29**(3), 333–349.
Elias, N. (1991). *The Society of Individuals*. Oxford: Basil Blackwell.
Elsbach, K.D. and R.M. Kramer (2003). Assessing creativity in Hollywood pitch meetings: evidence for a dual-process model of creativity judgments. *Academy of Management Journal* **46**(3), 283–301.
Evans, D.S. and B. Jovanovic (1989). An estimated model of entrepreneurial choice under liquidity constraints. *Journal of Political Economy* **97**(4), 808–827.
Fletcher, G.J.O. (1996). Realism versus relativism in psychology. *American Journal of Psychology* **109**(3), 409–429.
Gans, H.J. (1974). *Popular Culture and High Culture: An Analysis and Evaluation of Taste*. New York: Basic Books.
Gardner, H. (1988). Creativity: an interdisciplinary perspective. *Creativity Research Journal* **1**, 8–26.
Giorgi, A. (2004). A way to overcome the methodological vicissitudes involved in researching subjectivity. *Journal of Phenomenological Psychology* **35**(1), 1–25.
Goodman, J.P. (1994). What makes an entrepreneur. *Inc.* **16**(10), 29–30.
Granovetter, M. (1973). The strength of weak ties. *American Journal of Sociology* **78**(6), 1360–1380.
Granovetter, M. (1985). Economic action and social structure: the problem of embeddedness. *American Journal of Sociology* **91**(3), 481–510.
Granovetter, M. (1993). The nature of economic relationships. In R. Swedberg (ed.), *Explorations in Economic Sociology*. New York: Russell Sage Foundation, pp. 3–41.
Grant, P. and L. Perren (2002). Small business and entrepreneurial research: meta-theories, paradigms and prejudices. *International Small Business Journal* **20**(2), 185–211.
Gruber, H.E. and S.N. Davis (1988). Inching our way up Mount Olympus: the evolving-systems approach to creative thinking. In R.J. Sternberg (ed.), *The Nature of Creativity: Contemporary Psychological Perspectives*. Cambridge: Cambridge University Press, pp. 243–270.

Gruber, H.E. and D.B. Wallace (1999). The case study method and evolving systems approach for understanding unique creative people at work. In R.J. Sternberg (ed.), *Handbook of Creativity*. Cambridge: Cambridge University Press, pp. 93–115.
Gupta, A.K., S.P. Raj and D. Wilemon (1986). A model for studying R&D–marketing interface in the product innovation process. *Journal of Marketing* **50**, 7–17.
Harrington, A. (2001). *Hermeneutic Dialogue and Social Science: A Critique of Gadamer and Habermas*. London: Routledge.
Harrington, D.M. (1990). The ecology of human creativity: a psychological perspective. In M.A. Runco (ed.), *Theories of Creativity*. Newbury Park: Sage Publications, pp. 143–169.
Hart, S., E.J. Hultink, N. Tzokas and H.R. Commandeur (2003). Industrial companies' evaluation criteria in new product development gates. *Journal of Product Innovation Management* **20**, 22–36.
Hausman, C.R. (1964). Spontaneity: its arationality and its reality. *International Philosophical Quarterly* **4**, 20–47.
Heidegger, M. (1927/1962). *Being and Time*. Oxford: Blackwell.
Hekman, S. (1980). Phenomenology, ordinary language, and the methodology of the social sciences. *Western Political Quarterly* **33**(3), 341–356.
Hirsch, P.M. (1972). Processing fads and fashions: an organization-set analysis of cultural industry systems. *American Journal of Sociology* **77**(4), 639–659.
Hirsch, P.M. (2000). Cultural industries revisited. *Organization Science* **11**(3), 356–361.
Hirschman, E.C. (1983). Aesthetics, ideologies and the limits of the marketing concept. *Journal of Marketing* **47**(Summer), 45–55.
Hirschman, E.C. (1986). Humanistic inquiry in marketing research: philosophy, method and criteria. *Journal of Marketing Research* **23**, 237–249.
Jacobson, R. (1992). The 'Austrian' school of strategy. *Academy of Management Review* **17**(4), 782–802.
Janssen, S. (1999). Art journalism and cultural change: the coverage of the arts in Dutch newspapers 1965–1990. *Poetics* **26**, 329–348.
Jaspers, K. (1956). *Existenzphilosophie*. Berlin: Walter de Gruyter & Co.
Johansson, J.K. and I. Nonaka (2001). Market research the Japanese way. *Harvard Business Review* May–June, 16–22.
Kelley, T. (2001). *The Art of Innovation: Lessons in Creativity from IDEO, America's Leading Design Firm*. New York: Doubleday.
Kihlstrom, R.E. and J.-J. Laffont (1979). A general equilibrium entrepreneurial theory of firm formation based on risk aversion. *Journal of Political Economy* **87**(4), 719–748.
Kimble, G. (1996). *Psychology: The Hope of a Science*. Cambridge, MA: MIT Press.
Kirzner, I.M. (1973). *Competition and Entrepreneurship*. Chicago, IL: University of Chicago Press.
Kirzner, I.M. (1992). *The Meaning of Market Process: Essays in the Development of Modern Austrian Economics*. London, UK and New York, USA: Routledge.
Kirzner, I.M. (1997). Entrepreneurial discovery and the competitive market process: an Austrian approach. *Journal of Economic Literature* **35**(1), 60–85.
Kirzner, I.M. (1999). Creativity and/or alertness: a reconsideration of the Schumpeterian entrepreneur. *Review of Austrian Economics* **11**, 5–17.
Lauglaug, A.S. (1995). Technical-market research – get customers to collaborate in developing new products. In M. McDonald (ed.), *Marketing Strategies: New Approaches, New Techniques*. Oxford: Pergamon, pp. 15–24.
Leinbach, C. (2002). Managing for breakthroughs: a view from industrial design. In S. Squires and B. Byrne (eds), *Creating Breakthrough Ideas: The Collaboration of Anthropologists and Designers in the Product Development Industry*. Westport, CT: Bergin & Garvey, pp. 3–16.
Leonard, D. and S. Straus (1999). Putting your company's whole brain to work. *Harvard Business Review on Breakthrough Thinking*. Boston, MA: Harvard Business Review Paperbacks, pp. 57–86.
Lester, R.K. and M.J. Piore (2004). *Innovation: The Missing Dimension*. Cambridge, MA, USA and London, UK: Harvard University Press.

Lincoln, Y.S. and E.G. Guba (2003). Paradigmatic controversies, contradictions, and emerging confluences. In N.K. Denzin and Y.S. Lincoln (eds), *The Landscape of Qualitative Research: Theories and Issues*, Vol. 2. Thousand Oaks, CA: Sage Publications, pp. 253–291.
Locke, J. (1700/1975). *An Essay Concerning Human Understanding*. Oxford: Clarendon Press.
Lyons, W. (1995). Introduction. *Modern Philosophy of Mind*. London: Everyman.
Madison, G.B. (1990). Getting beyond objectivism: the philosophical hermeneutics of Gadamer and Ricoeur. In D. Lavoie (ed.), *Economics and Hermeneutics*. London: Routledge, pp. 34–60.
McCracken, G. (1988). *The Long Interview: Qualitative Research Methods*. Newbury Park, CA: SAGE Publications.
Meyer, J.-A. and R. Even (1998). Marketing and the fine arts – inventory of a controversial relationship. *Journal of Cultural Economics* **22**, 271–283.
Morgan, G. and L. Smircich (1980). The case for qualitative research. *Academy of Management Review* **5**(4), 491–500.
Narotzky, S. (1997). *New Directions in Economic Anthropology*. London, UK and Chicago, IL, USA: Pluto Press.
Noorderhaven, N.G. (2004). Hermeneutic methodology and international business research. In R. Marschan-Piekkari and C. Welch (eds), *Handbook of Qualitative Research Methods for International Business*. Cheltenham, UK and Northampton, MA, USA: Edward Elgar, pp. 84–108.
Oxford English Dictionary (1992). The Oxford English Dictionary, Second Edition. Oxford: Oxford University Press.
Packer, M.J. (1985). Hermeneutic inquiry in the study of human conduct. *American Psychologist* **40**(10), 1081–1093.
Penrose, E.T. (1959/1980). *The Theory of the Growth of the Firm*. Oxford: Basil Blackwell.
Perry, C., A. Reige and L. Brown (1999). Realism's role among scientific paradigms in marketing research. *Irish Marketing Review* **12**(2), 16–23.
Pettigrew, A.M. (1973). *The Politics of Organisational Decision Making*. London: Tavistock.
Piore, M.J. (1995). *Beyond Individualism: How Social Demands of the New Identity Groups Challenge American Political and Economic Life*. Cambridge, MA, USA and London, UK: Harvard University Press.
Poolton, J. and I. Barclay (1998). New product development from past research to future applications. *Industrial Marketing Management* **27**, 197–212.
Porter, M.E. (1980). *Competitive Strategy: Techniques for Analyzing Industries and Competitors*. New York: Free Press.
Prasad, P. (2005). *Crafting Qualitative Research: Working in the Postpositivist Traditions*. Armonk, NY: ME Sharpe.
Richards, R.J. (2002). *The Romantic Conception of Life: Science and Philosophy in the Age of Goethe*. Chicago, IL: University of Chicago Press.
Rickman, H.P. (1979). *Wilhelm Dilthey: Pioneer of the Human Studies*. London: Paul Elek.
Rogers, E.M. (2003). *Diffusion of Innovations*. New York: Free Press.
Rosen, S. (1997). Austrian and neoclassical economics: any gains from trade? *Journal of Economic Perspectives* **11**(4), 139–152.
Rothenberg, A. and C.R. Hausman (1976). Introduction: the creativity question. In A. Rothenberg and C.R. Hausman (eds), *The Creativity Question*. Durham, NC: Duke University Press, pp. 3–26.
Schumpeter, J.A. (1934). *The Theory of Economic Development: An Inquiry into Profits, Capital, Credit, Interest, and the Business Cycle*. Cambridge, MA: Harvard University Press.
Schumpeter, J.A. (1942). *Capitalism, Socialism, and Democracy*. New York: Harper Perennial.
Seymour, R.G. (2006). Hermeneutic phenomenology and international entrepreneurship research. *Journal of International Entrepreneurship* **4**(4), 137–155.
Shane, S. (2000). Prior knowledge and the discovery of entrepreneurial opportunities. *Organization Science* **11**(4), 448–469.

Shane, S. (2003). *A General Theory of Entrepreneurship: The Individual-Opportunity Nexus*. Cheltenham, UK and Northampton, MA, USA: Edward Elgar.

Shane, S. and S. Venkataraman (2000). The promise of entrepreneurship as a field of research. *Academy of Management Review* **25**(1), 217–226.

Shapero, A. (1984). The entrepreneurial event. In C.A. Kent (ed.), *The Environment for Entrepreneurship*. Lexington, KY: D.C. Heath & Co., pp. 21–40.

Shapiro, I. (2005). *The Flight from Reality in the Human Sciences*. Princeton, NJ: Princeton University Press.

Skinner, B.F. (1953/1965). *Science and Human Behavior*. New York: Free Press.

Skjervheim, H. (1974). Objectivism in Study of Man. *Inquiry* **17**, 213–245.

Srinivasan, V., W.S. Lovejoy and D. Beach (1997). Integrated product design for marketability and manufacturing. *Journal of Marketing Research* **34**, 154–163.

Sternberg, R.J. and T.I. Lubart (1996). Investing in creativity. *American Psychologist* **51**(7), 677–688.

Stewart, D. and A. Mickunas (1974). *Exploring Phenomenology*. Chicago, IL: American Library Association.

Swedberg, R. (2000). The social science view of entrepreneurship: introduction and practical applications. In R. Swedberg (ed.), *Entrepreneurship*. Oxford: Oxford University Press, pp. 7–44.

von Hayek, F.A. (1945). The use of knowledge in society. *American Economic Review* **35**(4), 519–530.

von Mises, L. (1949/1996). *Human Action: A Treatise on Economics*. San Francisco, CA: Fox & Wilkes.

Weinberg, D. (2002). Qualitative research methods: an overview. In D. Weinberg (ed.), *Qualitative Research Methods*. Malden: Blackwell Publishers, pp. 1–22.

Wind, J. and V. Mahajan (1997). Issues and opportunities in new product development: an introduction to the special issue. *Journal of Marketing Research* **34**, 1–12.

PART II

POSTURE

Part I of this *Handbook* introduced the issues surrounding the term 'social entrepreneurship' and set out how philosophies of science will impact upon researchers' understanding. It has highlighted how curiosity requires a strong grounding in the literature, in science and in personal passion.

Part II now turns our attention to the research postures. The term 'posture' has been chosen to include the overarching significance of research vision as well as research strategy: 'research strategy' implies that one will match one's resources and capabilities with the external context and phenomenon; and 'research vision' implies that one will look beyond the current and close.

Part II considers (in essence) three significant postures to be taken in any research activity: 'listening' to narrative (Chapter 3), participating in a project (Chapter 4) and bounding the project (Chapter 5).

Chapter 3 highlights the importance of listening to, and crafting, narratives. The novel approach taken by Chris Steyaert and Michel Bachmann requires us to re-examine and reconsider our data sources, our research processes, as well as our writing and engaging with various audiences. This requirement should be welcomed, as the significance of the narrative is typically underestimated and constricted by the research community. Steyaert and Bachmann contextualise the narrative approach within social entrepreneurship, providing insight into its value to the field. Equally importantly, they provide insight into how a researcher can gain and nurture their own sense of narrative competence. The detail of datapoints, methods and dissemination within an academic journal can quickly (or slowly) overwhelm a researcher. This chapter has particular relevance to all researchers, as mastering the art, craft and science of the narrative is a challenge that requires our constant observation and attunement.

Chapter 4 takes a radical approach, providing a supporting framework for researchers participating in research. It shows action research to have particular relevance for social entrepreneurship researchers and practitioners alike. The vast majority of research does not involve participation in the thing studied; nonetheless for all researchers the chapter will provide general and valuable insights into the processes of social entrepreneurship. This insight comes from the two lead authors, Mathew Tasker and Linda Westberg, who were part of a project team that included local teachers and community members. Their project was designed to recuperate the local indigenous Kichwa language and culture in the Ecuadorian Andean region of Cayambe. The Mushuk Muyu (meaning 'new seed') project provided a research environment rich in complexity, potential insights and opportunities for learning. Drawing on specific insights from the Mushuk Muyu project, the chapter documents an organising framework, the action research cycle, which is proposed to support the action researcher by providing an appropriate scaffold to manage and allow flexibility, complexity and recoverability of a research project. The chapter concludes with reflections on the strengths and weaknesses of the approach.

Chapter 5 covers the issues associated with the borders and boundaries of a research project. The authors, K. Kumar and Jarrod Ormiston, present a thorough summary of the case study approach, focussing our attention on understanding the dynamics present in single research settings (whether these utilise single or multiple cases). This is important for all researchers, as context confronts and challenges almost all social research projects. Case studies are shown to have particular relevance in the context of social entrepreneurship research. Kumar and Ormiston give clear advice on organising case design and selection, data collection and analysis, and writing up the analysis. As with each of the earlier chapters, the authors draw on their personal research practice in the context of social entrepreneurship. In conclusion, the chapter sets out a checklist for best practice.

3 Listening to narratives

Chris Steyaert and Michel Bachmann

The destiny of the world is determined less by the battles that are lost and won than by the stories it loves and believes in. (Goddard, 1965)

3.1 AND SO IT COULD START: AN INTRODUCTION

In this chapter, we will discuss various ways in which narrative approaches can be applied to research in social entrepreneurship. Though narrative approaches have been developed in the humanities and social sciences (Phelan and Rabinowitz, 2005), they have only more recently been applied in entrepreneurship studies where their possibilities have increasingly been acknowledged (Hjorth and Steyaert, 2004) and have even been considered 'a new path to the waterfall' (Gartner, 2010a). In the field of social entrepreneurship research, narrative approaches have not yet been exploited as a viable way to study and analyze the phenomenon. Many of the motives to apply narrative approaches to social entrepreneurship research are similar to those for studying entrepreneurship 'in general' (Steyaert and Bouwen, 1997; Gartner, 2010a), yet we see three particularly 'good' reasons why they should be applied in this fast-growing field. First, narrative approaches acknowledge the processuality and complexity of social entrepreneurial events; second, narratives as social practices are helpful in unfolding the social trajectories of such projects or enterprises; and third, narrative analysis contributes to a critical understanding of social entrepreneurship and can keep social entrepreneurship from being (re) presented as an unproblematic solution to social problems.

Throughout the chapter we will document how storytelling and narration is significant during all parts of the research process, namely while generating, analyzing and writing up stories, which form the bulk of narrative 'data'. Moreover, a narrative perspective also offers new possibilities for writing and engaging differently with various audiences, also in the context of the sometimes stiff genre of 'handbook'. In this text, we follow a conversational format to document our own research collaboration and to engage with other forms of narrating scientific texts. Applying methods is a multifaceted process of enactment, which is itself processual and complex, and requires a constant monitoring between research activities and the overall storyline of one's research project. In other words: research, too, is a narrative process, 'an inventive form of craftsmanship that is constantly engaged in adjusting and reconfiguring scientific protocols to meet the vagaries of each unique empirical situation' (Prasad, 2005, p. 6). Accordingly, every researcher needs to gain and nurture their own sense of narrative competence. Our conversational storytelling will unfold as a dialogue between a PhD student and his supervisor as they work together on studying and understanding the storied emergence of a new social entrepreneurial movement, which they had, for reasons of confidentiality, baptized 'neXus'. Thus begins their story.

3.2 OR SHOULD IT START LIKE THIS?

'Right', said the PhD student, a bit amused, as he closed *Storytelling Organizations*, David Boje's (2008a) book whose final chapter forms a Socratic storytelling symposium: Boje in dialogue with such eminent writers on narrative and language as Bakhtin, Dostoevsky, Heidegger, Ricoeur, Sartre and Stein. 'This narrative stuff makes a lot of sense but how am I going to apply that during my research project?' Like many before him, the PhD student became intrigued with what is usually called 'narrative approaches' to social science studies and considered using the related methodologies to study how a social entrepreneurship movement is (re)assembled. He had recently attended a course that encouraged him to rethink the very notion of method and was now a little confused about how to connect this to narrative approaches. John Law (2004) may have a point in his seminal book *After Method: Mess in Social Science Research*, when he writes that methods are inherently performative, that they help create the realities that they want to discover and that they are entangled with an immense 'hinterland' of pre-existing, interwoven stories, texts and materials that shape how research is being enacted.

But what did this mean for the enactment of his PhD project now? How should he go about collecting data, analyzing transcripts, and writing up an account that would respect the conventions of research practice while simultaneously challenging the very assumptions of these conventions? After all, he did want his work to get published and knew that he had to follow certain rules in order to do so. But what were those rules? Who created them? And might they be different for the kind of research he was going to undertake? Questions, questions. The only thing he knew for sure was that 'after method' is 'before method' and that he therefore needed to take proper stock of what had been written before him in the field of narrative research and how it had been applied to the study of social entrepreneurship. So when his supervisor presented him with an opportunity to co-author a book chapter about that very topic, he knew what he had to do.

PhD student: OK, so where do we start?

Supervisor: I guess in the middle, as there is already a long history of narrative research which cannot be easily summarised. Chase (2005) speaks of narrative research as 'a field in the making', which consists of 'a rich but diffuse tradition, multiple methodologies in various stages of development, and plenty of opportunities for exploring new ideas, methods, and questions' (p. 651). McHale (2005) doubts it is even possible to narrate the history of narrative theory, unless one accepts its ghostlike or even monstrous nature.

PhD student: Right. So how can we draw upon this 'elusive richness' then?

Supervisor: I started with (and returned many times to) Lyotard (1984) and Bruner (1990); in philosophical and psychological ways, respectively, they emphasized the importance of the narrative mode of knowing. Contrasting the paradigmatic (or logico-deductive) mode with the narrative mode of knowing, Bruner (1990) explains how narrative is intrinsic to human experience and key in the development of memory, the perception of time, the understanding of life events and the imagination of future lives. Lyotard (1984) furthermore underlined that narrative pervades almost every aspect of human knowledge, including legitimizing scientific knowledge. He argues that scientific knowledge, especially in the course of modernity, 'has sought to legitimate itself not by validating its own internal procedures but by appealing to narrative itself, a "grand narrative"' (Cobley, 2001, p. 187). By 'grand récits' or grand narratives – sometimes also called master or metanarratives – Lyotard (1992) thinks of 'narrations with a legitimating function' (p. 19). For example, he writes of 'the progressive emancipation of reason and freedom, the progressive or catastrophic emancipation of labor . . . [or] the enrichment of all humanity through the progress of capitalist technoscience' (p. 17); he says these narratives look for legitimacy 'not in an original founding act, but in a future to be accomplished' (p. 18). However, Lyotard believes that '[t]he grand narratives have become scarcely credible' (p. 29), and, instead, refers to the potential of little narratives.

PhD student: Sounds intriguing. So should I start reading Bruner and Lyotard then?

Supervisor: No, I don't think it makes much sense that you start where I did. You have to weave your own thread out of the ever-growing web of narrative research papers. On the other hand, I already began writing what I think could be the first section of the paper: ontological and epistemological dimensions of narrative research. Could you take a look?

3.3 WHEN THE EXCEPTION BECOMES THE RULE: ONTOLOGICAL AND EPISTEMOLOGICAL DIMENSIONS OF NARRATIVE APPROACHES

The potential of narrative approaches for the study of social entrepreneurship can be explicated by drawing upon both the epistemological and ontological dimensions of the ways research is framed. First, turning to a narrative study of social entrepreneurship involves researchers in a different epistemology of research, one that values knowledge as contextual, interpretive and local (Steyaert and Bouwen, 1997). Narrative knowledge is not about general laws or universal truths, but engages with what Geertz (1983) called generating local knowledge that can bring thick descriptions of unfolding processes of social complexity. This emphasis on the particular and the local becomes clear in Herman's (2007, p. 3) working definition; he says that: 'stories are accounts of what happened to particular people – and of what it was like for them to experience what happened – in particular circumstances and with specific consequences'.

Knowledge development, then, becomes a matter of differentiation, in which we do not treat the differences between bodies of knowledge as something to be avoided at all costs, but rather as an expression of the 'place-bound' nature of knowledge production. In other words, the exception becomes the rule. Geertz (1983) embraces the generative effect of an epistemology of local knowledge, which favours variety over generalizability, if only we can first succeed in teaching ourselves how to accept and apply so much detail and discretion:

> But it is from the far more difficult achievement of seeing ourselves amongst others, as a local example of the forms human life has locally taken, a case among cases, a world among worlds, that the largeness of mind, without which objectivity is self-congratulation and tolerance a sham, comes. If interpretive anthropology has any general office in the world, it is to keep reteaching this fugitive truth. (p. 16)

Especially as social entrepreneurship takes place in the most diverse contexts and localizations – whether rural or urban, developing or developed, North or South – this requires that our studies teach us how local and global elements cross with singular entrepreneurial projects. Narrative approaches can help to map this localized complexity as it responds to and is pervaded by globalization, in what can be called a 'globalization from below' (Appadurai, 1996; Steyaert et al., 2011).

This processual complexity could be called 'entrepreneuring', a verb to indicate that entrepreneurship is materialized in an ongoing creation process, in a world of 'becoming' (Steyaert, 2007a). In this perspective narratives are not just epistemological categories, but part of what Bruner (1991) calls 'world-making' and what Somers (1994, p. 614) sees as a shift towards an ontological narrativity, which gives narratives an ontological force:

> Before this shift, philosophers of history had argued that narrative modes of representing knowledge (telling historical stories) were representational forms imposed by historians on the chaos of experience. Recently, scholars are postulating instead that social life is itself storied and that narrative is an ontological condition of social life. Their research shows that stories guide action, that people construct identities by locating themselves or being located within a repertoire of emplotted stories. Experience, in other words, is constituted through narratives. People make sense of what has happened and is happening to them by attempting to integrate these happenings within one or more narratives. People are guided to act in certain ways and not others on the basis of the projections, expectations and memories derived from a repertoire of available social, public and cultural narratives.

Second, as a consequence of the above epistemological and ontological arguments, narrative helps to highlight the meaning of the social in social entrepreneurship in a double sense (see Steyaert and Hjorth, 2006). Narrative practice is compatible with a social ontology of entrepreneurship and argues that much of the complexity is related to the various social actors and their worlds. Drawing upon actor network theory (Latour, 2005), we could say that a narrative study consists of reconstructing the narrative trajectory of a social entrepreneurship project and tracing how the many human and non-human actors are assembled. Thus a study of social entrepreneurship is never the study of one person, the social entrepreneur. Even if one focuses intensively on one person's life story or autobiography, the analysis should attempt to reconstruct the various social and material worlds this person is drawing upon to position themself and the others who take part, directly or indirectly, in this entrepreneurial project.

Third, social entrepreneurship is social because it has an interest in social change; this has been emphasized by practitioners (Bornstein, 2007) and academics (Nicholls, 2008) alike. Narrative analysis enables us to consider ethical and political consequences, as 'narratives explicitly or more often implicitly establish their own ethical standards in order to guide their audiences to particular ethical judgments' (Phelan, 2005, p. 325). Far too often, social entrepreneurship is narrated in a merely positive light, as something that is inherently good (Cho, 2006), as if it had no shadow sides and did not produce any negative effects. We believe that social entrepreneurship needs critical analysis and that narrative approaches can be vital in establishing such critical perspectives through several processes: unmasking some of the master narratives and their typical interpellations that are worked into the story of social entrepreneurship, providing counter-narratives, and investing in empirically based, prosaic stories that reveal the ambiguities, paradoxes, and open-endedness in the projects, processes and outcomes of many entrepreneurial endeavours in the social realm (Dey and Steyaert, 2010).

PhD student: These are interesting theoretical – and even philosophical – threads, but I am still wondering, as a novice at narrative research, how this could be applied more concretely to social entrepreneurship studies.

Supervisor: I guess the best way to find out is to experiment a little and jump right into the middle of your empirical setting. So why don't you start by writing down your experiences of co-shaping neXus during the past year?

PhD student: Interesting. So narrative data would then be constructed by writing up my own story-in-the-making and how it is interwoven with the narrative trajectory of this emerging social entrepreneurship movement?

Supervisor: Exactly. And in parallel, you could read more about how narrative can be used to enter and participate in the field of research. That would allow you to reflect upon, and improve, your own data generation methods in the process of enacting your research project.

PhD student: Very well then. So let me dig into the existing literature on narrative research and start writing little vignettes of my own experience as entrepreneur-researcher. That could even become the basis for our book chapter: going beyond the linear format of the text you have written so far and instead demonstrating the richness of narrative genres and styles that can be applied in writing. Walking the talk, so to say.

3.4 HEAD OVER HEELS INTO THE FLUX

He never thought that getting involved in this social entrepreneurship movement would be so demanding. He had worked at a big management consulting company and was sure that he had reached his limits in terms of working hours back then. He was sorely mistaken. neXus had become his life, consuming every minute of his waking hours and even finding its way into his dreams. Always more to be done, never time for a break. Quite ironic, he thought. All this talk about sustainability and radically changing the world and then this: working to the point of utter exhaustion, sacrificing personal relationships, and not even really getting paid.

Something was clearly wrong with this picture. How could this be 'social'? On the other hand: tons of passion, mind-blowing energy, a sense of real purpose, riding the wave at the cutting edge of society. Certainly worth it. Or one could also say: dangerously addictive. How much longer until the wave broke down? Would he hit the hidden reef underneath the dazzling surface or find his way back to the shore unharmed? What about the others that he had talked into joining the ride, just as he himself had become seduced by the promise of 'another world happening'? Questions, questions. The only thing he knew for sure was that he wasn't alone, that many social entrepreneurs were experiencing a similar story. Different facets maybe, but essentially the same pattern. So something had to be inherently wrong with the grand narrative of harmonious social change that was constructed around the fast-moving phenomenon of social entrepreneurship. The next bubble about to burst?

He was determined to find out. To prove that it could work. Luckily he had a safe space to experiment and fall back upon if things broke apart: his PhD. From the very beginning of his studies, he was intrigued by Tsoukas and Chia's (2002) argument that: 'only by placing ourselves at the center of an unfolding phenomenon can we hope to know it from within' (p. 571). So here was his chance: to immerse himself into the assembling of a social entrepreneurship movement and reflect on the various tensions, paradoxes and ambiguities that this experience would bring along. Not from the outside, but from within.

But how could he do that? How could he trace the narrative trajectory that seemed to connect the various actors shaping this movement while acknowledging that he himself had become an active force in the interweaving of this unfolding story? How should he engage in the ambivalent dance along the hyphen as researcher-entrepreneur? Or put more simply: how would he go about collecting data? Could it be that by writing down his own stories he was already creating narrative data? Maybe the vast amount of literature on narrative research would offer some answers.

3.5 GENERATING NARRATIVE DATA

As scholars enter the field of narrative research, they often set out to collect interesting stories that they can then analyze to answer their research questions. The notion of 'collecting stories' may be misleading, however. As Czarniawska-Joerges (2004a) points out in reference to Boland and Tenkasi (1995): 'Stories do not lie around – they are fabricated, circulated, and contradicted . . . Nor is a story collector, in this case a researcher, a mushroom picker: he or she listens selectively, remembers fragmentarily, and re-counts in a way that suits his or her purpose' (p. 45). In other words, stories are produced rather than collected, and the researcher takes an active part in the co-production of the narratives that he or she seeks to gather. So we should speak of 'data generation' rather than 'data collection' and acknowledge that data are not so much 'givens' as 'mades', arrived at by mutual agreement between the researcher and the researched (Steyaert and Bouwen, 1997). Bearing this in mind, we can look at various ways that narrative data may be generated for social entrepreneurship research and beyond. Gabriel (2000) points out that an important choice must be made at the outset of the narrative research process: 'whether to elicit the stories by asking appropriate questions and explaining the point of the research or whether to collect them as and when they occur' (p. 137). The latter can be achieved through participant-observation or by drawing upon secondary data, the former through so-called 'storytelling interviews'. As a consequence, we can elaborate on three distinct methods of generating stories: secondary data, participant observation and interviews.

First, we will turn to the collection – here we can actually apply the term – of stories through secondary data. Stories can be 'found' almost anywhere: in books, newspapers, scientific articles, fashion magazines, advertisements, websites and even YouTube videos; they all tell stories that want to be heard, reproduced and circulated. As narrative researchers, we can thus select a sample of stories that catch our interest and may help us explore our research questions. Dempsey and Sanders (2010), for instance, took a critical look at three popular autobiographies from social entrepreneurs and demonstrated how these self-portrayals celebrate a troubling account of work–life balance that is centered on self-sacrifice, underpaid labor and the privileging of organizational commitment at the expense of health and personal relationships. Autobiographies can thus be seen as a promising source to investigate how people narrate their own journey towards becoming a social entrepreneur and to reflect critically on the meta-narratives that are evoked to position this journey. The main problem with stories from secondary data is that they are often taken out of context and tend to hide the multiplicities, paradoxes and complexities that the 'real story' has to offer. Accordingly, many narrative researchers prefer to explore how stories are produced 'in situ' through participant observation.

A pioneer in this field is David Boje. Boje (1991) wanted to go beyond the study of 'story-as-text' and thus focused on the organizational context in which stories are 'performed'. To do so, he recorded various social scenes that make up the discursive environment of an organization, for example meetings in conference rooms, training sessions and informal conversations. He used field notes to supplement the recordings. He concluded that stories are frequently challenged, reinterpreted and revised as they unfold in conversations, and are rarely told from beginning to end when performed in an organizational setting: they are fragmented, terse, discontinuous, polysemic and multi-authored. We can therefore research the emergence of social enterprises as collective storytelling systems in which the continuous performance of stories is a key part of organizational sense-making. For this work, the method of participant observation is particularly conducive as it facilitates exploring how stories are performed in their everyday context where the researcher becomes part of the storytelling process itself. Gubrium and Holstein (2009) call this ethnographic study of stories 'narrative ethnography', as it is concerned with how the circumstances of storytelling 'mediate what is said and how that is assembled for the telling' (p. 21). Thus, an observing researcher is sensitive to the contingent conditions of how accounts are assembled. A narrative ethnography considers questions 'such as who produces particular kinds of stories, where are they likely to be encountered, what are their purposes and consequences, who are the listeners, under what circumstances are particular narratives more or less accountable, how do they gain acceptance, and how are they challenged' (ibid., p. 23). Such an approach to data generation has the advantage that researchers have 'access' to the ongoing and everyday production of storytelling and its social organization, namely who is participating and in what kinds of ways. However, this data generation practice is quite time-consuming, as it requires both taking part in a specific social context for a longer period, and then analyzing a large amount of experiences, notes and transcripts.

Therefore, many narrative researchers choose to generate their data through interviews, which make it possible to probe more deeply into a particular research subject in an effective way, though they also have the disadvantage of eliciting stories that are not encountered in their 'natural state' but are performed for the benefit of an outsider, that is, the researcher. Storytelling interviews are usually fairly unstructured and give the interviewees much space to tell their story after being prompted by a few opening questions. A popular technique is to ask the interviewees for 'critical incidents' that best describe their organizations, lives or any other subject the researcher is interested in (Gabriel, 2000). This has the advantage of triggering a natural storytelling mode as the interviewee reflects on the most important events that led to the present situation. Once such incidents are described, rcsearchers can prompt for more detail with processual questions such as, 'Can you give an example?' 'How did this happen?' or 'How did others respond?' As interviewees might respond with rather factual statements, the interviewer sometimes needs to employ various forms of activation (Gabriel, 2000). For instance, interviewees can be prompted to describe the flow of events in the form of 'book chapters' (see Gubrium and Holstein, 2009) to describe their involvement in a social endeavour (for example 'Can you tell me how you first got involved with this project and share your experience of how it has evolved up to today, and maybe even how you see it unfolding in the near future? You can make as many chapters as you feel you need'). As this is not always an easy task, the interviewer might continuously bring in supporting questions.

This technique of book chapters is often used to conduct the so-called 'life story interview', a conducive method for learning more about how social entrepreneurs reconstruct their lives. As Johansson (2004) points out:

> our personal identity can be seen as the fabrication of an emerging story. We are in the middle of our stories and do not yet know what the end will be. Therefore we continually revise the plot as we pass through new experiences. Life stories are then a way of articulating and explaining who we are, not only to others but also to ourselves. (p. 275)

To elicit these stories, the research subjects can be asked to tell a story of their life up until the moment of the interview, focusing on the most important episodes that have shaped their personal experience; for example how they got involved in their project of social entrepreneurship. In life stories, the past is reconstructed and the future anticipated simultaneously, albeit strongly embedded in and actualized from the present context (Thisted and Steyaert, 2006). Life and stories are thus internally related, which 'implies that life is both more and less than a story. It is more in that it is the basis of a variety of stories, and it is less in that it is unfinished and unclear as long as there are no stories told about it' (Widdershoven, 1993, p. 19).

Supervisor (email to PhD student): I read your text. Many thanks for taking the time to dig into the literature even though you must be heavily invested in keeping neXus going, if I understand your last vignette correctly. This could actually be an interesting case study: how a social entrepreneurship movement reassembles itself during episodes of turmoil. So if the worst comes to the worst, you should have some interesting data at least. But back to your text on narrative data generation: I find it especially important that you stress the use of secondary data. We live in a narrative society where people continuously produce a variety of smaller and larger stories about themselves, the activities they undertake, and the movements or organizations they identify with. This increase in story production is of course related to new technological possibilities and the rise of social media in particular. In this sense, I think it is important not to miss out on 'the multiple stylistic modes of telling that are very telling' (Boje, 2008a, p. 207), such as visual and even gestural forms of storytelling. Interestingly, most of these stories are distributed and consumed in public arenas, and are meant to position the storyteller with a specific (positive) image, be it on Facebook, Twitter, or YouTube. This form of imagineering can be called 'spinning', as many people and organizations invest in the kind of stories they want to circulate and how they need to be concocted for their audience to consume them (Boje, 2008b).

The other important point that you mention is Gabriel's distinction between limited participation through interviews and engaging more actively through ethnography for data generation. I think we should keep doing both. I believe that in addition to autobiographies, we need studies of social entrepreneurship that are reconstructed around life stories. I know we are always served the same names, such as Mohammed Yunus and Bill Drayton (though we know very little about the intricacies of their life stories beyond what they themselves have made public), while instead we should turn to the life stories of other, less known people. However, this focus on individuals again increases the cult status of entrepreneurial heroes – stories can easily become hagiographies – and takes attention away from the social complexity and communities they are embedded in. That is a little ironic if one takes seriously the social in social entrepreneurship.

Therefore, I applaud the turn to the performative side of stories, the storytelling process itself. Could you not find any examples of narrative ethnographies in entrepreneurship studies? The three-year ethnographic study by Simon Down (2006) comes to mind, but he focused more on the emergence of a small industrial business rather than a case of social entrepreneurship. So could it be that you are one of the first scholars making an ethnography in the context of social entrepreneurship? Even if, in your case, you arc more doing auto-ethnography. So how do you reflect upon your own (auto)ethnographic practice? By the way, please find attached what I wrote on narrative analysis. I am curious to hear your thoughts!

3.6 NARRATIVE ANALYSIS

3.6.1 Narrative Processes of Identity Formation

A variety of narrative studies in entrepreneurial contexts have analyzed stories as a way to understand the construction of social identities (see for example Down, 2006; Johansson, 2004; Jones et al., 2008). This is one of the important outcomes of narrative studies as the focus on identity formation offered entrepreneurship scholars an alternative to the dead end of personality studies (Steyaert, 2007b). Somers (1994) argues that:

> it is through narrativity that we come to know, understand, and make sense of the social world, and it is through narratives and narrativity that we constitute our social identities . . . [A]ll of us come to *be* who we *are* (however ephemeral, multiple, and changing) by being located or locating ourselves (usually unconsciously) in social narratives *rarely of our own making*. (p. 606)

That is, a narrative identity approach assumes that social action can only be intelligible if we recognize that people are guided by an evolving web of stories in which they are embedded and through which they constitute their identities. We can therefore study the emergence of social entrepreneurship by taking a closer look at how social entrepreneurs construct their identity to become a social entrepreneur in the first place.

To illustrate this, we can draw on the study by Jones et al. (2008); they analyzed the narrative process through which a social entrepreneurial identity can be constructed. They build on the life story of a 'social-activist entrepreneur' with the pseudonym of 'Pat' who founded an organization in Australia to support migrants seeking refugee immigration status there. Pat was encouraged to tell the researchers about his organization and his beliefs and motivations for undertaking this type of work; thus he was prompted to engage in identity work through a narrative response. Here is an excerpt of the narrative they recorded:

> I came to Australia as a migrant at four years old. My dad was from [South American country] . . . At that time the military took over, there was a dictatorship, we weren't directly affected in the political sense, we were not refugees or anything. So my dad felt that this country is going to the shit, I want to get out of here and take my family, because there is no future here at the moment . . . we came out in seventy-seven. So I went through the whole experience of going through migrant hostels like [a local] detention centre. We stayed there, we were in public housing for the first three or four years . . . so I have had that sort of experience. I have also had that experience of being a migrant and the racism at the hands of a whole range of people . . . being a migrant, being from a working class background.

So my family, they are not political, they are working class, they hate communists, even though they hate capitalists at the same time. My parents sent me off to the local working class Catholic school. So from there I guess, I have got to admit it, because I am an atheist, but a lot of the core humanistic principles of Christianity, you know, treat other people how you would like to be treated, you not hurting others, sort of the core little humanistic principles. I think I learnt a lot at that stage, becoming interested, my parents bought another thing to improve our life, it was encyclopaedia wall books . . . and from there I was really keen on reading so I started from A and read pretty much to Z . . . And at about K I came across a whole section on Martin Luther King and the US civil rights movement. And I was really quite interested by that, and that sort of . . . informed me. So I had that upbringing, you know, at home we had that social justice where we were treated fair. So yes, I saw the experiences my parents had, they were injured at work, and they had all those issues, how they were treated by their employers and all that kind of stuff, so they were really informed and their experience informed me . . . I was interested in doing anything that would be of benefit to the general community . . .

I guess my whole life ended up being around social enterprise . . . just because I feel that need . . . from a very libertarian perspective . . . I am informed by Leninism, Marxism and whatever, but I don't believe that we should be organised around the state, but we need to be organised at a much more local level. So libertarian . . . the word is not used that much, anarchist sort of principles. If you look at the co-ops and Mondragon they come from anarchist, you know philosophy, and very much I personally am about that. And that we need to have communities control the means of production. I don't want to help people, I want people to help themselves. You need to be able to do it yourself. You need to take that power back.

Bearing in mind that this is only a fragment of a larger story, how can we analyze this excerpt? Put differently: how should we read and interpret this (partial) story? For instance, we could study how Pat emplots his whole life as a journey towards becoming a social entrepreneur, from his experience as an underprivileged migrant to taking action for the benefit of the wider community. Or we could investigate which meta-narratives Pat locates himself in, to account for this journey and how he interweaves his own narrative with the story of Martin Luther King, for example. Better still, we could compare Pat's life story with the narratives of other social entrepreneurs to search for common patterns in constructing their identities as social entrepreneurs, for example the need to account for some sort of epiphany. There are many ways to read, analyze and interpret a story. In their analysis, Jones et al. identify three gerund processes of 'positioning through divisioning' that are enmeshed in Pat's identity construction: dividing, undividing and suppressing. This builds on Burke's (1980) argument that people define their identity (who am I?) in relation to their counter-identities (who am I not?) and adds a third element of 'suppressing' that which is absent in the narrative of the self. Consequently, they show how a social entrepreneurial identity can be constructed through the joint crafting of the narration of 'Me' (Pat's undividing discourses, endorsing local, participative, grass-roots community initiatives), 'Not-Me' (Pat's dividing discourses, rejecting mainstream practices and philosophies) and 'Suppressed-Me' (Pat's suppressed discourses, sidelining certain elements such as financial failure). We can therefore explore how social entrepreneurs negotiate the tension of lacing together potentially contrasting discourses while maintaining the overall integrative nature of their self-narrative.

Other narrative studies go beyond the investigation of self-identity construction and focus instead on the exploration of collective identity formation. These studies view organizations as discursive spaces where 'the very fabric of organization is constantly being created and re-created through the elaboration, contestation and exchange of narratives' (Brown, 2006, p. 8). Organizations are thus in a perpetual state of becoming as their collective identities are constructed through 'continuous processes of narration where both the narrator and the audience formulate, edit, applaud, and refuse various elements of the ever-produced narrative' (Czarniawska-Joerges, 1994b, p. 198).

An illustrative example of collective identity-building is Polletta's (1998) study of narrative in the constitution of social movements. Polletta argues that social movements are 'moments when agency explodes structure, the taken for granted becomes precarious, when old "words lose their meaning" (White, 1984) . . . In that context, narratives may serve to contain the disruptive within a familiar form to turn the anomalous into the "new"' (p. 422). In this sense, narratives may be employed strategically to strengthen a collective identity but they also may precede and make possible the development of a coherent community or collective actor: 'where there are neither established organizations nor coherent ideologies in place, narratives may be a prominent mode of talk on account of their capacity to turn confusing events into a suspenseful story of overcoming, and to turn a threatened sense of self and group into a powerfully mobilizing identity' (ibid., p. 429). To illustrate this, Polletta draws on various social movements such as the student sit-ins in 1960 or the movement around Martin Luther King, and shows how such movements construct their own stories of origin, defeat and victory in order to create a collective identity that mobilizes the masses when the cracks of society become too large to ignore. We may thus turn to narrative precisely when we cannot explain the unexplainable as we engage in the ambiguity of our collective sense-making.

3.6.2 Embedding Narratives: On the Importance of Intertextuality

An important way to analyze stories is by looking at their intertextual conception. Intertextuality refers to the principle that 'all writing and speech – indeed, all signs – arise from a single network: what Vygotsky called "the web of meaning"' (Porter, 1986, p. 34); thus it points to the explicit and implicit ways in which texts refer to one another. In other words: there are no stand-alone texts but only entangled conversations that perpetually weave and reweave the very fabric of social reality. We therefore need to take the 'con-text' of our research seriously and acknowledge how we, as researchers, also become part of the social which is being explored.

To illustrate this, we can draw on an interesting narrative study conducted by Ellen O'Connor (2004). O'Connor explored how a high-tech start-up company – originally one with a social purpose – built legitimacy through the pursuit of intertextuality, that is, the 'grafting of the story line of the new company onto existing relevant, generally accepted, and taken-for-granted story lines' (p. 106). Immersing herself as a participant-observer in the early days of the venture, that started out with the idea of empowering frustrated customers by aggregating their voices on an online platform to exert pressure and effect positive change, she documented how the founders' story of the company changed from a 'romantic, epic-heroic plot about changing the world' (p. 113) to a profit-seeking business story about a customer relationship management (CRM) product that would facilitate communication between companies and consumers.

What had happened? According to O'Connor, the original story line failed to attract the necessary funds to finance the venture and thus a new storyline had to be written that resonated more strongly with potential venture capitalists in order to achieve legitimacy. As Suchman (1995) points out, accounts about a company's activities 'must mesh both with the larger belief system and with the experienced reality of the audience's daily life' (p. 582). O'Connor (2004) refers to this 'meshing' as a verbal process of intertextuality and emphasizes that 'entrepreneurs operate in a world of long-standing conversations. To achieve legitimacy, their conversations must engage with these pre-existing, ongoing, and encompassing conversations' (p. 105). In this case, what the company needed was an embedded narrative about building a profit-seeking business rather than assembling a critical mass of activists to effect positive social change. Accordingly, (social) entrepreneurship does not happen within an empty space but needs to connect to an existing conversation in order to become legitimate, respecting the principle of intertextuality.

This is interesting because social entrepreneurship has often been depicted as a 'disruptive force' that 'breaks with tradition' in order to bring about 'radical social change' (see for example Dees et al., 2001; Bornstein, 2007). Indeed, the grand narrative of social entrepreneurship is infused with a rhetoric of 'newness' that emphasizes the necessity of a fertile 'rupture with the past' (Dey and Steyaert, 2010). So how can we resolve this paradox? Or, as Nicholls and Cho (2008) put it: 'How should social entrepreneurs negotiate the need to be single-minded and disruptive with the need to pursue inclusive and sustainable processes?' (p. 106). A potential way out of this seeming contradiction is to conceive of social entrepreneurship as 'boundary work' (see Lindgren and Packendorff, 2006) rather than 'disruptive innovation'. That is, it is less about breaking with the past than about forging an (intertextual) bridge that connects the old with the new, never quite resolving the tension but holding on to the ambiguity of the 'in-between', the transitional space where the unthinkable becomes entirely possible.

Social entrepreneurship then becomes an intermediary act that seeks to change the way we understand and deal with ourselves by upholding and thus transforming the tension between the strange and the familiar, the marginal and the dominant, as well as the hidden and the overt (see Spinosa et al., 1997). Social entrepreneurship can thus be seen as 'a process of socially constructing deviations and belongings in a certain world and maintaining these tensions long enough for historical changes to materialize' (Lindgren and Packendorff, 2006, p. 212). Accordingly, we can study how 'entrepreneurial action can be embedded in local history and tradition at the same time as it challenges and stretches these taken-for-granted boundaries' (ibid., p. 211). The narrative approach appears particularly suitable here as it allows us to conceive of the world as an entangled web of intertextual storylines that unfold in a perpetual process of becoming, and thus remain open for the new while respecting the past.

3.6.3 Genres of Narrating

A third way to analyze stories is through genre analysis. Social entrepreneurship itself can be analyzed as a narrative that is created to address, in specific ways, societal issues such as poverty, injustice and exclusion; we can also look at how it provides a new and different take on social change (Dey and Steyaert, 2010). However, nothing we confront is ever entirely fresh, since 'texts come before us as the always-already-read' (Jameson, 1981, p. 9). This requires that we learn to read and analyze narratives on social entrepreneurship in critical ways. As Boddice (2009, p. 134) emphasized, social entrepreneurship is a concept that has not yet been understood appropriately in terms of its 'origins, the traditions it draws on and the kinds of ideology employed, sometimes unconsciously, in its execution'. Therefore, Dey and Steyaert (2010, p. 87) emphasize that 'if we want to understand – to use Jameson's expression – the political unconscious contained in social entrepreneurship stories', we must accept that narrations, including those in academia, 'have far-reaching consequences, not least because they imply a certain priority setting and narrative closure' (Lyotard, 1993 p. 87). In their analysis, drawing on the work of Lyotard (1984), Dey and Steyaert (2010) distinguish between three genres of narrating. First, they indicate that social entrepreneurship is constructed as a grand narrative through such distinct interpretive repertoires as utility, rationality, progress and individualism, which hinge on the ideal of performativity (Lyotard, 1984). These alignments stabilize social entrepreneurship as a societal actor that confirms the modernist, Western notion of order and control, while contributing to the impression that social change can be achieved without causing debate, tensions or social disharmony. As a consequence, social entrepreneurship is inscribed in an account that engenders a depoliticization of social change.

Second, Dey and Steyaert point at another genre of narrative, namely the counter-narrative which tempers the earlier optimist genre, and tries to counter the monological aspect of current narrations of social entrepreneurship. For instance, in an earlier illustration, we pointed out that the analysis of Dempsey and Sanders (2010) provides an alternative reading of the dominant story that social entrepreneurs try to convey in their autobiographies. Their counter-narrative emphasizes the precarious financial, social, and health situation of these entrepreneurs:

> Even as popular US-based representations of social entrepreneurship offer a compelling vision of meaningful work, they celebrate a problematic account of work/life balance centred on extreme self-sacrifice and the privileging of organizational commitment at the expense of health, family and other aspects of social reproduction. By drawing upon the notion of the calling, these portrayals help naturalize and further justify a reliance on unpaid labour and the payment of survival wages within the nonprofit sector. (p. 3)

As another illustration of a counter-narrative, we can refer to Dey and Steyaert (2010) who deconstruct the usual ways in which the practice of microfinance is represented as an unproblematic solution to development aid. Contrary to the immaculate representation of microcredit in (Western) public discourse, they point at other narrations which indicate how microcredit programs (whether run by profit or non-profit organisations or cooperatives) have had detrimental effects. For instance, microcredit has destroyed some established social relations by replacing traditional modes of exchange and bonds of solidarity with more formalized and conditional exchange relations. Most alarmingly, there are reports of people, mainly women, who have turned to suicide because they could not repay their loans (Padmanabhan, 2001).

As a third genre of narration, Steyaert and Dey return to 'the little narrative [which] remains the quintessential form of imaginative invention' (Lyotard, 1984, p. 64). Their proposal to invest in the study of little narratives makes the circle round as it encourages researchers to invest in, for instance, life stories of less famous entrepreneurs or narrative ethnographies of social entrepreneurial projects.

PhD student (email reply to Supervisor): Thanks for your elaborate feedback and reflections on narrative analysis! Your last point, on the importance of 'little narratives' for the study of social entrepreneurship, especially caught my attention as it links quite nicely to what I am trying to do with my research project. I very much agree that we need to go beyond the grand narrative of harmonious social change when investigating the phenomenon of social entrepreneurship and should instead engage in 'probing discussions of the relational paradoxes, complexities and dilemmas that come to the fore in the pragmatic context of everyday practice and the political and ethical consequences thereof', as you argue in your recent publication (Dey and Steyaert, 2010). In this sense, I will try to trace the multiplicity of little narratives that contest neXus's dominant story of being the world's fastest-growing social entrepreneurship movement and show how this opens up a much-needed space for the re-negotiation of the movement's narrative trajectory – as it appears to have become trapped in its own success story. My only concern is how I can make all of this visible when writing up my dissertation, especially as I have become an active force in the shaping of this movement. Do you have any suggestions?

3.7 WRITING AND CHANGING STORIES

3.7.1 Enacting the Multiple

Latour (2005) makes a strong case that, above all, 'good sociology has to be well written; if not, the social doesn't appear through it' (p. 124). So how can we achieve that? How can we translate our narrative data into an account that goes beyond being 'just a story' (ibid., p. 127). Latour is quite explicit: 'A good ANT [actor network theory] account is a narrative or a description or a proposition where all the actors do something and don't just sit there' (ibid., p. 128). That is, we need to treat the actors in our story as active mediators and not just as passive intermediaries who happen to be in there, in order to render the movement of the social visible, so that 'each of the points in the text may become a bifurcation, an event, or the origin of a new translation' (ibid., p. 128). This means that instead of constructing a common plot where the social entrepreneur becomes the sole hero in his journey towards effectuating positive change, we should focus on making the other actors and the corresponding complexities visible, and thus take seriously the social in social entrepreneurship. Only then will we manage to go beyond writing the same old story of the lone hero figure that evokes the grand narrative of harmonious social change, a story that has little to offer but a comforting account of how the world is being saved by a new (male) messiah (Dey and Steyaert, 2010).

So how can we do that? How can we (re)present, or rather enact, the multiple, the entangled and the ambivalent in our stories, as we acknowledge that 'much of the world is vague, diffuse or unspecific, slippery, emotional, ephemeral, elusive or indistinct, changes like a kaleidoscope, or doesn't really have much of a pattern at all' (Law, 2004, p. 2)? Law contends that 'method always works not simply by detecting but also by amplifying a reality' (p. 116). That is, when we listen carefully to what our data are telling us, when we tune out the noise of the louder voices and instead seek to detect the hidden patterns that resonate, we amplify them and thus help bring them to the forefront of our reality while silencing others. So we have to find ways that surface the hidden complexities of our stories while leaving space for multiple readings to materialize. This can be achieved through non-linear narration (as exemplified in this text), by letting different actors speak for themselves, or by drawing upon other forms than written texts (such as pictures, videos and so on) to recreate the most compelling account our story can offer.

While doing so, we must not forget that we as researchers are actors too, and therefore need to render our involvement visible when writing up our stories. Essers (2009), for instance, skillfully illustrates how she actively co-produced the life stories of the female entrepreneurs of Moroccan and Turkish origin that she investigated; she reminds us that 'researchers are not freed from taking responsibility for the power that is played out in the making and writing of narratives' (p. 176). We therefore need to explicate the process around which the narrative emerges and make visible how our own story feeds into it, taking into account the affective entanglements that go beyond words. This reflexive capability becomes even more important when we deliberately intervene in the course of the stories that we investigate.

3.7.2 From Stories of Change to Changing Stories

Social entrepreneurship is usually embedded in and constructed through a 'story of change', an elaborate account of transforming the status quo into something 'better'. When researchers reproduce this story and give it an interpretive twist, they actively intervene in the shaping of the story and may trigger a fundamental shift in the unfolding of the story itself. Intervention then becomes invention. For instance, researchers engaging in critical narrative inquiry often dedicate their work to uncovering the grand narratives that dominate how social reality is constructed, for example by giving voice to the marginalized who have been silenced for the sake of 'harmonious social change' (Dey and Steyaert, 2010). This, in turn, may help destabilize the grand narratives and thus open up the possibility for radical social change. Life stories from the marginalized are particularly powerful in this regard as they may reveal the oppressive forces of unquestioned metanarratives and provide alternative storylines for people to reconfigure their identities:

> Life histories are helpful not merely because they add to the mix of what already exists, but because of their ability to refashion identities. Rather than a conservative goal based on nostalgia for a paradise lost, or a liberal one of enabling more people to take their places at humanity's table, a goal of life history work in a postmodern age is to break the stranglehold of metanarratives that establishes rules of truth, legitimacy, and identity. The work of life history becomes the investigation of the mediating aspects of culture, the interrogation of its grammar, and the decentering of its norms. (Tierney, 2002, p. 546)

Some researchers decide to go one step further, acknowledging the enactive power of research in shaping social reality. The notion of 'enactive research' (Johannisson, 2011) embraces the insight that the social sciences '*participate in*, *reflect upon*, and *enact* the social in a wide range of locations' (Law and Urry, 2004, p. 392), that is, that they are performative and thus far from innocent. Put differently: research methods 'have effects; they make differences; they enact realities; and they can help to bring into being what they also discover' (ibid., p. 393). We therefore need to concern ourselves with the 'ontological politics' that our methods enact and ask ourselves this question: if research produces realities, which worlds do we want to co-create?

The researcher then becomes an active agent in the shaping of social reality and deliberately moves from recounting stories of change to changing the stories themselves. This can be achieved through a form of 'autoethnography' which has been advocated as a valid form of doing research that 'make[s] the researcher's own experience a topic of investigation in its own right' (Ellis and Bochner, 2000, p. 733). However, in order to move beyond the genre of 'confessional tales' and thus avoid the pitfall of getting caught up in a narcissist account of one's own story, Alvesson (2003) proposes the notion of 'self-ethnography' which locates the researcher in their native context but focuses more on what happens around them rather than an elaborate account of their own experience. In either case, personal involvement is seen as a resource rather than a liability as it allows unique access to how social reality is constructed. So we can think of a narrative research methodology where the researcher moves beyond being a 'participant observer' towards becoming an 'observing participant' who immerses themself in the flux of the unfolding storyline(s) and thus takes seriously the notion of enactive research. This can be particularly conducive in the field of social entrepreneurship studies where the complexities, tensions and ambiguities of 'reassembling the social' (Latour, 2005) might be best traced from within the phenomenon itself. But the hyphen between researcher and entrepreneur has to be carefully managed, as the entrepreneurial experience may completely capture the researcher. In the end, then, the researcher may be forced to step out of the flux in order to understand better what happened within.

3.8 WORKING THE HYPHEN

At one point, not too long ago, he was proud to answer every email within a few hours. Now there were 853 emails in his inbox and counting – most of them unanswered. Ever since he became part of the global leadership team to transition neXus into a new organizational model, his daily digest of emails had tripled. People from all over the world were writing him with their opinions on how things should be done differently, how the old needs to die before the new can emerge, why the founder needs to exit immediately, why he should stay, why everyone is frustrated, why we need a revolution now. 'At least I'm getting good data', the PhD student thought, as he carefully documented the most interesting email conversations that were floating around in the network.

At first he had tried to keep a diary but he quickly gave up as he simply didn't have the energy to write down all the experiences he was having. Luckily, his colleague had the brilliant idea of doing a video interview with him every six weeks to document how the narrative of his project was evolving. It already felt like a ritual. They would come together, install the camera, get some coffee, and then switch to English to reduce the time spent translating when transcribing the interviews. He would then narrate the most important events of the preceding weeks: what had moved him, what excited him, and what kept him awake at night. Stories of following his calling, of passionate self-sacrifice, of frustrating Skype calls, of emotionally loaded network gatherings, of censoring communication, of hostile takeover attempts and of systemic burnout. Who would have thought so much politics was involved in social entrepreneurship? Then again, it wasn't so surprising. Reassembling the social is an intrinsically political endeavour after all. It just felt a little odd after all this talk of 'deep democracy', 'co-creation' and a 'radically better world'. But he hadn't given up on believing that it could be done. It had to be. The key question was how. At least that's what he kept telling himself.

Experiencing all the different tensions first hand had one big benefit: it had made him more critical. At first he was worried that immersing himself into the unfolding story of a social entrepreneurship movement would endanger his ability to reflect critically on what was happening. It had certainly captured him – in every sense of the word. But at the same time he grew more and more aware of the various paradoxes that came with the notion of social entrepreneurship and was already looking forward to the time where he could step out of this project to reflect on his experiences and conduct interviews to generate multiple accounts of the story he himself was both witnessing and shaping. After all, he was really quite happy with his double role as researcher-entrepreneur. Working the hyphen of the in-between had opened many avenues for further exploration and offered great material to assemble his dissertation. If only he had the time to write. Someday he would, he was sure. But for now, a different story was waiting to be written: the future of neXus. And he felt called to become a co-author in shaping this story, remembering the promise that resonated so strongly with him: That another world was happening. That history was to be made. An unfolding story yet to be written.

Supervisor: Well done! Your narrative vignettes appear to come together quite nicely. They are still a little bit too focused around your own experience, so it will be interesting to see how you interweave them with the accounts of other actors to make the assembling of neXus visible. But this will be the next step as you reconstruct the narrative trajectory of this social entrepreneurship movement. For now, it is more important that you continue documenting the multiple threads that spin this movement without getting lost in the spinning yourself.

PhD student: What do you mean by that?

Supervisor: Well, narrative trajectories can become quite powerful as they inscribe a certain reality and the people who take part in it. You may see yourself as the author or at least co-author of this story-in-the-making, but think about it: is that really so? Stories often take on a life of their own as they grow into a complex web of heterogeneous actants who move in various directions simultaneously and thus cannot be easily traced. At the same time, the illusion of a single, grand narrative may emerge and keep everyone prisoner – until the cracks along the storyline grow big enough to make space for alternative, little narratives that show a variety of possible realities and thus contest the hegemony of the dominant story. So stay alert; be careful not to become too entangled with the seductive calling of this movement and try to listen to the little voices that may open up a space for the new to emerge – especially as the dominant story appears to falter anyway.

PhD student: I see. Well, it would be interesting to find out what happens if the narrative trajectory falters or even falls apart and thus witness how the movement would reassemble itself. It certainly wouldn't be the end of the story, rather a kind of transition or even a new beginning.

Supervisor: Exactly. That's the beauty of little narratives: they open up to new connections and stories. So, just as we started right in the middle of this unfolding story, we shall stop in the middle and leave the end to the imagination of our readers. A thousand potentialities yet to be dreamed into reality.

3.9 AND THUS IT COULD ~~END~~ BEGIN

A narrative 'must advance to its end whilst simultaneously delaying it, and in lingering, as it were, a narrative occupies a "space"' (Cobley, 2001, p. 12). Most academic texts anticipate their endings by way of rather standardized formats for constructing text. The increasing demands of journal ranking systems and the pressures by publishers for quick-fix handbooks and textbooks might make us less mindful of the rich ways in which we can give form to this space in both writing and publishing, and the associated ethical responsibilities (Rhodes and Brown, 2005). Scholarly writing is concerned with the reflexive and creative engagement with the 'ongoing project of saying the ethical' (Rhodes, 2009, p. 653). Considering the ethical dimension of social entrepreneurship – with its emphasis on enduring social change that favours the weakest and poorest in our societies – we think scholars in social entrepreneurship should not rush to the end but should instead pause and linger. They can then critically reflect upon and experiment with how they occupy and position themselves in the spaces of academic 'freedom'. This is also why we have disrupted the habitual script of chapter-writing and made visible some of the ongoing choices and possibilities available as we engaged in co-authoring this chapter.

In the narrative format we adopted and the lingering we hope it brought along for readers, we have discussed the possibilities and problems with applying narrative approaches during the generation, analysis and writing up of empirical research on social entrepreneurship. While there is a solid repertoire of narrative analyses within entrepreneurship studies in the form of edited books (Hjorth and Steyaert, 2004), special issues (Gartner, 2007), prominent journals (Martens et al., 2007) and new journal experiments – the new journal *Enter* (*Entrepreneurial Narrative Theory Ethnomethodology and Reflexivity*) (Gartner, 2010b) comes to mind – it is fair to say that narrative research can still be considered a 'new' path within the mainstream of entrepreneurship studies (Gartner, 2010a), and at most a fragile but promising opening for studies of social entrepreneurship.

However, we have argued that there are three particularly valuable reasons to engage with and invest extensively in narrative approaches in the context of social entrepreneurship: namely, its possibilities to engage with processuality, sociality and criticality. First, narrative studies move beyond the tendency to represent social enterprises, social entrepreneurial projects and social business as 'fait accompli stories': success stories where the complexity and ongoing open-endedness of an entrepreneurial endeavour becomes a black box rather than being made visible and explained. Narrative approaches bring forward an extensive conceptual vocabulary to analyze processes of social entrepreneuring and the ways we create chronology and coherence, yet not closure (Steyaert, 2007b). Narrative analysis thus allows us to detect and understand the rich variety of media, genres and styles through which entrepreneurial narratives are scripted and distributed.

Second, narrative is a social practice that steers us away from individualistic analyses and interpretations and gives us chances to map how the social is reassembled in narrative trajectories. Narratives are social practices, as the storytelling is performed in social interaction. When we tell stories, we do not follow fixed structures; instead we form 'dynamic and evolving responses to recurring rhetorical situations, as resources more or less strategically and agentively drawn upon, negotiated and reconstructed anew in local contexts' (De Fina and Georgakopoulou, 2008, p. 383). In reconstructing the narrative of neXus, for instance, we found various transitional moments where the multiple small stories were confronted with the dominant story that had been told so far and that, as a consequence, came under pressure and was renegotiated.

Finally, narrative analysis responds to the growing call for a critical understanding of entrepreneurship studies, and social entrepreneurship in particular. For example, if 'the field of inquiry is to flourish, it needs to be approached from a more critical perspective, instead of merely accepting normative, or even strongly ideologically driven, standpoints dominant in so many studies' (Blackburn and Kovalainen, 2009, pp. 127–148).

Entrepreneurship is currently rewritten out of the economic growth paradigm (Steyaert and Katz, 2004) into one of emancipation (Rindova et al., 2009) and social change (Calás et al., 2009); we believe that narrative studies of social entrepreneurship can play a crucial role in paving the roads towards (more) complexity, sociality and criticality.

In this sense, this rather abrupt ending will hopefully trigger the multiplication of narrative research projects in the still nascent field of social entrepreneurship studies. After all, there are many stories yet to be told – and in their multiplicity, they may actually change the world.

REFERENCES

Alvesson, M. (2003). Methodology for close up studies: struggling with closeness and closure. *Higher Education* **46**(2), 167–193.

Appadurai, A. (1996). *Modernity at Large: Cultural Dimensions of Globalization*. Minneapolis, MN: University of Minnesota Press.

Blackburn, R. and A. Kovalainen (2009). Researching small firms and entrepreneurship: past, present and future. *International Journal of Management Reviews* **11**(2), 127–148.

Boddice, R. (2009). Forgotten antecedents: entrepreneurship, ideology and history. In R. Ziegler (ed.), *An Introduction to Social Entrepreneurship: Voices, Preconditions, Contexts*. Cheltenham, UK and Northampton, MA, USA: Edward Elgar, pp. 133–152.

Boje, D.M. (1991). The storytelling organization: a study of story performance in an office-supply firm. *Administrative Science Quarterly* **36**(1), 106–126.

Boje, D.M. (2008a). *Storytelling Organizations*. London: SAGE.

Boje, D.M. (2008b). Spin. In D. Barry and H. Hansen (eds), *The SAGE Handbook of New Approaches in Management and Organization*, London: SAGE, pp. 203–212.

Boland, R.J. and R.V. Tenkasi (1995). Perspective making and perspective taking in communities of knowing. *Organization Science* **6**(3), 350–372.

Bornstein, D. (2007). *How to Change the World: Social Entrepreneurs and the Power of New Ideas*. Oxford: Oxford University Press.

Brown, A.D. (2006). A narrative approach to collective identities. *Journal of Management Studies* **43**(4), 731–753.

Bruner, J.S. (1990). *Acts of Meaning*. Cambridge, MA: Harvard University Press.

Bruner, J.S. (1991). Self-making and world-making. *Journal of Aesthetic Education* **25** (1), 67–78.

Burke, P. (1980). The self: measurement requirements from a symbolic interactionist perspective. *Social Psychology Quarterly* **43**(1), 18–29.

Calás, M.B., L. Smircich and K.A. Bourne (2009). Extending the boundaries: reframing 'entrepreneurship as social change' through feminist perspectives. *Academy of Management Review* **34**(3), 552–569.

Chase, S.E. (2005). Narrative inquiry: multiple lenses, approaches, voices. In N.K. Denzin and Y.S. Lincoln (eds), *The SAGE Handbook of Qualitative Research*. London: Sage, pp. 651–679.

Cho, A.H. (2006). Politics, values, and social entrepreneurship: a critical appraisal. In A. Nicholls (ed.), *Social Entrepreneurship*. New York: Palgrave Macmillan, pp. 34–56.

Cobley, P. (2001). *Narrative*. London: Routledge.

Czarniawska-Joerges, B. (2004a). *Narratives in Social Science Research*. London: SAGE.

Czarniawska-Joerges, B. (2004b). Narratives of individual and organizational identities. In M.J. Hatch and M. Schultz (eds), *Organizational Identity: A Reader*. Oxford: Oxford University Press, pp. 407–435.

De Fina, A. and A. Georgakopoulou (2008). Analysing narratives as practices. *Qualitative Research* **8**(3), 379–387.
Dees, J.G., J. Emerson and P. Economy (2001). *Enterprising Nonprofits: A Toolkit for Social Entrepreneurs*. New York: John Wiley & Sons.
Dempsey, S.E. and M.L. Sanders (2010). Meaningful work? Nonprofit marketization and work/life imbalance in popular autobiographies of social entrepreneurship. *Organization* **17**(4), 437–459.
Dey, P. and C. Steyaert (2010). The politics of narrating social entrepreneurship. *Journal of Enterprising Communities: People and Places in the Global Economy* **4**(1), 85–108.
Down, S. (2006). *Narratives of Enterprise: Crafting Entrepreneurial Self-Identity in a Small Firm*. Cheltenham, UK and Northampton, MA, USA: Edward Elgar.
Ellis, C. and A.P. Bochner (2000). Autoethnography, personal narrative, reflexivity: researcher as subject. In N. Denzin and Y. Lincoln (eds), *The Handbook of Qualitative Research*, 2nd edn, Thousand Oaks, CA: Sage, pp. 733–768.
Essers, C. (2009). Reflections on the narrative approach: dilemmas of power, emotions, and social location while constructing life-stories. *Organization* **16**(2), 163–181.
Gabriel, Y. (2000). *Storytelling in Organizations: Facts, Fictions, and Fantasies*. Oxford: Oxford University Press.
Gartner, W.B. (2007). Is there an elephant in entrepreneurship? Blind assumptions in theory development. *Entrepreneurship Theory and Practice* **25**(4), 27–39.
Gartner, W.B. (2010a). A new path to the waterfall: a narrative on a use of entrepreneurial narrative. *International Small Business Journal* **28**(1), 6–19.
Gartner, W.B. (ed.) (2010b). An issue about The Republic of Tea. Enter, **1**, 1–210.
Geertz, C. (1983). *Local Knowledge: Further Essays in Interpretive Anthropology*. New York: Basic Books.
Goddard, H. (1965). *The Meaning of Shakespeare*. Chicago, IL: University of Chicago Press.
Gubrium, J.F. and J.A. Holstein (2009). *Analyzing Narrative Reality*. London: Sage.
Herman, D. (2007). *The Cambridge Companion to Narrative*. Cambridge: Cambridge University Press.
Hjorth, D. and C. Steyaert (2004). *Narrative and Discursive Approaches in Entrepreneurship*. Cheltenham, UK and Northampton, MA, USA: Edward Elgar.
Jameson, F. (1981). *The Political Unconscious: Narrative as a Socially Symbolic Act*. Ithaca, NY: Cornell University Press.
Johannisson, B. (2011). Towards a practice theory of entrepreneuring. *Small Business Economics* **35**(2), 135–150.
Johansson, A.W. (2004). Narrating the entrepreneur. *International Small Business Journal* **22**(3), 273–293.
Jones, R., J. Latham and M. Betta (2008). Narrative construction of the social entrepreneurial identity. *International Journal of Entrepreneurial Behaviour and Research* **14**(5), 330–345.
Latour, B. (2005). *Reassembling the Social: An Introduction to Actor-Network-Theory*. New York: Oxford University Press.
Law, J. (2004). *After Method: Mess in Social Science Research*. New York: Routledge.
Law, J. and J. Urry (2004). Enacting the social. *Economy and Society* **33**(3), 390–419.
Lindgren, M. and J. Packendorff (2006). Entrepreneurship as boundary work: deviating from and belonging to community. In C. Steyaert and D. Hjorth (eds), *Entrepreneurship as Social Change: A Third Movements in Entrepreneurship Book*. Cheltenham, UK and Northampton, MA, USA: Edward Elgar Publishing, pp. 210–230.
Lyotard, J.F. (1984). *The Postmodern Condition: A Report on Knowledge*. Minneapolis, MN: University of Minnesota Press.
Lyotard, J.F. (1992). Answer to the question, what is the postmodern? *The Postmodern Explained*. Minneapolis, MN: University of Minnesota Press, pp. 1–16.
Lyotard, J.F. (1993). *Libidinal Economy*. London: Athlone.
Martens, M.L., J.E. Jennings and P.D. Jennings (2007). Do the stories they tell get them the

money they need? The role of entrepreneurial narratives in resource acquisition. *Academy of Management Journal* **50**(5), 1107–1132.
McHale, B. (2005). Ghosts and monsters: on the (im)possibility of narrating the history of narrative theory. In J. Phelan and P.J. Rabinowitz (eds), *A Companion to Narrative Theory*. Oxford: Blackwell Publishing, pp. 60–72.
Nicholls, A. (2008). *Social Entrepreneurship: New Models of Sustainable Social Change*. Oxford: Oxford University Press.
Nicholls, A. and A.H. Cho (2008). Social entrepreneurship: the structuration of a field. In A. Nicholls (Ed.), *Social Entrepreneurship: New Models of Sustainable Social Change*. Oxford: Oxford University Press, pp. 99–118.
O'Connor, E. (2004). Storytelling to be real: narrative, legitimacy building, and venturing. In D. Hjorth and C. Steyaert (eds), *Narrative and Discursive Approaches in Entrepreneurship* Cheltenham, UK and Northampton, MA, USA: Edward Elgar, pp. 105–124.
Padmanabhan, K.P. (2001). Poverty, microcredit, and Mahatma Gandhi: lessons for donors. *International Social Science Journal* **53**(169), 489–499.
Phelan, J. (2005). Narrative judgments and the rhetorical theory of narrative: Ian McEwan's Atonement. In J. Phelan and P.J. Rabinowitz (eds), *A Companion to Narrative Theory*. Oxford: Blackwell Publishing, pp. 322–336.
Phelan, J. and Rabinowitz, P.J. (2005). *A Companion to Narrative Theory*. Oxford: Blackwell Publishing.
Polletta, F. (1998). Contending stories: narrative in social movements. *Qualitative Sociology* **21**(4), 419–446.
Porter, J.E. (1986). Intertextuality and the discourse community. *Rhetoric Review* **5**(1), 34–47.
Prasad, P. (2005). *Crafting Qualitative Research: Working in the Postpositivist Traditions*. Armonk: ME Sharpe.
Rhodes, C. (2009). After reflexivity: ethics, freedom and the writing of organization studies. *Organization Studies* **30**(6), 653–672.
Rhodes, C. and A. Brown (2005). Writing responsibly: narrative fiction and organization studies. *Organization* **12**(4), 467–491.
Rindova, V., D. Barry and D. Ketchen (2009). Entrepreneuring as emancipation. *Academy of Management Review* **34**(3), 477–491.
Somers, M.R. (1994). The narrative constitution of identity: a relational and network approach. *Theory and Society* **23**(5), 605–649.
Spinosa, C., F. Flores and H.L. Dreyfus (1997). *Disclosing New Worlds: Entrepreneurship, Democratic Action, and the Cultivation of Solidarity*. Cambridge, MA: MIT Press.
Steyaert, C. (2007a). 'Entrepreneuring' as a conceptual attractor? A review of process theories in 20 years of entrepreneurship studies. *Entrepreneurship and Regional Development* **19**, 453–477.
Steyaert, C. (2007b). Of course that is not the whole (toy) story: entrepreneurship and the cat's cradle. *Journal of Business Venturing* **22**(5), 733–751.
Steyaert, C. and R. Bouwen (1997). Telling stories of entrepreneurship. In R. Donckels and A. Miettinen (eds), *Entrepreneurship and SME Research: On Its Way to the Next Millennium*. Aldershot: Ashgate, pp. 47–62.
Steyaert, C. and D. Hjorth (2006). *Entrepreneurship as social change*. Cheltenham, UK and Northampton, MA, USA: Edward Elgar.
Steyaert, C. and J. Katz (2004). Reclaiming the space of entrepreneurship in society: Geographical, discursive and social dimensions. *Entrepreneurship and Regional Development* **16**(3), 179–196.
Steyaert, C., A. Ostendorp and C. Gaibrois (2011). Multilingual organizations as 'linguascapes': negotiating the position of English through discursive practices. *Journal of World Business* **46**(3).
Suchman, M.C. (1995). Managing legitimacy: strategic and institutional approaches. *Academy of Management Review* **20**(3), 571–610.
Thisted, L.N. and C. Steyeart (2006). Voicing differences and becoming other: life stories of immigrants in an organizational context. *Advances in Organization Studies* **16**, 152.

Tierney, W.G. (2002). Get real: representing reality. *Qualitative Studies in Education* **15**, 385–398.
Tsoukas, H. and R. Chia (2002). On organizational becoming: rethinking organizational change. *Organization Science* **13**(5), 567–582.
White, J.B. (1984). *When Words Lose their Meaning: Constitutions and Reconstitutions of Language, Character, and Community*. Chicago, IL: University of Chicago Press.
Widdershoven, G. (1993). The story of life. *The Narrative Study of Lives* **1**, 1–20.

4 Participating in research

*Mathew Tasker, Linda Westberg and Richard G. Seymour**

Academics are increasingly choosing research environments that are rich in complexity and that provide an opportunity for learning. Furthermore, academics are realising that in some of these environments their active participation rather than passive observation would be beneficial. This chapter describes one such research setting, the project Mushuk Muyu.

The Mushuk Muyu (meaning 'new seed') project was designed to recuperate the local indigenous Kichwa language and culture in the Ecuadorian Andes. The project was initially developed over the course of a 14-month period in the Ecuadorian Northern Andean area of Cayambe. A team of local teachers and community members worked with volunteers (including two authors of this chapter) to create a range of products. These outputs include 67 experimental multimedia classes for bilingual local schools, and four textbooks that were accepted for publication on a national scale by the Ministerio de Educación del Ecuador (MEE) and the Dirección Nacional de Educación Intercultural Bilingüe del Ecuador (DINEIB). Though the project continues to grow and develop in new and innovative ways, this chapter focuses on the initial 14-month period of activity.

This chapter is motivated and initiated by the engaged practice of two of the authors, who developed and applied action research (AR) methods to understand the processes building the Mushuk Muyu social entrepreneurship project. AR is an important approach appropriate for tackling the complexity of community-based initiatives and ventures. It has only rarely been applied in the context of social entrepreneurship, even though the combination of research and participator-led action promises not only to generate new knowledge, but also to solve real problems.

In undertaking this project, we have concurrently developed and applied a theoretical framework, the action research cycle (ARC), which is proposed to consist of five episodes and a dynamic of project ebb and flow. This organising framework is proposed as a means of supporting, without limiting, the action researcher. Specific insights regarding the individual episodes of the ARC are then elaborated upon with reference to the project. The chapter concludes with the strengths and weaknesses of AR in the context of social entrepreneurship, with the conclusion that the framework provides an appropriate scaffold to allow a researcher to manage for flexibility, complexity and recoverability of an action research project in the context of social entrepreneurship.

4.1 CATALYSTS FOR THEORY DEVELOPMENT

Undertaking research while at the same time dealing with the difficulties associated with a complex social entrepreneurship project proved to be a catalyst to theory development.

4.1.1 The Mushuk Muyu Project

The Mushuk Muyu project was set in a very complex social environment:[1] it involved multiple participants (community leaders, teachers from four community schools, a well-respected Kichwa linguist who ran a local non-governmental organisation (NGO), students from two community schools, parents from three communities, one local indigenous activist, various indigenous individuals working with the Kichwa culture in Quito, three local NGOs, and DINEIB), multiple activities (planning, brainstorming, writing, negotiating, recording, photographing, compiling and presenting the material), and multiple locations (schools, communal buildings, private residences in three different communities in Cayambe, and the offices of NGOs, DIPEIB-P[2] and DINEIB in Cayambe and Quito).

Mushuk Muyu initially developed workshops that taught Kichwa to adults and children outside the classroom, as well as multimedia publications and lessons for use in schools as part of Las Unidades Educativas del Milenio (UEM) initiative[3] and publication on the DINEIB website.[4] The project has continued to grow: multimedia classes are now used to teach Kichwa to adults through a local NGO, Centro de Investigaciones Interculturales y Desarrollo Ecológico Cultural Guanchuro, with revenue raised to be shared with teachers involved in the project. Additionally, Microsoft Ecuador is in discussions with local members to see how they can utilise the multimedia material in their One Laptop per Child (OLPC) initiative.

Clear impacts and benefits were noted for a number of stakeholders. Students enjoyed increased awareness of, and interest in, their historical and cultural roots. Teachers were able to exercise greater agency over issues that had previously been considered beyond their capabilities, developing pedagogical repertoires to enhance Kichwa teaching and learning. Teachers also developed the confidence to approach and engage with government representatives. Outside the classroom, local people found the project materials far more accessible and engaging than traditional educational material. The creation of Kichwa workshops outside the classroom also demonstrated the increased interest and pride that families had for their local culture and language, which also led to increased self-confidence in other social and political arenas. Finally, the project was awarded the prize of most innovative educational material in the Ecuadorian national competition El Segundo Concurso Nacional Docentes Innovadores.[5]

We consider Mushuk Muyu to be an example of social entrepreneurship as it sought to generate change (by creating social and cultural value) through the development and sale of its new language 'products'. As such, the project provided an immensely complex purpose and setting that threatened to overwhelm stakeholders.

4.1.2 Social Entrepreneurship as a Challenging Research Setting

There are multiple understandings of 'the social' in social entrepreneurship: many researchers consider the creation of social value as core to the concept (see for example Austin et al., 2006; Nicholls, 2006; Perrini and Vurro, 2006; Weerawardena and Mort, 2006; Jones et al., 2008). Other scholars allude to 'the social' in social mission (Nicholls, 2006), social objectives (Henry, 2007; Tapsell and Woods, 2008), social goals (Rhodes and Donnelly-Cox, 2008), social aims (Haugh, 2006), social purpose (Pearce, 2003) and social transformation. Unfortunately, these 'socials' are typically treated either as an obvious quality that does not require explanation, or as an exogenous factor (Cho, 2006).

For this chapter, we build on the Organisation for Economic Co-operation and Development (OECD) Entrepreneurship Indicators Project definitions (Ahmed and Seymour, 2008), with pragmatic definitions of the concepts as follows:

> Social Entrepreneurs are those persons (key stakeholders) who seek to generate change (creating social, cultural or natural value), through the creation or expansion of economic activity, by identifying and exploiting new products, processes or markets.
>
> Socially Entrepreneurial Activity is the enterprising human action in pursuit of the generation of change (creating social, cultural or natural value), through the creation or expansion of economic activity, by identifying and exploiting new products, processes or markets.
>
> Social Entrepreneurship is the phenomena associated with socially entrepreneurial activity.

These definitions indicate why AR can be a valuable approach to research in the context of social entrepreneurship: First, the multiple stakeholders and their multiple perspectives, objectives and opinions will challenge a researcher. Second, in contrast to the typical commercial entrepreneurial project which can be evaluated by a profit and loss statement or balance sheet, the success of a social entrepreneurial initiative is difficult to measure and control (the generated value can be economic, social, cultural or natural). The numerous participants, dialogical processes and community contexts further raise the complexity of such value recognitions. Third, social entrepreneurship projects are not simple activism or lobbying, but include a commercial aspect of activity. Complex social exchanges, gifts and other transactions must coexist with the pecuniary flows of sales, donations and grants. Finally, the projects include the 'novel', whether that be introducing new products, entering new markets or changing organisations' activities. Social entrepreneurs are change-makers, taking a different approach to the established players (whether they be NGOs, government agencies or commercial organisations).

'Traditional' or 'established' research methods and methodologies will not fit well with these complexities and intersubjectivities. Action research was initially proposed as an appropriate approach to study and activate the field of social entrepreneurship. Developing a framework for the perspective quickly became a focus of activity.

4.2 THE PERSPECTIVE OF ACTION RESEARCH

Researchers have for a long time recognised that traditional positivistic sciences provide inadequate tools for the resolution of critical social problems (Lewin, 1946/1988; Berkowitz and Donnerstein, 1982) and that the artificial dichotomies of theory versus practice, and researcher versus researched (Borda, 2006) do not typically result in the systematic development of practical knowing. The term 'action research' (AR) is widely attributed to Kurt Lewin (1946/1988). Influenced by the social philosopher Moreno and driven by the concern that traditional positivistic sciences were proving inadequate in the resolution of critical social problems (Susman and Evered, 1978), Lewin developed his conception of research leading to social action. AR has grown into a science of praxeology, which brings together what Dewey (1930) argued was an artificial dichotomy of theory and practice, through a participatory democratic process that is concerned with systematic development of practical knowing.

4.2.1 Grounding Researchers and Subjects

Practitioners of AR have increasingly recognised the importance of grounding both researcher and subject in a participative and democratic relationship, based on discourse that is open, reciprocal and reflexive (Bradbury and Reason, 2006). AR can be seen as a science of experiential qualities, moving away from the inadequate reductionism of an empirical-positivistic worldview. The combination of research, action, participation and self-reflection (Webb, 1996; Zuber-Skerritt, 1996) generates new forms of knowledge that help to instigate change, both to solve real problems and to generate democratic changes in social processes (Greenwood and Levin, 2007).

Unlike the sterile conditions of laboratory-controlled experiments, AR is dealing with social environments that are governed by complex relationships in which the generation of knowledge is always intersubjective and socialised (Schutz, 1962). For researchers, this 'reality' is a messy place to work, leading to debate within the field as to whether a framework is appropriate and practical for directing processes and their associated methods (Ebbutt, 1985; Kemmis, 1988; Elliott, 1991; Hopkins, 1993; Race, 1993). AR does, however, promise rich insights for the complex settings associated with social entrepreneurship.

4.2.2 Undertaking AR in the Context of Social Entrepreneurship

There are a number of issues that confront a researcher undertaking AR in the context of social entrepreneurship: flexibility, complexity and recoverability. First, flexibility is required because of social entrepreneurship's and AR's emphasis on participation and the cogeneration of knowledge through collaborative communicative processes (Greenwood and Levin, 2007). AR is by its nature unpredictable, and its processes must remain flexible and adaptable in order to function effectively in different social settings. For this reason, Kemmis and McTaggart's (1988) earlier work has been criticised for the over-representation of AR as a series of fixed and predictable steps. For example, Hopkins (1993) warns of the dangers of representing in a prespecified way what are essentially intended to be free and open courses of action. However, Elliott's (1991) argument for a more complex approach that engages the dynamic, unfolding and mutually reinforcing processes of AR is in danger of what Ebbutt (1985) highlighted were unduly complex frameworks leading to mystification, rather than clarification. A balance must therefore be struck between the need for flexibility and the need for a workable framework.

Second, the action researcher is confronted by a vast (overwhelming) array of methods, compounded by the complexity of the phenomenon of social entrepreneurship. AR must be multidisciplinary, multimethod, contextual and holistic, in order to 'respect the multidimensionality and complexity of the problems people face in everyday life' (Greenwood and Levin, 2007, p. 53). In this pluralistic landscape of AR, there are inevitably a vast number of methods that are available to any researcher. Researchers must maintain flexibility and adaptability when choosing and utilising methods, as it will become more evident which are effective and which provide few results over the course of the project. It is important to utilise quantitative, qualitative and mixed methods for data collection and analysis throughout the entire duration of the project. By utilising a variety of different methods, a framework should give the opportunity to gain a deeper understanding of the subjects involved in the project and will strengthen the validity of the project's findings (Tacchi et al., 2003). No single method should be used exclusively or independently, as individual methods will not provide an accurate enough picture of a particular social context. Instead, they need to be chosen and combined in a contextually sensitive manner to ensure that a wide range of information is obtained, and that an accurate portrayal of a particular social context, its problems, and particular solutions, can be made.

Third, action researchers exploring social entrepreneurship must seek to ensure recoverability to enable the research processes to be replicated by interested outsiders (Checkland and Holwell, 1998). The underlying concepts, methodological processes and assumptions must be made clear so that the procedures undertaken are made explicit and the AR process as a whole is transparent. Traditional scientific criteria emphasising replicability and generalisability are not applicable or a useful gauge of the environment that AR processes take place in (Burns, 2005). Knowledge derived from AR processes is contextually dependent and internally valid, and while it may hold utility in other social contexts, this knowledge does not hold true for all social contexts (Cook and Campbell, 1976; Berkowitz and Donnerstein, 1982). A process allowing recoverability to be built into the methodology will offer greater opportunities for learning and insight into the context of social entrepreneurship.

4.3 ACTION RESEARCH CYCLE (ARC) AS AN ORGANISING FRAMEWORK

Recognising the complexity of the task and to address the above, we worked to develop a framework: the action research cycle (ARC). This framework incorporates a hybrid methodology of 'loose' and 'tight' designs, the merits of which have been extensively illustrated by Miles and Huberman (1994). As can be seen from Figure 4.1, there are two important components of this framework: the five episodes of the cycle, and the project dynamics of ebb and flow.

4.3.1 Action Research Cycle

The ARC is based on a broad stream of literature (Schön, 1983, 1991; Grundy, 1988; Taba and Noel, 1988; Race, 1993; Hall, 1996; McNiff et al., 1997; Punch, 1999; Cherry, 2002; Tacchi et al., 2003; Kemmis and McTaggart, 2005; Reason and Bradbury, 2006; Greenwood and Levin, 2007).

Episodes of the cycle

We have identified five key episodes of an AR project that can guide a researcher and participants of an action research project:

- Problem arena – initiate discussion and encourage communication of the issue confronting the participants in the communicative arena.
- Fundamental themes – organise the mass of information generated in the problem arena into themes, see the emerging relationship between problem(s) and actions.
- Strategic action planning – start shaping strategies and creating an action plan to address the fundamental themes that have been brought to the forefront in previous discussions.
- Action – actively implement strategies in order to transform the project from a set of ideas and themes into a functioning entity.
- Reflection-on-action – review the way the project was carried out; the results and consequences of the action taken; the projected vision achievement(s); and the types, quality and sustainability of value produced.

Each of these five episodes of the ARC includes communicative arenas (CAs) consisting of four key stakeholders: the researcher(s) and/or social entrepreneur(s); influential community members; the wider community members and groups; and interested external members and external institutions (such as universities, government departments, NGOs, and so on). Each of these come together and work through the many possibilities open to them (see Figure 4.2).

The CA highlights that in many AR projects there are active participants comprising different groups not necessarily from the community

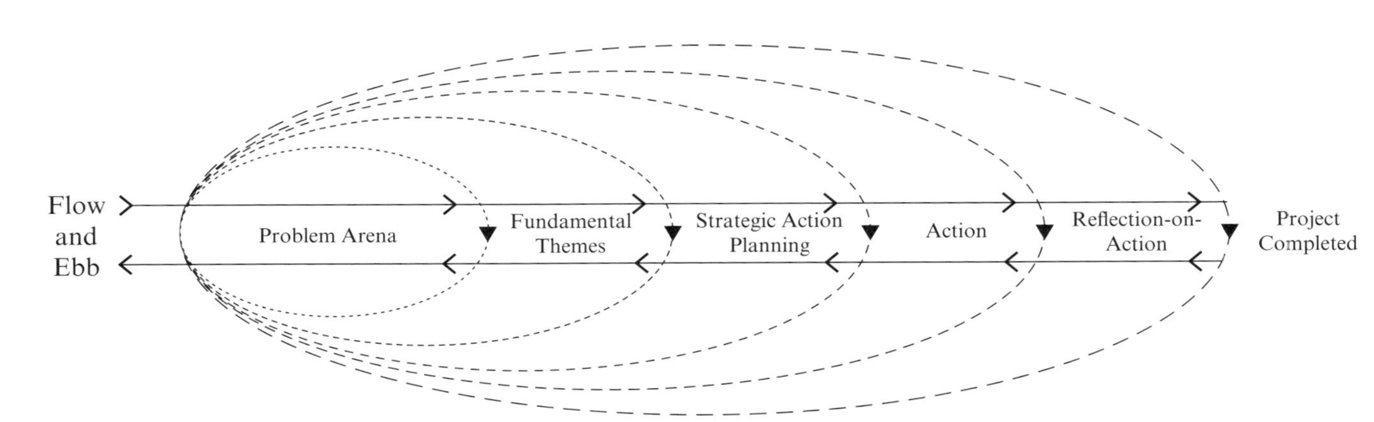

Figure 4.1 Action research cycle (ARC), and project ebb and flow

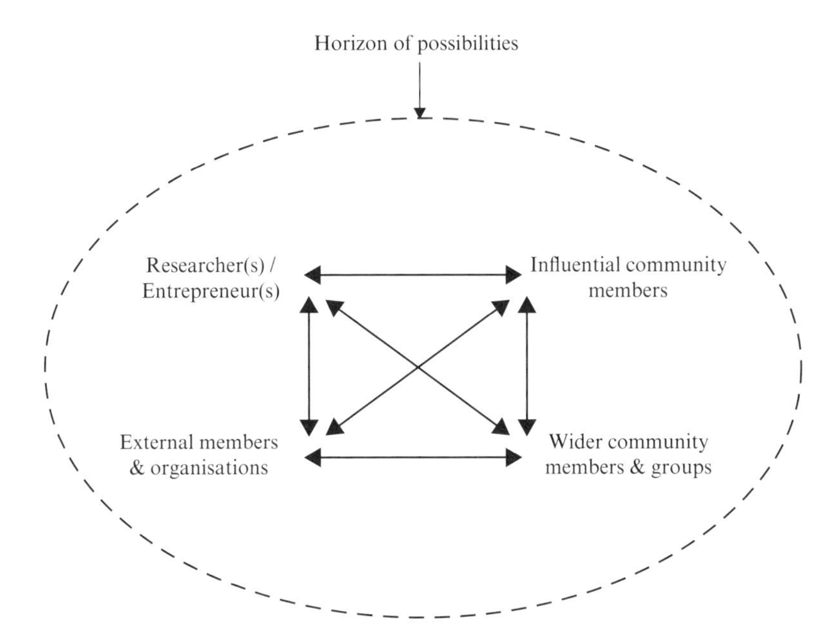

Figure 4.2 Communicative arena of the five episodes of the ARC

or set of communities in which the project is taking place. We avoid using the concept of 'community' as a homogenous container of a discrete cultural unit, but instead acknowledge the embeddedness of different groups in any 'community'. Participants will hold varying degrees of power and influence, and will bring differing perspectives, beliefs, values and knowledge to any project. An important objective of AR is, therefore, to foster open, collaborative and egalitarian communication between these participants (Ludema et al., 2006). This democratic co-generation of knowledge is an underlying feature of AR, and is concerned with providing opportunities for all participants to contribute and actively influence their social and intellectual reconstruction (Kemmis, 1988; Gustavsen, 2006).

The democratic process highlights the need for the cogeneration of knowledge and information through collaborative communication arenas, where all participants' contributions are taken seriously (Winter, 1996; Greenwood and Levin, 2003, 2007; Gustavsen, 2006). Rather than seeing the researcher's professional knowledge as superior to local knowledge, AR highlights that it is instead complementary, as 'local knowledge, historical consciousness and everyday experience of the insiders complements the outsider's skills in facilitating learning processes, technical skills in research procedures and comparative and historical knowledge of the subject under investigation' (Greenwood and Levin, 2007, p. 64).

It should also be noted that the channels of discourse between participants and groups in the communicative arena are artificial constructions, created by the researchers in order to facilitate the project. This is important, as it highlights that a researcher is never able to examine a social sphere in its 'natural' context (his or her presence and the creation of the project inevitably changes the context of the participants' everyday activities). This lends further support to the use of AR practices because they acknowledge the change of environment that a researcher inevitably induces, and thereby attempt to record how the presence and involvement of any researcher brings about certain changes in practices and behaviour.

Furthermore, the ARC episodes, and the CAs of which they are comprised, do not refer to a specific point in time or space where all participants or community members come together to converse and ultimately move forward. This concept, while it would be ideal for AR, is highly unrealistic, as it fails to take into account the functioning of most communities (in which people have differing occupations, schedules, priorities, availabilities and resources). This is made even more difficult when external members and institutions are also involved. These episodes, therefore, represent geographies and time that transform with people's coming and goings. The researcher must be sensitive to the different community contexts and individual members. Each community will have differing degrees of social cohesion, political complexities and cultural diversities, and each member will have different times and places that will allow for participation and engagement.

The dynamics of ebb and flow

A constant dynamic throughout the ARC is the relationship between ebb and flow. Within and between each of these episodes, participants will grapple with their individual as well as the project's ebb and flow.

A sense of flow is usually experienced when perceived challenges are at an optimal level. By optimal, we mean when challenges stretch (but do not break) the abilities and skills of the participants. These challenges encourage the participants to persist at, and return to, an activity because of the promised rewards and the continual development and growth of their own skills (Csikszentmihalyi, 1991). With a sense of flow, participants are completely engaged in the task at hand, mastering challenges and continually developing greater levels of ability and skill. This is an optimal experiential mode that has the potential to drive participants to overcome foreseeable challenges and develop a successful project.

In contrast, periods of ebb may negatively affect and destabilise a project. These moments disturb the collective confidence of the project, impacting the momentum and work ethic. Events can initially have a negative impact on a project team if they feel that the challenge exceeds their capabilities. Momentum and enthusiasm can dissipate, with the whole process becoming stagnant to the point where the project may look as if it would collapse.

Ebbs and flows are symbiotic: they are not simply oscillating forces, but rather they are woven into one continuum (albeit one that is comprised of a complex layering of externally and internally generated interactions) that has the potential to influence perceptions, emotional states, behaviours, and rational constructions. The key is to address these issues and adapt and innovate accordingly. This may result in readdressing a particular episode and in the possibility of the project needing to be modified to take heed of new developments both externally and internally.

Throughout the ARC and relating to this ebb and flow, we identify three interrelated themes that indicate how the project ebbs and flows: (1) reflection-in-action; (2) social value production; and (3) projected vision.

The term 'reflection-in-action' is typically ascribed to Schön (1983, 1991), and has proved to be an elusive category receiving much critical attention (see for example Court, 1988; Van Manen, 1991; Eraut, 1994). It has been criticised for its undertone of instrumental reasoning (Van Manen, 1991) but it is not a deductive or instrumental reasoning process. The substance of reflexivity, such as feelings, emotions and thoughts, are naturally occurring processes which are integral to understanding the many ways participants may perceive the activities related to the project and the people they are dealing with. Therefore, participants should actively attempt to record their reflections in a medium that best suits them, for example through group or individual discussions, interviews, journals, questionnaire-based sample surveys, or an anonymous project log book open to all participants. Reflection-in-action allows for a continual assessment and reappraisal of the project, including its processes, its participants and its environment. If a problem is identified, or if it is discovered that a particular issue was not recognised or sufficiently elaborated on, the researchers must revisit one of the previous episodes until they are satisfied that the issue has been resolved (see Figure 4.1). If an issue is identified in the action episode, researchers may choose to return to the strategic action planning episode to alter the strategies, or alternatively, they could revisit the problem arena episode to redefine the problems the project is attempting to address. The revisiting of any episode depends on the insights gained from the reflection-in-action process, and will always be highly contextual and specific to particular projects.

Social value production is the process by which value is created and captured by, or shared with, the targeted social group. It should be recognised that there are different types as well as different layers of value that may be produced. Rather than narrowing the focus to overarching goals of systemic change, Young (2006) has developed a detailed framework of social value that includes: social added value; empowerment and social change; social innovation; and systemic change. Young (2006) recognises that social values are dynamic and flexible in nature as they are inseparable from the social context producing them, and as such, are contingent on their negotiation and reappraisal. The importance of such a multilayered spectrum is that it recognises and enables different types of social value to be addressed and negotiated in relation to the project. The aim of this method of recording value throughout the course of the ARC is to emphasise that value creation should be seen both as the means and the end of the AR project, ensuring that benefits are gained throughout the different ARC episodes. Even if the AR initiative does not meet its overall 'objective' or achieve its 'social mission', it will have created different forms of value along the way that may have an important impact on a community, and may be useful for shaping future initiatives.

As with social value, the grand themes or 'projected vision' that may be envisioned by the community and researchers are not static objects, but should be continuously evolving. Therefore, constant feedback records what type of grand projected visions are envisioned by those involved in the project, and how these themes are discarded, modified or completely changed over the course of the project. Due to the complexity of interactions between participants and the open-ended nature of AR, the vision and mission of a particular project must be flexible, as well as continuously open to reappraisal, evaluation and redefinition. Each of these three themes can give insight into how a project ebbs and flows through the differing episodes of the ARC.

4.4 EPISODES, FLOWS AND EBBS: INSIGHTS FROM AN ACTION RESEARCH PROJECT

We will draw on the events and processes of our Andean-based project Mushuk Muyu in order to illustrate the dynamics of the five ARC episodes, and the project ebb and flows.

4.1.1 Action Research Cycle

The ARC episodes were all clearly identifiable and manageable within the project. The significance of the communicative arenas was also present. For example, many community members we encountered were initially cautious and suspicious of our presence. They recounted previous situations where 'outsiders' claiming some form of expert status had simply entered their communities to take photos, record data, and interview people, and left without explaining the purpose of their actions. In contrast, we focused on gradually building trust through a democratic research process that was transparent and open to all community members. As the project developed, we continually asked for suggestions and critiques from community members who were not directly involved. We actively engaged with the community as a whole, from living with local families and participating in community events, to helping with daily activities such as the milking of cows. This holistic approach recognises that each individual possesses unique and valuable knowledge about their communities, their lives, their experiences and their aspirations. As such, the community members' participation is integral to the successful generation of both knowledge and action in the AR process: participation and input allowed for a thorough understanding of the contextual basis of the situation, as well as for ensuring that participants had sufficient understanding and control over the new processes. This will facilitate the continued use of the ARC practices, ensuring that changes result in permanent shifts and transformations rather than temporary alterations.

Problem arena

The objective for us was to open up and strengthen the channels of communication between the participants comprising the CA. This was an essential foundation enabling us to explore (through a process of discussion, negotiation and argumentation) the social dynamics and influences behind what different participants perceived to be the problems facing their communities. It also gave the different groups and participants an insight into what the others thought about the situation. This was especially important in breaking the previous situation in which limited communication and coordination between many of the participants and groups was evident.

We continuously adapted our methods to fit the ever-changing environment and found that attempts to use formal interviews were not well received by participants and tended to hinder the flow of information due to their artificial nature. We learnt that while questionnaire-based sample surveys were not very useful for understanding the situation in depth, they were useful reference guides detailing the types of questions and themes we had discussed in the meetings for participants to take with them when they returned to their respective communities to speak with other community members. We also found that the informal medium of individual and group discussions and transect walks with community members yielded far richer and more candid insights when discussing the possible problems associated with the state of Kichwa instruction in the educational arena and community at large.

This first episode highlights the complexity of problem definitions, and the disparate views, opinions and interpretations that different participants hold. The problem arena (PA) acknowledges that conclusions will not be reached with simple consensus, but instead that the process is dialectical, and that by opening up and connecting all those concerned through participative communication, an understanding of the various problems and their differing interpretations, may be reached. In this sense, we developed the general theme of education and stimulated an environment in which we gave voice to the many contextualised issues and perceived problems that the different participants held. By observing how participants acted when they were alone or within small and large groups, we were able to see first-hand the dynamics of the power relations and struggles between participants and how this impacted the situation. This episode was very much a period that brought all the underlying issues, problems and power relations to the surface so that we could document them for future reference.

During this episode we found considerable apprehension to tackling a complex issue such as indigenous education, and there was initially a negative response from much of the community. Many perceived the challenges as too great for their present abilities or positions. While this initial atmosphere of ebb fostered a sense of futility and stagnation, it also helped to clarify the issues that had previously never been rigorously addressed by the community, and fuelled a sense of flow as certain participants saw that there was potential and value in expounding what exactly the major issues, challenges and needs of the community were.

A projected vision began to manifest as the potential for social value became clearer for many participants through reflexively reviewing the dynamics of the issues that we were able to clarify and bring to the surface through the transformation of ebb into flow.

Fundamental themes

Here, the participants aim to organise the mass of information generated in the problem arena into a coherent picture, identifying the thematic groups that underlie the many problems and concerns that were discussed. From a host of group meetings, ranging from two to 60 participants, we were able to gain a more holistic grounding of a matrix of issues that permeated the social discourse at the local level. While some thought the teaching of Kichwa was important, but not essential, the majority thought the Kichwa language and culture was integral to affirming their autonomy in the Ecuadorian state. The general perception of the current situation was that most parents no longer had the ability to speak Kichwa or remember much of their histories. Even though some hinted that they thought Kichwa was simply a language of their grandparents and did not matter any more, they did share a similar feeling of shame regarding the loss of much of what previous indigenous activists had fought extremely hard to promote. There was a general consensus that the situation could be rectified through community-based Kichwa workshops, and the majority of ideas focused on the creation of better material and practices for teaching the Kichwa language and culture at schools. This process also was very useful in teaching us first-hand the dynamics of the power relations between certain participants, the general suspicion of 'outsiders', the lack of faith in the government to provide adequate teaching resources, and how these affected the way people interacted with the above mentioned issues.

The fundamental themes established were: the lack of government responsibility; general shame at the current loss of the Kichwa language and culture; and that while the role of the modern institution of primary bilingual schools is central to the process of revitalising the language and culture, they are in desperate need of new and more innovative resources and practices to achieve this.

This episode helped the group to reinforce the major issues that connected many of the problem sets that had been raised and may at first have seemed disparate. It ultimately brought greater clarity and order to a mass of thoughts, perceptions and ideas regarding problem issues. This enabled the group to navigate through a large amount of information focusing on the emerging patterns that signified the fundamental themes and values, while discarding other issues that after further discussion and consideration were deemed to have little significance. The fact that these fundamental themes transcended any one piece of information gave them more weight, and ultimately, after lengthy discussion, interpretation and negotiation, made them catalysts for a basic consensus. This was vitally important since it gave the group the momentum to move forward with the project in a coordinated fashion, while allowing each participant to express the particular way they perceived these fundamental themes and the impact they had on them and their communities.

In this episode there was a considerable amount of discussion and clarification of the challenges that we would face. To effectively address possible moments of ebb that had the potential to destabilise the morale of the group and exaggerate internal conflict, we devoted our attention to long periods of discussion, negotiation and sometimes argumentation. This was an important process where we could navigate a host of emotional states relating to the issues, hurdles and pressures that the project presented.

It created a cathartic space where participants had the opportunity to express their concerns and views. A greater sense of flow only manifested within the group once we all felt that we were given the opportunity to express ourselves and directly shape the projected mission and the social values that would result from our actions.

Strategic action planning

The objective of the strategic action planning (SAP) episode is to start shaping strategies and creating an action plan that addresses the fundamental themes that have been brought to the forefront in previous discussions.

This episode was initially stagnant as participants found it difficult to move from talking about the issues to actually planning strategies that they thought they could feasibly implement. It became apparent that the teachers' lack of formal training, and the fact that they had never taken a leading role before, caused anxiety and low morale. Arguments frequently erupted and a feeling of futility led to the constant shifting of blame for the inadequacies of the educational system, where teachers blamed the MEE and parents, parents blamed the teachers and the MEE, and the MEE blamed the parents and teachers. This general reluctance to accept any responsibility meant that no one was prepared to take action and attempt to change the situation.

We used a series of group workshops to instigate a movement away from simply discussing ideas into an arena in which the participants could start focusing on tangible outcomes through the coordination of activities relating to the development of the project. To help with this we brought in the idea of using audio technology to create classes in Kichwa. While the technology is not new, nor is it particularly innovative, it was a novelty in the local context and acted as a trigger that opened up the horizon of possibilities for the group. This process stimulated an atmosphere of innovative and imaginative thinking as the participants began to break from the status quo of their educational context.

This promoted one of the most creative periods in the whole project, as the group explored these new possibilities and began brainstorming ways in which the technology could be adapted and remoulded into a contextually relevant and culturally innovative product. They soon developed an idea that went well beyond anything we had originally thought of, as they modified the use of the technology to include a visual medium that would promote a better didactic learning environment and stimulate the capacities of both visual and auditory learning preferences. This whole process helped to shape an innovative and contextually relevant educational concept for Kichwa language instruction in the Cayambe region.

It was through the introduction of audio technology that the group realised they now had the tools to develop something new, and could break from the constraints of their present context. The projected vision and potential social value at this point changed dramatically as their horizon of possibilities expanded. The anxiety and fear of the failure to create change that had held the project in a state of ebb turned to flow as the participants began to create a radically different and innovative approach that was unlike any previous one. It was the novelty of this approach to education and the creation of educational materials that manifested this flow, as participants realised that they were not just creating another version of existing materials, but something completely new and fresh.

Action

The action episode is primarily concerned with the active implementation of strategies in order to transform the project from a set of ideas into a functioning entity. This episode was the most difficult and challenging since the group had to produce tangible outcomes and interact with government departments and various other bodies in order to expand the scope of the project. The more ownership the participants felt in relation to the material and the project, the harder they were willing to work through the challenges. To help maintain momentum and avoid becoming overwhelmed, we found that setting clear, achievable (relatively short-term) goals was a good way to create a steady path forward. For us the goal of a launch date for a pilot version of the project consisting of one textbook and 12 multimedia classes, open to the members of the surrounding local communities, government officials and NGOs, was a pivotal moment in the project and served a number of important functions: (1) it acted as a focal point that all the participants could make a coordinated drive towards and therefore injected new momentum into the project; (2) the launch gave the participants the opportunity to present the project as they had experienced it, take responsibility and at the same time take complete ownership of the work and the product; and (3) It was an important reflexive platform that presented the project to the wider community and authorities through an open forum in which they could voice their opinions, suggestions and critiques regarding the work. It was also an opportunity for people who were unable or unwilling to join the team to give some productive input.

The feedback from the many attending local community, NGO and government members and representatives clearly confirmed that the greater community were genuinely concerned about the state of Kichwa instruction in the bilingual schools and were very passionate about the recuperation of their language, culture and history. They also emphasised the importance of stimulating interest among the youth with such an innovative form of educational material that combined the ancient oral language and culture with modern multimedia technology. Not only was staging a public event to present the project in pilot form a great way to gauge whether the project was in fact reflecting the needs of the community and the situation, but it also allowed us to gain invaluable insights and suggestions from the wider community on how further to develop the project. The feedback, unlike that generated within the group through open discussion and reflective processes, came from people who were 'outsiders' and had no vested interest in the work already done, and therefore were less biased towards the project. With community support and the financial support of DINEIB, we were able to deduce that we had created a unique and valuable educational resource. From this point on, we had the motivation and support to develop the project into one of national proportions.

As with the SAP episode, we found that the anxiety and fear of not possessing the skills and capacity to create a project that could surpass the challenges made this episode extremely difficult to drive forward. Here, more than in any other episode, the expectations and feedback from external organisations and people had a direct impact on the morale and sense of ebb or flow that the group experienced. At this stage in time, the project was at a threshold of either collapsing under the weight of criticism or expanding rapidly if it was well received. For us the positive feedback reinforced the participants' belief in their abilities and further expanded the possibilities of the projected vision and the evolution of the prospective social values. Without this wider reflexive process and the resulting positive feedback the flow would have been drastically stunted and we would have had to readdress the project in light of the criticism.

It is important to note that particular actions had different impacts on the various participants, which created numerous patterns of ebb and flow. For example, the launch justified and validated some of the participants' time and effort, and gave them renewed energy to move forward with the project. However, despite their satisfaction and pride in the launch and the materials produced, other participants saw this success as a demotivating factor. Even though two participants felt they had achieved something special with the launch, their limited proficiency in Kichwa meant that they had struggled to produce the material for the pilot, and they did not have the ability or energy required for scaling the project up to a level at which DINEIB could justify producing the material at a national level. Shortly after the launch they notified the rest of the group that they had decided to end their involvement in the project.

Reflection-on-action

The reflection-on-action (Schön, 1983, 1991) episode is primarily concerned with the evaluation of four key variables: (1) the way the project was carried out; (2) the results and consequences of the action taken; (3) the projected vision achievement(s); and (4) the types, quality and sustainability of social values produced. We gauged the success of the project in relation to these variables through the perspectives of the participants. To do this we decided to maintain a relaxed and casual atmosphere and primarily used group and individual discussion sessions and semi-structured interviews. Since the participants preferred discussion over writing or formal interviews, this was a far more conducive and natural platform for the participants to speak freely and candidly about their experiences.

Participants highlighted that group and individual discussions and workshops fostered a comfortable and casual atmosphere that had helped them to find confidence in their ideas and abilities to contribute to the project. It was also a time when the participants felt that the most innovative and productive ideas and activities were able to come to fruition.

As for the final product, they were very proud of what we had collectively achieved. The fact that we had created a set of multimedia classes that were innovative enough to gain the support of DINEIB and the wider community was indicative of the calibre of the project to address the problems in a new and effective manner.

For the members of the group the projected vision had been completely surpassed with the late inclusion of DINEIB's support and financing. While the projected vision had changed over the course of the project as we built momentum and gained more confidence due to the positive feedback from the launch, it had always maintained a grounded scope of local proportions. So the prospect of this project setting the agenda for the use of this educational technology at a national level was very satisfying for all concerned.

It was clear to the participants that in the wake of Mushuk Muyu new forms of value were being generated within the local communities. They had been contacted after the launch by some of the school directors and teachers who were increasingly thinking about the issues of the loss of Kichwa and were enquiring how they could get more material for their schools. One of the directors of the largest bilingual schools in the area was using our material to start teaching herself Kichwa. One of the participants also believed he had learnt valuable skills from working on the project and was putting them to use in both his political involvement and his new focus on teaching Kichwa at the preschool level. He was also taking the initiative in his community to raise awareness on the loss of

Kichwa and had already begun to make some very promising progress in motivating the parents to begin speaking more Kichwa in the home. In the community of La Chimba, some of the group members had also begun running a series of popular Kichwa cultural identity workshops. This was all spontaneously developing in, and self-generated by, the communities themselves. Even if Mushuk Muyu is not published, we believe that this would not have a serious impact on the sustainability of the residual value that was at first associated with the emergence of Mushuk Muyu, but is now independently manifesting in these community-based Kichwa revival initiatives.

At the completion of this stage, there are different paths for the researchers, participants and associated communities. If it is agreed upon during this process that the goals of the project have not been met, or that the processes have not been adequately understood, the ARC may overcome this momentary ebb and recommence at any of the previous episodes depending on the extent of the problem, and build flow once again. For example, if the actions were deemed to have been ineffective the group may choose to return to the SAP stage to reassess their strategies or, if they wish to redefine the problems in relation to events that may have encroached on the project or the emergence of new residual social values, they may start the whole cycle again. However, in our case the participants felt that we had finished the project and we felt that the project was in a state of flow and already functioning beyond our direct involvement with the support of DINEIB and the emergence of the community initiatives, and therefore we were able to end the cycle and leave the project.

4.4.2 The Dynamics of Ebb and Flow

Clear dynamics of ebbs and flow were experienced in the project. There were clear periods of flow, in which the project grew and advanced at a rapid rate.

An example of one critical ebb in the project related to the reaction of a very senior member of a key stakeholder who had originally publicly praised and pledged support for the project. In private, however, he took an increasingly negative and defensive attitude, later withdrawing all organisational support as well as individual contact. Meetings with junior staff highlighted that the merits of the project were well known, but lack of seniority precluded any reappraisal of involvement. Further questioning revealed that the director of the stakeholder organisation disliked the fact that the project was an initiative created and driven by local community members and teachers, and that it had succeeded in creating an innovative and popular product where his organisation had failed.

All the participants expressed a sense of futility in continuing without the key stakeholder organisation's support. This depressed state fuelled and exacerbated internal conflict. These feelings were strong enough to affect the projected visions of the project. With the onset of such a tepid and unproductive atmosphere we all decided to put the project on hold so that we could take some time to refresh and reenergise. At this point we were unsure whether the project would continue.

After this break, a strategy was devised to bypass the organisation at the provincial level and liaise directly with the national office. What had effectively derailed the project, and held the potential to stop it altogether, had stimulated us to take a giant leap outside normal protocol and develop the project on a much larger and more ambitious scale. Once again, the flow of the project returned, and people engaged on a clearer and strengthened basis.

4.5 REFLECTIONS ON METHOD ADAPTABILITY AND FLUIDITY

This project confirmed that the implementation of the ARC episodes acted as focal points that not only orientated the many activities, ideas and participating members, but also promoted a sense of stability and direction for the project as a whole.

Care was taken not to impede the creativity or freely evolving nature of the project by artificially 'pushing' between episodes, or announcing a new episode. Furthermore, we never specifically announced a method that we wanted to attempt within an episode. We found that the participants were more comfortable with, and effective at completing, different methods when we managed to join appropriate methods seamlessly to the way activities and discussions were unfolding. For example, when we were discussing ideas or generating problems we would simply begin writing them down with the group, or begin asking which were the most pressing issues, and by doing so we were able to create a natural entrance in the discussion for ranking or affinity diagram methods (Berkun, 2005). This helped to break down any semblance of a researcher–researched subject relationship, and helped to give a more natural quality to methods as they were no longer perceived as simply research tools or unnatural activities, but as intrinsically important parts of the progression of the discussion or activity.

This approach also meant that our methods had to be flexible and we needed to adapt to the continually changing circumstances of the project. An example of this was when we spoke with local family members: as soon as we tried to take any form of notes we saw how uncomfortable they were with this. Once we put our pens and notepads away, the conversation became relaxed again and we were able to gain much more detailed and candid information about the community. In regards to note taking, using a Dictaphone or any type of structured interview was deemed ineffective and obtrusive, so we focused on utilising individual and group discussion where we were able to maintain an informal and natural atmosphere, and instead took notes in private, afterwards. It is important to recognise that few AR methods are set in stone – they can be altered and adapted to fit better the social context in which research is being conducted. Researchers need to be flexible and ready to adapt and adjust their methods, maintaining sensitivity to local cultural and social conditions as well as the particular dynamics of continuously shifting contexts.

4.5.1 Strengths and Weaknesses of Approach

As with any research methodology, there are inherent strengths and weaknesses that must be taken into consideration. Here we conclude with an outline of the principal strengths and weaknesses of AR in the context of social entrepreneurship.

Strengths

AR is dynamic and highly flexible with a wide range of methods that can be continuously adapted to suit the evolving context of a social entrepreneurial initiative. Unlike the traditional scientific concept of non-interference, AR instigates complete interaction between researchers and participants, which enables researchers to gain a much better understanding of the subjects and their environment. This research ethic also promotes democratic dialogue and information sharing where all participants are given the opportunity to discuss a wide array of issues and ideas, which in turn stimulates the collective development of innovative concepts and possible solutions to problems.

The fact that AR allows local participants to decide what the problem is, and shape the initiative in search of innovative solutions, ensures that a social entrepreneurial initiative is addressing the actual needs and wants of the local population who drive and shape the initiative. The equal participation of stakeholders ensures a greater sense of ownership and strengthens the prospect of their continued involvement in developing the project after the researcher exits. AR is a very productive and pragmatic approach to social entrepreneurship as it attempts not only to understand the local situation and the participants, but develop a solution to the problems identified by the participants.

Weaknesses

There is always a danger that AR can become overly subjective if researchers become heavily embroiled in what they are attempting to study. It is important that researchers maintain a balance between active participation and the ability to continuously assess the project objectively. With so much happening and the researcher right at the heart of the situation, there can be a tendency to focus more on the action at hand, while sacrificing the development and documentation of good-quality research data.

Even with complete transparency, the fact is that all action is combined with the process of data collection for research purposes, and the researcher may find it difficult to explain what the documentation and research is for and why it is needed. This situation can be taxing on the relationship and has the potential to cause friction between the local participants and the researcher.

The lack of structure and rigidity inherent in what AR attempts to research can make the planning of a project very difficult. You cannot have a strict plan with methods and steps to follow in an exact order, and results are more unpredictable and difficult to hypothesise. This means that researchers have to be far more reflexive and take more time and care to document the way the project was carried out and the assumptions and epistemology they carried with them into the project.

Finally, AR can be painstakingly slow and seem quite inefficient precisely because it strives to offer all interested participants a chance to become involved and have an equal space to share their ideas, air their grievances and negotiate solutions. A by-product of this democratic discourse is that conflicts between participants, or between participants and non-participants, are inevitable and therefore participants may need to spend a considerable amount of time dealing with conflict resolution. This is an issue that many organisations, such as NGOs, government ministries, community groups and universities, who often operate on tight budgetary and funding-led timelines, may find difficult to accommodate.

4.6 CONCLUSION

Social entrepreneurship is a complex and dynamic force that is difficult to study. Because of the complex and intricate nature of the social component, the methods used must be flexible and adaptable, and the researcher must be highly aware of the dynamic nature of the social environment where research is being conducted. AR, with its multidisciplinary, contextual, holistic and flexible approach, is ideally suited for the study of this phenomenon. AR is not the right method for all research studies, but for social entrepreneurial initiatives, particularly ones involving active local participation, AR can provide not only solid insight and knowledge generation, but also practical solutions to the problems identified. This framework provides an appropriate scaffold to allow a researcher to manage for flexibility, complexity and recoverability of an action research project in the context of social entrepreneurship.

NOTES

* This chapter originally appeared as Tasker M., Westberg L. and Seymour R.G. (2010). Action research in social entrepreneurship: a framework for involvement. *International Journal of Action Research* **6**(2–3), 223–255, reprinted with the friendly permission of Hampp Verlag (http://www.Hampp-Verlag.de).

1. Despite the Ecuadorian constitution recognising the plurinational dynamic of the state, and the increasing political power of larger indigenous groups, a long history of violence towards and repression of indigenous peoples by the Inca Empire, Spanish conquistadores and wealthy landowners through the feudal *hacienda* period of the nineteenth century has had a profound impact on the cultural and historical identities of many indigenous people in Ecuador. In the area where the authors worked, many families expressed concern over the loss of their cultural history and their inability to pass on their mother tongue, and saw bilingual schools as a key environment for their children. As a result of this the Ecuadorian government has played a pioneering role in designing an intercultural bilingual educational system whereby indigenous children are able to attend schools offering both Spanish and their respective language. However, as we found in Cayambe, in practice the ability of many schools to run a bilingual curriculum effectively is limited by a lack of financial and human resources as well as political support.
2. DIPEIB-P is the provincial bilingual office for Pichincha.
3. UEM is an Ecuadorian government initiative to modernise schools and raise the calibre of education through the use of experimental and pedagogically innovative technologies.
4. See the DINEIB website: http://www.dineib.gov.ec/pages/interna.php?txtCodiInfo=193.
5. This competition was organised by Alianza por la Educación de Microsoft and Escuelas Inter@ctivas de Fundación ChasquiNet.

REFERENCES

Ahmad, N. and R.G. Seymour (2008). Defining entrepreneurial activity: definitions supporting frameworks for data collection. OECD Statistics Working Papers Series. Paris: OECD Publications.

Alvord, S.H. and L.D. Brown (2002). Social entrepreneurship and social transformation: an exploratory study. The Hauser Center for Nonprofit Organizations and The Kennedy School of Government, Harvard University, USA.

Austin, J.E. (2006). Three avenues for social entrepreneurship research. In J. Mair, J. Robinson and K. Hockerts (eds), *Social Entrepreneurship*. New York: Palgrave Macmillan, pp. 22–33.

Austin, J., H. Stevenson and J. Wei-Skillern (2006). Social and commercial entrepreneurship: same, different, or both? *Entrepreneurship Theory and Practice* **30**(1), 1–22.

Berkowitz, L. and E. Donnerstein (1982). External validity is more than skin deep: some answers to criticisms of laboratory experiments. *American Psychologist* **37**(3), 245–257.
Berkun, S. (2005). *The Art of Project Management*. Beijing: O'Reilly.
Borda, O.F. (2006). Participatory (action) research in social theory: origins and challenges. In P. Reason and H. Bradbury (eds), *Handbook of Action Research*. London: Sage Publications, pp. 27–37.
Bradbury, H. and P. Reason (2006). Conclusion: broadening the bandwidth of validity: issues and choice-points for improving the quality of action research. In P. Reason and H. Bradbury (eds), *Handbook of Action Research*. London: Sage Publications, pp. 343–351.
Burns, A. (2005). Action research: an evolving paradigm? *Language Teaching* **38**(2), 57–74.
Checkland, P. and S. Holwell (1998). Action research: its nature and validity. *Systemic Practice and Action Research* **11**(1), 9–21.
Cherry, N. (2002). *Action Research: A Pathway to Action, Knowledge and Learning*. Melbourne: RMIT University Press.
Cho, A.H. (2006). Politics, values and social entrepreneurship: a critical appraisal. In J. Mair, J. Robinson and K. Hockerts (eds), *Social Entrepreneurship*. New York: Palgrave Macmillan, pp. 34–56.
Cook, T.D. and D.T. Campbell (1976). Four kinds of validity. In M.D. Dunnette (ed.), *Handbook of Industrial and Organizational Psychology*. Chicago, IL: Rand McNally, pp. 224–246.
Court, D. (1988). Reflection-in-action: some definitional problems. In P.P. Grimmett and G.L. Erickson (eds), *Reflection in Teacher Education*. New York: Teachers' College Press, pp. 143–146.
Csikszentmihalyi, M. (1991). *Flow: The Psychology of Optimal Experience*. New York: Harper & Row Publishers.
Dewey, J. (1930). *Individualism, Old and New*. New York: Minton Balch & Co.
Ebbutt, D. (1985). Educational action research: some general concerns and specific quibbles. In R. Burgess (ed.), *Issues in Educational Research: Qualitative Methods*. Lewes: Falmer.
Elliott, J. (1991). *Action Research for Educational Change*. Milton Keynes: Open University Press.
Eraut, M. (1994). *Developing Professional Knowledge and Competence*. London: Falmer Press.
Greenwood, D.J. and M. Levin (2003). Reconstructing the relationships between universities and society through action research. In N.K. Denzin and Y.S. Lincoln (eds), *The Landscape of Qualitative Research: Theories and Issues*. Thousand Oaks, CA: Sage Publications.
Greenwood, D.J. and M. Levin (2007). *Introduction to Action Research: Social Research for Social Change*. Thousand Oaks, CA: Sage Publications.
Grundy, S. (1988). Three modes of action research. In S. Kemmis and R. McTaggart (eds), *The Action Research Reader*. Geelong, Victoria: Deakin University Press, pp. 353–364.
Gustavsen, B. (2006). Theory and practice: the mediating discourse. In P. Reason and H. Bradbury (eds), *Handbook of Action Research*. London: Sage Publications, pp. 17–27.
Hall, S. (1996). Reflexivity in emancipatory research: illustrating the researcher's constitutiveness. In O. Zuber-Skerritt (ed.), *New Directions in Action Research*. London: Falmer Press, pp. 28–48.
Haugh, H. (2006). Social enterprise: beyond economic outcomes and individual returns. In J. Mair, J. Robinson and K. Hockerts (eds), *Social Entrepreneurship*. New York: Palgrave Macmillan, pp. 180–206.
Henry, E. (2007). Kaupapa Maori entrepreneurship. In Leo Paul Dana and R.B. Anderson (eds), *International Handbook of Research on Indigenous Entrepreneurship*. Cheltenham, UK and Northampton, MA, USA: Edward Elgar, pp. 536–548.
Hopkins, D.J. (1993). *A Teacher's Guide to Classroom Research*. Buckingham: Open University Press.
Jones, R., J. Latham and M. Betta (2008). Narrative construction of the social entrepreneurial identity. *International Journal of Entrepreneurial Behaviour and Research* **14**(5), 339–345.

Kemmis, S. (1988). Action research in retrospect and prospect. In S. Kemmis and R. McTaggart (eds), *The Action Research Reader*. Geelong, Victoria: Deakin University Press, pp. 27–40.
Kemmis, S. and R. McTaggart (eds) (1988). *The Action Research Reader*, Geelong, Victoria: Deakin University Press.
Kemmis, S. and R. McTaggart (2005). Participatory action research: communicative action and the public sphere. In N.K. Denzin and Y.S. Lincoln (eds), *The Sage Handbook of Qualitative Research*. Thousand Oaks, CA: Sage Publications, pp. 559–603.
Lewin, K. (1946/1988). Action research and minority problems. In S. Kemmis and R. McTaggart (eds), *The Action Research Reader*. Geelong, Victoria: Deakin University Press, pp. 41–46.
Ludema, J.D., D.L. Cooperrider and F.J. Barrett (2006). Appreciative inquiry: the power of the unconditional positive question. In P. Reason and H. Bradbury (eds), *Handbook of Action Research*. London: Sage Publications, pp. 155–166.
McNiff, J., P. Lomax and J. Whitehead (1997). *You and Your Action Research Project*. London: Routledge.
Miles, M.B. and A.M. Huberman (1994). *Qualitative Data Analysis: An Expanded Sourcebook*. Newbury Park, CA: Sage Publications.
Nicholls, A. (2006). *Social Entrepreneurship: New Models of Sustainable Social Change*. Oxford and New York: Oxford University Press.
Pearce, J. (2003). *Social Enterprise in Anytown*. London: Calouste, Gulkenian Foundation.
Perrini, F. and C. Vurro (2006). Social entrepreneurship: innovation and social change across theory and practice. In J. Mair, J. Robinson and K. Hockerts (eds), *Social Entrepreneurship*. New York: Palgrave Macmillan, pp. 57–86.
Punch, K.F. (1999). *Introduction to Social Research: Quantitative and Qualitative Approaches*. London: Sage Publications.
Race, P. (1993). Never mind the teaching – feel the learning. *SEDA Paper 80*. Birmingham.
Reason, P. and H. Bradbury (2006). Introduction: inquiry and participation in search of a world worthy of human aspiration. In P. Reason and H. Bradbury (eds), *Handbook of Action Research*. London: Sage Publications, pp. 1–14.
Rhodes, M.L. and G. Donnelly-Cox (2008). Social entrepreneurship as a performance landscape: the case of 'front line'. *Emergence: Complexity and Organization* **10**(3), 35–50.
Schön, D.A. (1983). *The Reflective Practitioner: How Professionals Think in Action*. New York: Basic Books.
Schön, D.A. (1991). Concluding comments. In D.A. Schön (ed.), *The Reflective Turn: Case Studies in and on Educational Practice*. New York: Teachers College Press, pp. 343–360.
Schutz, A. (1962). *Collected Papers*. The Hague: Nijhoff.
Susman, G.I. and R.D. Evered (1978). An assessment of the scientific merits of action research. *Administrative Science Quarterly* **23**(4), 582–603.
Taba, H. and E. Noel (1988). Steps in the action research process. In S. Kemmis and R. McTaggart (eds), *The Action Research Reader*. Geelong, Victoria: Deakin University Press, pp. 67–74.
Tacchi, J.A., D. Slater and G. Hearn (2003). *Ethnographic Action Research: A User's Handbook*. New Delhi: UNESCO.
Tapsell, P. and C. Woods (2008). A spiral of innovation framework for social entrepreneurship: social innovation at the generational divide in an indigenous context. *Emergence: Complexity and Organisation* **10**(3), 25.
Van Manen, M. (1991). Reflectivity and the pedagogical moment: the normativity of pedagogical thinking and acting. *Journal of Curriculum Studies* **23**(6), 507–536.
Webb, G. (1996). Becoming critical of action research for Development. In O. Zuber-Skerritt (ed.), *New Directions in Action Research*. London: Falmer Press, pp. 137–164.
Weerawardena, J. and G.S. Mort (2006). Investigating social entrepreneurship: a multidimensional model. *Journal of World Business* **41**, 21–35.
Winter, R. (1996). Some principles and procedures for the conduct of action research. In O. Zuber-Skerritt (ed.), *New Directions in Action Research*. London: Falmer Press, pp. 13–27.

Young, R. (2006). For what it is worth: social value and the future of social entrepreneurship. In A. Nicholls (ed.), *Social Entrepreneurship: New Models of Sustainable Change*. Oxford: Oxford University Press, pp. 56–73.

Zuber-Skerritt, O. (1996). Emancipatory action research for organisational change and management development. In O. Zuber-Skerritt (ed.), *New Directions in Action Research*. London: Falmer Press, pp. 83–105.

5 Bounding research settings

K. Kumar and Jarrod Ormiston

Case study research focuses on 'understanding the dynamics present within single settings' (Eisenhardt, 1989, p. 533) and can involve either single or multiple cases. Case studies can be employed retrospectively or prospectively, and utilise quantitative or qualitative data or both (Zucker, 2009). As a research strategy, case study research is appropriate when the phenomenon has been underexplored or when dominant theoretical discourse requires re-evaluation (Ghauri, 2004). As noted by Yin (2003, p. 1): 'case studies are the preferred strategy when "how" or "why" questions are being posed, when the investigator has little control over events and when the focus is on a contemporary phenomenon within some real-life context'. The strategy should therefore be considered appropriate when 'thick description' is required to elucidate meaning (Lincoln and Guba, 2002).

The case study has much to offer the nascent field of social entrepreneurship given the current stage of theoretical underdevelopment. Additionally the complex nature of social entrepreneurship and the dynamic environments in which it takes place raises the importance of rich description and contextual depth, both of which are qualities of case study research. The flexibility and iterative nature inherent in case study research supports the study of social phenomena such as social entrepreneurship that are emerging outside of the dominant organisational frameworks.

This chapter provides researchers with the basics for using case studies as a research strategy. The first part of this chapter will present a brief overview of case study literature and insights from specialists in the field. We then look briefly at the relevance of using case studies in the context of social entrepreneurship research, and provide researchers with a set of guidelines drawing on examples from our social entrepreneurship research projects.

5.1 THE CASE STUDY AS RESEARCH STRATEGY

A case study aims to appreciate the complexity of a single context and explore in detail the interactions and particularities within it (Stake, 1995). Despite the widespread use of case studies in academia, however, a great deal of ambiguity surrounds the term 'case study' – it is variously defined as a method, methodology, research design, research strategy or heuristic (van Wynsbeghe and Khan, 2007). To some extent this lack of clarity can be explained through the confusion which exists in distinguishing the above categories from each other (Verschuren, 2003). The distinctive features of a case study are the detailed and intensive investigation of a phenomenon, in its context, using multiple data collection methods and acquiring a multiplicity of contextualised perspectives (Ghauri, 2004; Snape and Spencer, 2003; Stake, 1995; Yin, 2003). This highlights the fact that a case study is more than a research method.

We consider the use of case studies to be a research strategy (or research approach) which takes a holistic approach to exploring the cases selected, appreciating context, obtaining multiple perspectives and utilising multiple methods of data collection in order to challenge theory with empiricism (George and Bennett, 2004; Hartley, 1994; Piekkari et al., 2009; Vennesson, 2008; Verschuren, 2003). Essentially, the purpose of the case study research is not to represent the world, but to represent the case (Stake, 2000a). In representing the case, or an aspect of an historical episode, the researcher intends to develop or test historical explanations that may be generalizable to other events (George and Bennett, 2004).

As a research strategy, the case study is widely utilised in biography and history, psychology, sociology, political science, management and medical research. Looking more closely at areas of relevance to social entrepreneurship, the case study has been used widely in strategy, entrepreneurship, organisation behaviour, third sector and development research. Best practice associated with case study methods are, however, typically not codified (George and Bennett, 2004), and have yet to be explored deeply in social entrepreneurship literature despite their common use.

5.1.1 The Diversity of Case Studies and Theoretical Underpinnings

Before deciding upon a research strategy, it is important to understand the myriad of factors that lead to the choice of the research strategy, design and methods. As introduced in earlier chapters, these factors include the ontological and epistemological positions and the theoretical perspectives adopted by the researcher. These positions are influenced by the purpose and goals of the research, traditions within the field, and the position and environment of the researcher (Snape and Spencer, 2003). To ensure a sound research approach with credible outcomes, an understanding of how these perspectives influence the holistic research process is required (Crotty, 1998). Clarity in the philosophical and theoretical positions adopted ensures the necessary base for the choice of an appropriate research strategy and accompanying research methods.

Case study research is generally qualitative in nature and is better suited to more subjectivist or interpretivist approaches; however more positivist approaches to case study research have been applied with impressive results (most notably by Yin, 2003). Regardless of the philosophical positions taken by the researcher, attention should be drawn to the assumptions that are embedded within these differing philosophical and theoretical assumptions. The case study research strategy should be chosen when it provides coherence between the research questions and these perspectives.

5.1.2 Why are Case Studies Useful in a Social Entrepreneurship Context?

For social entrepreneurship researchers, case studies promise rich insights but also threaten difficulties. This section will briefly review the various methodological strengths and weaknesses of case study research in the field of social entrepreneurship.

Whilst there are many criticisms of qualitative case studies from within the positivist school of thought (Ghauri, 2004), their use is supported by strong traditions of effectiveness in the fields of corporate entrepreneurship (Liu et al., 2007), social entrepreneurship (Short et al., 2009; Weerawardena and Mort, 2006) and strategic management (Eisenhardt and Graebner, 2007). Case studies are generally strong when statistical methods and formal models are weak (George and Bennett, 2004):

> When explanation, propositional knowledge and law are the aims of an inquiry, the case study will often be at a disadvantage. When the aims are understanding, extension of experience and increase in conviction in that which is known, the disadvantage disappears. (Stake, 2000b, p. 21)

Strengths of case study research from which social entrepreneurship research can benefit include: (1) allowing a researcher to identify and measure the indicators that best represent the theoretical concepts intended; (2) facilitating the identification of new variables and derivation of new hypotheses; (3) permitting the exploration of causal mechanisms in detail; and (4) being relatively accommodating as regards complex causal relations (George and Bennett, 2004). The case study as research strategy is appropriate for social entrepreneurship research when these strengths are utilised and when the researcher seeks to adapt and probe areas of original and emergent theory (Gruber, 1988; Gruber and Wallace, 1999; Hartley, 1994; Stake, 2000b).

The main criticisms of case study research concern the lack of validity of predictions and generalisations which emerge, and thus it is argued that qualitative research through case studies is of a lower quality than more quantitative methodologies (Verschuren, 2003). Critics argue that case studies are too contextualised and therefore not appropriate for generalisation. Indeed, there have been calls within the field of social entrepreneurship research to advance more generalisable methods to counter the common excessively contextual case study research (Short et al., 2009).

The specific trade-offs, limitations and weaknesses associated with the case study as research strategy include: (1) selection bias that can understate or overstate the relationship between dependent and independent variables; (2) the limitation of only tentatively being able to present conclusions; (3) the problem of overgeneralising to types or subclasses of cases unlike those actually studied; and (4) the potential lack of independence of cases (George and Bennett, 2004). Whilst high-order generalisations are not the aim of case study research, the question of generalisability remains central to most critiques. Generalisability is an appealing concept, note Lincoln and Guba (2000, p. 28), as:

> when a generalization has been devised, no member of that class, kind or order can escape its pervasive influence . . . the concept oozes determinism, and seems to place the entire world at the feet of those persons who can unlock its deepest and most pervasive generalities.

Generalisation is significant for case study researchers in two respects: (1) it is one means by which researchers argue for the general relevance of their findings; and (2) much case study research involves generalisation within the case(s) researched, with the researcher seeking both what is common and what is particular about a case. However, these calls for generalisability must be tempered by the recognition that this research approach has as its purpose the refinement and development of theory, and the recognition of the importance of the particular:

> Case studies are of value for refining theory and suggesting complexities for further investigation, as well as helping to establish the limits of generalizability . . . the purpose of the case report is not to represent the world, but to represent the case. (Stake, 2000a, p. 448).

Assuming the researcher does not attempt to achieve generalisability, we believe case study research is well suited to social entrepreneurship: it allows the interactions between a phenomenon and its context to be explored in great depth (Ghauri, 2004). We argue that the advantage of depth offered by case studies far outweighs any disadvantages of scale, especially in the context of an emerging complex phenomenon. We now turn our attention to the question of how one undertakes case study research.

5.2 HOW TO UNDERTAKE CASE STUDY RESEARCH

This section endeavours to provide the required foundations to allow you to undertake case study research in social entrepreneurship contexts. These guidelines have emerged from the literature and the authors' experiences with case study research. To highlight issues of relevance and practice, they are supplemented by evidence and examples from actual studies undertaken.

This section draws upon a research project which explored how Latin America social enterprises understand their social impacts. The study developed a conceptual framework to consider the cyclical process of value creation in social entrepreneurship. The three case studies undertaken exemplify the diversity of social entrepreneurial missions and the breadth of intended social impact, as exemplified by the following descriptions: (1) Language Venture, which was founded by two young Australian social entrepreneurs to recuperate the Kichwa language and traditions throughout the Andean region in Ecuador by developing language class podcasts; (2) Youth Venture, a Chilean social enterprise facilitating access to healthcare, education and employment for marginalised youth in greater Santiago; (3) Finance Venture, an American-based multinational social enterprise which aims to alleviate poverty through the delivery of microfinance to developing regions in Mexico and Argentina. Throughout this section this study will be referred to as 'the Latin American study'.

5.2.1 Single-versus Multiple-Case Designs and Case Selection

The first issues to confront are the decisions about which, and how many, cases to study. You must decide between a single-case design which focuses on an in-depth exploration of an extreme or unique case, or a multiple-case design which aims to investigate similar, or predictably contrasting, outcomes (Zucker, 2009). In choosing which design to follow, you should not equate the number of cases with the notion of a statistically representative sample. Theoretical or case selection should determine the number and type of cases whereby 'cases are selected because they are particularly suitable for illuminating and extending relationship and logic among constructs' (Eisenhardt and Graebner, 2007). The design chosen will influence the process of case selection, as illustrated in the following discussion.

Single-case design

In a single-case design, the researcher should ignore criticisms of small sample size and instead focus on selecting a case which is unusual, extreme or something to which access is rarely granted (Eisenhardt and Graebner, 2007). Take Siggelkow's (2007) analogy of the 'talking pig', for example:

> imagine the following scenario, adapted from Ramachandran (1998): You cart a pig into my living room and tell me that it can talk. I say, 'Oh really? Show me.' You snap with your fingers and the pig starts talking. I say, 'Wow, you should write a paper about this.' You write up your case report and send it to a journal. What will the reviewers say? Will the reviewers respond with 'Interesting, but that's just one pig. Show me a few more and then I might believe you'? I think we would agree that that would be a silly response. (Siggelkow, 2007, p. 20)

This somewhat extreme example stresses the power of single case studies and should encourage social entrepreneurship researchers to search out their own 'talking pig' when conducting single-case research.

Multiple-case design

Alternatively, a multiple-case design allows for interaction with multiple research settings and provides a framework for multiple perspectives to be gathered both inside and across cases. Generally speaking, multiple case studies provide a greater opportunity for theory development (Eisenhardt and Graebner, 2007). The rationale for studying multiple cases, rather than a single one, is to achieve replication across cases to improve the robustness of the findings (Eisenhardt, 1989; Yin, 2003). It is important to understand that the multiple-case design seeks 'analytical generalisation' through comparing findings to theory, rather than making statistical generalisations (Yin, 2003). Given this theoretical logic, probability sampling is largely inappropriate and therefore the multiple-case design should not be a sampling decision. Rather, individual cases should be purposefully selected with the intention of achieving a rich, textured understanding of the phenomena identified in the literature review. The relevant theory (or organising framework) is therefore 'used as a template with which to compare the empirical results of the case study' and possibly evaluate rival theories (Yin, 2003, p. 32).

Cases within a multiple-case design should be selected to exhibit particular features which enable detailed exploration of the phenomena and yet should be sufficiently heterogeneous to allow for common central themes to be identified (Lewis, 2004; Patton, 1990). This approach to case selection is consistent with the primary objective of case study research, which is to understand individual cases in great detail and then draw conclusions which may apply to cases operating in similar contexts (Stake, 1995). This design provides an opportunity to study each case within many dimensions and then to draw various elements together in a cohesive interpretation (Ghauri, 2004).

In summary, the choice of case design largely depends on the nature of the study itself and its theoretical underpinnings. Typically, though, several elements will critically influence your choice of single versus multiple case design, including: (1) the research question; (2) philosophical underpinning of the research; (3) the theoretical domain; and (4) time, budget and access constraints.

Example

In the Latin American study, particular attention was directed at gaining an insight into how social entrepreneurs understand value creation across a variety of social enterprises. To do so, multiple cases were selected to represent the breadth of economic models in social entrepreneurship. This need was contrasted against time and budget constraints and the depth of qualitative data sought. Ultimately three cases were chosen, each internationally recognised for the entrepreneurial efforts within the Latin American region. A case logic was developed, and structured around organisational contexts rather than a series of individual participants. Multiple international bodies recognising social entrepreneurs – including Ashoka, Skoll Foundation, the United Nations Children's (Emergency) Fund (UNICEF) and the United Nations Educational, Scientific and Cultural Organization (UNESCO) were accessed to avoid a focus on one classification system. This ensured replication amongst the cases so that similar issues could be explored and triangulation achieved through guaranteeing exposure to multiple perspectives (Ghauri, 2004). Though the central focus remained the social entrepreneur, multiple perspectives were obtained from inside and outside the venture, allowing for deep understanding and unbiased perspectives.

Now, imagine you are interested in researching funding models in social entrepreneurship. If you are interested in understanding how social entrepreneurs decide between different funding options, the appropriate choice would be a multiple-case design in which cases are selected which have implemented diverse funding models. Alternatively, if you are interested in looking at the implications of combining impact investing with government grant funding, you may choose a single-case design and select a case which embodies the interactions which you seek to explore. The focus of your research project will thus greatly inform your choice regarding which approach should be followed throughout your study, and will in turn influence the nature of your results.

5.2.2 Data Collection

Undertaking the data collection, management, analysis and reporting of multiple case studies is a complex task (Patton, 2002). The first step is to decide which research methods will be used within the case study research. Multiple data sources from multiple participants should be accessed within each case to allow for deeper understanding through accessing multiple realities, and to provide triangulation between the different sources and perspectives, thus leading to more valid conclusions through corroboration (Ghauri, 2004; Yin, 2003).

Collecting 'naturally occurring' and 'generated' data will ensure that the research phenomena are sufficiently illuminated, detailed, accurate and complete (Lewis, 2004). Naturally occurring data sources include: annual reports, emails, formal business documents, website information and performance history. Generated data sources include interviews, surveys, focus groups and any other method where the researcher intervenes in the social world of the research participants. These data can be qualitative or quantitative in nature. The following sections provide brief summaries of how these different methods can be utilised in case study research, and also discuss the additional benefits of mixing qualitative and quantitative research methods.

Qualitative data collections

The main source of qualitative data utilised in case study research is the interview. Other examples include archival documents, observation, focus groups and reflective journals.

Interviews Interviews are commonly used in case study research in appreciation of the importance of language in illuminating meaning (Legard et al., 2004). Further, in-depth interviews are arguably the most suitable method when the researcher wants to comprehend the behaviour of decision-makers in different cultures, as understanding can be confirmed through asking clarifying questions (Ghauri, 2004). The purpose of using interviews is to see the phenomenon from the perspective of the interviewees and understand how and why they reached their opinions (King, 2004). A wide range of participants that are internal and external to the cases can be sought to reflect differing interests in the activities of the social entrepreneur. This allows multiple perspectives to be gathered and compared, and allows for triangulation of evidence (King, 2004). Those interviewed should be selected with the intention of providing multiple perspectives.

There are three main types of interviews: structured, semi-structured and open-ended. Structured interviews are useful when the researcher is interested in answers to specific questions (contained in an interview guide), and are generally more appropriate in studies that are directed at theory testing rather than theory generation. Semi-structured interviews are the most commonly used type of interview as they combine the benefits of structure with flexibility. Similar to structured interviews, they are guided by prepared interview guides, yet allow for probing and exploration of emergent issues raised within the interview (Legard et al., 2004). Open-ended interviews could appear as a friendly unstructured conversation (Fontana and Frey, 2003; Seidman, 1998), with the interviewer adopting an empathic style (as opposed to passive, rational type interviewing) (Fontana and Frey, 2003). These are useful when the researcher is exploring an area in which theory has not been developed and when the researcher is interested in exploring complexity amongst seemingly unrelated constructs.

The main sources in developing an interview guide should be your literature review, the researcher's personal knowledge of the phenomenon, and preliminary discussions with experts and practitioners within the field (King, 2004). A conscious effort should be made when conducting the interviews to ask open-ended questions to ensure that holistic detail is given and that answers are not overly influenced by the questioning technique. Further, in bilingual interviews in which interpreters are used, question phrasing should be streamlined to cater to the language capabilities of both the interpreter and the participant (Wilkinson and Young, 2004).

Document analysis Relevant documents and archival data can be collected before, after and at the time of the interview to provide triangulation of reference material for later analysis and to gain insights which are not raised through questioning in the interview (Creswell, 2003). These can range from public to procedural and personal documents, including business publications, newspaper articles, internet sources, corporate materials, internal reports, letters and emails. The selective bias in using this method should be noted and thus the potential usefulness of documents should be judged in advance to ensure timely analysis of data gathered and avoid reliance on documentary data (Stake, 1995). The analysis of documents allows the artefacts of social entrepreneurs to complement the information obtained within the interviews and thus solidify the opinions formed by the researcher (Yin, 2003).

Reflective journals The role of the researcher should be taken into consideration in the analysis of the interviews (Legard et al., 2004). The following steps can be taken to ensure reflexivity in the interview process with regard to awareness of the impact of the researcher. The researcher's presuppositions should be regularly noted and reflected upon throughout the research process (King, 2004). A reflective journal can be kept throughout the research process, and interviews listened to during the fieldwork to review the researcher's own performance. The reflective journal itself, and the contextual experiences expressed within, are viewed as valid sources of data and can help to foster the researcher's understanding of local viewpoints (Grisar-Kasse, 2004).

Quantitative data collections

The most commonly used quantitative data in case study research are survey data. Note, however, that quantitative analysis can be applied to many forms of numerical or categorical data in case study research through the use of descriptive or inferential statistics. More detail on survey data is provided in Chapter 8 of this *Handbook*.

Mixed data collections

Research which combines at least one qualitative method with at least one quantitative method describes the emerging trend of 'mixed methods research' (Greene, 2008). Mixed methods research is considered appropriate when researchers are confronted by different frameworks or integrating different fields of study, common issues in the context of social entrepreneurship (Hohenthal, 2006).

Onwuegbuzie and Leech (2005) argue that quantitative and qualitative methods are not independent of each other; that both are required to gain an understanding of unexplored phenomena. They note the similarities: both are considered to involve observations to answer questions, safeguards to minimise bias, analytical techniques to give maximal meaning, attempts to explain complex relationships, techniques to verify data, and place an importance on the role of data reduction techniques and the central role of theory.

The main rationale for adopting mixed methods research is to support generality and idiosyncrasy by providing research that communicates magnitude and dimensionality at the same time as providing contextualised stories (Greene, 2008). There are a number of motivations to conduct mixed methods research (Greene et al., 1989): (1) triangulation, which aims to corroborate results from different methods to increase validity in data analysis; (2) complementarity, which aims to elaborate on results from one method with those from another; (3) development, which aims to use the results from one method to inform another method; (4) initiation, which aims to discover contradictions by analysing results from a different perspective; and (5) expansion, which aims to increase the breadth of inquiry by selecting different methods based on the appropriateness for different inquiry components.

If you are to mix methods, it is important that it is done for the right reasons and not just for the sake of it. The methods 'mixed' must be compatible and complement each other. Examples of compatible mixed methods would include a survey of all employees of a large social enterprise accompanied by in-depth interviews with key staff. Another example could involve using mixed methods at differing levels of analysis, for example conducting interviews within cases then conducting an industry analysis using quantitative data at the macro level.

Examples

In the Latin American study, qualitative research was undertaken given both the expertise of the research team and the difficulties of conducting surveys and using other quantitative methods in bilingual research settings. Semi-structured interviews were the main source of data and these were conducted with multiple participants within each of the three cases. An interview guide, that was developed in line with a conceptual framework for understanding value creation, directed these interviews. Local interpreters were used in the interview process when participants did not speak English to ensure that meaning was not lost or obscured in translation. Documentary analysis was conducted to provide verification and triangulation of information garnered in the interviews, but also to produce insights which did not arise in the interview process. Finally, a reflective journal of time in the field was compiled, allowing for contemplation and self-orientation (especially considering the researcher's 'foreignness' in the cultural context of the study).

5.2.3 Data Analysis

Data should be analysed by compiling information within the cases and conducting cross-comparisons through the lens of theory or an organising framework.

The historical accounts

The first task is to construct case descriptions and histories to give a background of understanding (Ghauri, 2004). This involves simple storytelling (independent of any theoretical analysis) of the cases and their environments to produce a chronological or longitudinal explanation (Ghauri, 2004). The intention is to improve the external consistency of the data (George and Bennett, 2004), and to make the first approach of 'sensemaking' (Langley, 1999). This term 'sensemaking' is used to imply the possibility of a variety of 'senses' or theoretical understanding that may legitimately emerge from the data, and that the process can begin with either data or theory, or a combination of both (Langley, 1999). The analysis does not, however, strip the individual's perspectives or views: the bulk of the insight will be sourced from personal data.

Data reduction and use of qualitative software

Following the storytelling stage, data should be rearranged into more conceptual categories to allow for conclusions to be drawn (Ghauri, 2004). All data should be analysed inductively and deductively through generating themes within the data pertinent to the research questions, and through reviewing the data with constant comparison to the relevant literature (Osmond and O'Connor, 2006). Coding should be used in the analysis of the data, which allows them to be reduced into analysable categories. Both theoretically derived codes, which are constructed from existing knowledge underpinning the research, and *in vivo* codes, based on the indigenous terms used by informants, can be used to ensure that pragmatic illustrations of theory are acknowledged and that meaning is not excessively imposed on the participants by the researcher (Patton, 1990). The coding process should be recursive and involve constant iterations as new codes are developed, to determine whether earlier material should be recoded (Osmond and O'Connor, 2006).

Due to the in-depth nature of qualitative research, case study analysis can become very complex and voluminous. In interpreting large volumes of data, data management software can be used to facilitate the process of coding data to ensure a robust approach. The use of computer-assisted qualitative data analysis software (CAQDAS), such as NVivo, affords an ease of evaluation in making comparisons between different actors within single cases, between cases, and between groups across cases (Lewis, 2004). Utilising CAQDAS also assists with the development of higher-order classifications and categories, to formulate propositions and to test such propositions. NVivo has a high standing and usage within the academic community (Weitzman, 2003), yet other CAQDAS options are available.

Examples

In the Latin American study, the first stage of the data analysis involved writing up atheoretical historical descriptions of the cases: the social entrepreneurs and the contexts within which they operate. This was preceded by a process of conceptual coding which began by compiling a coding frame underpinned by literature and the organising frame. The data were then coded using the theoretical codes from the coding frame and *in vivo* which emerged in the data itself. Given that there were over 100 000 words of data to code, the process was facilitated through the CAQDAS, NVivo, to allow for a robust and streamlined approach to the iterative analysis process. Finally, the data and findings from the analysis were written up in a parsimonious manner which was enabled through reducing complex and in-depth descriptions into easy-to-understand figures and tables which assisted in simplifying the analysis.

5.2.4 Writing up the Analysis

The final stage of data analysis involves displaying and concisely conveying the data and insights gained through coding. The central challenge of case study data composed of events is: 'moving from a shapeless data spaghetti toward some kind of theoretical understanding that does not betray the richness, dynamism, and complexity of the data but that is understandable and potentially useful to others' (Langley, 1999, p. 694).

McCracken (1988) cites two key objectives to writing up case study data analysis: (1) the 'herding' objective, allowing rich and abundant data to speak to the reader without losing the writer's or reader's way in a mass of detail; and (2) the 'landing' objective, providing a clear and vivid sense of the particulars while also showing the general formal properties and theoretical significance of data.

Robustness

As mentioned, qualitative research through case studies is often criticised for its lack of generalisability due to its contextual nature. Generalisability refers to the relevance of the study beyond the cases themselves and their specific context, and relies on the reliability and validity of the research conducted (Golafshani, 2003). Whilst these concepts originated in the natural sciences, an extension of these theories to qualitative research can ensure the adequacy of the research conducted (Patton, 1990). Taking reliability and validity at their widest conception, as sustainability and well-groundedness respectively, qualitative research can be strengthened through striving to meet these requirements (Lewis and Ritchie, 2004).

Reliability

Reliability in case study research can be achieved through reference to ideals such as 'trustworthiness', 'consistency' and 'dependability' (Lewis and Ritchie, 2004; Lincoln and Guba, 1985). The following steps should be taken to ensure the reliability of the analysis. Consistency in the fieldwork can be achieved through allowing all participants sufficient time and opportunities to portray and clarify their experiences. This can be ensured through scheduling extra time than necessary for the interviews, contacting participants a month after the interview to explain any confusion, and allowing for additional inputs in the form of documents. Dependency and trustworthiness can be ensured through a systematic and comprehensive analysis and interpretation of the data. This may involve using CAQDAS to allow for an audit trail to be maintained and also through constant iterations of the coding and interpretation process, referring to the original data throughout the entire process. Further, a sound case logic which aims to gather multiple perspectives will ensure that the data gathered are not overly influenced by the values of the social entrepreneurs.

Validity

Similarly to reliability, the concept of validity, which is usually taken to mean 'correctness', takes on a new understanding when considered in case study research (Alvesson and Deetz, 2000). Given that reality is understood through meaning and language, 'credibility' and 'plausibility' are of the greatest concern in determining the validity of interpretation (Creswell, 2003; Lewis and Ritchie, 2004). Validity is thus defined as: 'how accurately the account represents participants' reality of the social phenomena and is credible to them' (Creswell and Miller, 2000, pp. 124–125). The main measures used to ensure the validity of the interpretation should be a constant comparative method, labelling methods and triangulation. Through the constant comparative method, hypotheses can be derived in the data, then applied to different areas or cases; this is useful in developing descriptive and explanatory accounts (Ragin, 1987). Using CAQDAS, coding can be carried out attributing theoretical and indigenous labels to the data to ensure that the phenomena are appropriately identified and meaning is not misconstrued. Finally, triangulation should be used to ensure validity in three main ways (Lewis and Ritchie, 2004): 'triangulation of sources', through the use of multiple research methods; 'triangulation of perspectives', through accessing multiple research participants from within and outside of the cases; and 'theory triangulation', through looking at the data from the perspectives of multiple theories.

Examples

In the Latin American study, reliability was ensured through multiple means. The case logic of interviewing participants both inside and external to the social enterprises proved critical in gaining an honest perspective of the cases. When conducting the fieldwork, a decision was made to conduct only one or two per day, thereby allowing for interviews to run their course (for example, although interviews were estimated to take only 45 minutes, one interview with an entrepreneur went on for three and a half hours). Following the interviews, transcripts were sent to participants to allow them to correct any statements that were not clear or had been taken out of context. Documentary analysis was also conducted to verify where possible the information discussed in interviews. To ensure dependency and trustworthiness of the analysis, the CAQDAS NVivo was used in the coding process to create an audit trail of the coding and ensure that the original data were not spliced into different sections.

Reliability was assured through using the constant comparative method by iterating between theory, data and across the cases throughout the data analysis process. Labelling methods were facilitated through NVivo by attributing theoretical and *in vivo* codes to the data. Finally, triangulation was achieved: in 'sources' through using interviews and documentary accounts; in 'perspectives' through conducting interviews and obtaining documents from participants within and outside the social enterprises; and of 'theory' through using an organising framework which coalesced thinking from entrepreneurship and strategic management literature.

5.3 CHECKLISTS FOR BEST PRACTICE

Table 5.1 provides a checklist for social entrepreneurship researchers utilising the case study as their research strategy. The checklist incorporates

Table 5.1 The case study checklist

Moment	Protocols
Rationale and research questions	Underdeveloped theory 'How?' and 'Why?' questions Contemporary, real-life phenomena Contextual understanding
Research design and case selection	Single vs. multiple cases Theoretical sampling Single case – extreme or unusual case Find the talking pig Multiple case – similar or purposefully contrasting cases
Data collection	Qualitative – interviews, document analysis, reflective journal Quantitative – surveys Mixed methods
Data analysis	Historical storytelling Coding – theoretical and *in vivo* CAQDAS Parsimony in data display key – figures and tables
Robustness	Validity – timing, participant verification, multiple perspectives Reliability – constant comparative method, labelling methods and triangulation CAQDAS

the main issues raised in this chapter and is based on a case study protocol developed by Zucker (2009).

5.4 CONCLUSION

We hope this chapter has provided you with a solid overview of what is required to undertake case study research in the context of social entrepreneurship. Though the chapter has summarised the key considerations for conducting case study research, we encourage you to explore the seminal writings of Yin (2003), Eisenhardt (1989) and Stake (1995) in depth before embarking on your own study.

REFERENCES

Alvesson, M. and S. Deetz (2000). *Doing Critical Management Research*. London: Sage.

Creswell, J.W. (2003). *Research Design: Qualitative, Quantitative and Mixed Methods Approaches*, 2nd edn. Thousand Oaks, CA: Sage.

Creswell, J.W. and D.L. Miller (2000). Determining validity in qualitative inquiry. *Theory into Practice* **39**(3), 124–130.

Crotty, M. (1998). *The Foundations of Social Research*. London: Sage Publications.

Eisenhardt, K.M. (1989). Building theories from case study research. *Academy of Management Review* **14**(4), 532–550.

Eisenhardt, K.M. and M.E. Graebner (2007). Theory building from cases: opportunities and challenges. *Academy of Management Journal* **50**(1), 25–32.

Fontana, A. and J.H. Frey (2003). The interview: from structured questions to negotiated text. In N.K. Denzin and Y.S. Lincoln (eds), *Collecting and Interpreting Qualitative Materials*, 2nd edn, Vol. II. Thousand Oak, CA: Sage Publications, pp. 61–106.

George, A.L. and A. Bennett (2004). *Case Studies and Theory Development in the Social Sciences*. Cambridge, MA, USA and London, UK: MIT Press.

Ghauri, P. (2004). Designing and conducting case studies in international business research. In R. Morschan-Pickker and C. Welch (eds), *Handbook of Qualitative Research Methods for International Business*. Cheltenham, UK and Northampton, MA, USA: Edward Elgar, pp. 109–124.

Golafshani, N. (2003). Understanding reliability and validity in qualitative research. *Qualitative Report* **8**(4), 597–607.

Greene, J.C. (2008). Is mixed methods social inquiry a distinctive methodology? *Journal of Mixed Methods Research* **2**(1), 7–22.

Greene, J.C., V.J. Caracelli and W.F. Graham (1989). Toward a conceptual framework for mixed-method evaluation designs. *Educational Evaluation and Policy Analysis* **11**(3), 255–274.

Grisar-Kasse, K. (2004). The role of negative personal experiences in cross-cultural case study research: Failure or opportunity? In R. Morschan-Pickker and C. Welch (eds), *Handbook of Qualitative Research Methods for International Business*. Cheltenham, UK and Northampton, MA, USA: Edward Elgar, pp. 144–160.

Gruber, H.E. (1988). The evolving systems approach to creative work. *Creativity Research Journal* **1**, 27–59.

Gruber, H.E. and D.B. Wallace (1999). The case study method and evolving systems approach for understanding unique creative people at work. In R.J. Sternberg (ed.), *Handbook of Creativity*. Cambridge: Cambridge University Press, pp. 93–115.

Hartley, J.F. (1994). Case studies in organizational research. In C. and G.S. Cassell (eds), *Qualitative Methods in Organizational Research: A Practical Guide*. London: SAGE Publications, pp. 208–230.
Hohenthal, J. (2006). Integrating qualitative and quantitative methods in research on international entrepreneurship. *Journal of International Entrepreneurship* **4**(4), 175–190.
King, N. (2004). Using interviews in qualitative research. In C. Cassell and S. Gillian (eds), *Essential Guide to Qualitative Methods in Organizational Research*. London: SAGE Publications, pp. 11–22.
Langley, A. (1999). Strategies for theorizing from process data. *Academy of Management Review* **24**(4), 691–710.
Legard, R., J. Keegan and K. Ward (2004). In-depth interviews. In J. Ritchie and J. Lewis (eds), *Qualitative Research Practice*. London: Sage Publications, pp. 138–169.
Lewis, J. (2004). Design issues. In J. Ritchie and J. Lewis (eds), *Qualitative Research Practice: A Guide for Social Science Students and Researchers*. London: SAGE Publications, pp. 47–76.
Lewis, J. and J. Ritchie (2004). Generalising from qualitative research. In J. Ritchie and J. Lewis (eds), *Qualitative Research Practice: A Guide for Social Science Students and Reseachers*. London: Sage Publications, pp. 263–286.
Lincoln, Y.S. and E.G. Guba (1985). *Naturalistic Inquiry*. Beverly Hills, CA: Sage.
Lincoln, Y.S. and E.G. Guba (2000). The only generalization is: there is no generalization. In R. Gomm, M. Hammersley and P. Foster (eds), *Case Study Method*. London: SAGE Publications, pp. 27–44.
Lincoln, Y.S. and E.G. Guba (2002). Judging the quality of case study reports. In A.M. Huberman and M.B. Miles (eds), *The Qualitative Researcher's Companion*. Thousand Oaks, CA: Sage Publications, pp. 205–216.
Liu, T.-H., S.-C. Hung and Y.-Y. Chu (2007). Environmental jolts, entrepreneurial actions and value creation: a case study of Trend Micro. *Technological Forecasting and Social Change* **74**(8), 1432–1445.
McCracken, G. (1988). *The Long Interview: Qualitative Research Methods*. Newbury Park, CA: SAGE Publications.
Onwuegbuzie, A.J. and N.L. Leech (2005). On becoming a pragmatic researcher: the importance of combining quantitative and qualitative research methodologies. *International Journal of Social Research Methodology* **8**(5), 375–387.
Osmond, J., and I. O'Connor (2006). Use of theory and research in social work practice: implication for knowledge-based practice. *Australian Social Work* **59**(1), 5–19.
Patton, M.Q. (1990). *Qualitative Evaluation and Research Methods*. Newbury Park, CA: Sage Publications.
Patton, M.Q. (2002). *Qualitative Research and Evaluation Methods*, 3rd edition. Thousand Oaks, CA: Sage Publications.
Piekkari, R., C. Welch and E. Paavilainen (2009). The case study as disciplinary convention: evidence from international business journals. *Organizational Research Methods* **12**(3), 567–589.
Ragin, C.C. (1987). *The Comparative Method*. Berkeley, CA: University of California Press.
Ramachandran, V.S. (1998). *Phantoms in the Brain*. New York: Harper Collins.
Seidman, I.E. (1998). *Interviewing as Qualitative Research: A Guide for Researchers in Education and the Social Sciences*, 2nd edn, New York: Teachers College Press.
Short, J.C., T.W. Moss and G.T. Lumpkin (2009). Research in social entrepreneurship: past contributions and future opportunities. *Strategic Entrepreneurship Journal*, **3**(2), 161–194.
Siggelkow, N. (2007). Persuasion with case studies. *Academy of Management Journal* **50**(1), 20–24.
Snape, D. and L. Spencer (2003). The foundations of qualitative research. In J. Ritchie and J. Lewis (eds), *Qualitative Research Practice: A Guide for Social Science Students and Researchers*. London: Sage Publications, pp. 1–23.
Stake, R. (1995). *The Art of Case Study Research*. Thousand Oaks, CA: Sage Publications.

Stake, R.E. (2000a). Case Studies. In N.K. Denzin and Y.S. Lincoln (eds), *Handbook of Qualitative Research*, 2nd edition. Thousand Oaks, CA: Sage Publications, pp. 435–454.
Stake, R.E. (2000b). The case study method in social inquiry. In R. Gomm, M. Hammersley and P. Foster (eds), *Case Study Method*. London: SAGE Publications, pp. 19–26.
van Wynsbeghe, R. and S. Khan (2007). Redefining case study. *International Journal of Qualitative Methods* **6**(2), 1–10.
Vennesson, P. (2008). Case studies and process tracing: theories and practices. In D. Della Porta and M. Keating (eds), *Approaches and Methodologies in the Social Sciences: A Pluralist Perspective*. Cambridge: Cambridge University Press, p. 223.
Verschuren, P. (2003). Case study as a research strategy: Some ambiguities and opportunities. *International Journal of Social Research Methodology* **6**(2), 121–139.
Weerawardena, J., and G.S. Mort (2006). Investigating social entrepreneurship: a multidimensional model. *Journal of World Business* **41**(1), 21–35.
Weitzman, E.A. (2003). Software and qualitative research. In N.K. Denzin and Y.S. Lincoln (eds), *Collecting and Interpreting Qualitative Materials*, Vol. 2. Thousand Oaks, CA: SAGE Publications, pp. 310–339.
Wilkinson, I., and L. Young (2004). Improvisation and adaptation in international business research interviews. In R. Morschan-Pickker and C. Welch (eds), *Handbook of Qualitative Research Methods for International Business*. Cheltenham, UK and Northampton, MA, USA: Edward Elgar, pp. 207–223.
Yin, R.K. (2003). *Case Study Research: Design and Methods*, 3rd edn. Thousand Oaks, CA: Sage Publications.
Zucker, D.M. (2009). How to do case study research. In M. Garner, C. Wagner and B. Kawulich (eds), *Teaching Research Methods in the Social Sciences*. Aldershot: Ashgate Publishing, pp. 171–182.

PART III

GATHERING

Part III of this *Handbook* focuses on the tasks associated with garnering data and insight in a systematic and methodical manner. The chapters address discourse analysis, social network analysis, and large surveys and data sets. Of course, these activities also closely relate to Part II, and as such these chapters should not be read in isolation.

Before turning to the specifics of these chapters, I divert to the biggest challenge associated with gathering data and insight: that of managing data. Dealing with masses of information increases the risk of suboptimal assessments which could arise from a variety of issues, including misperception, misaggregation and defective inferences. These cognitive limitation biases appear to be linked to our natural processes of cognition, and methods of reducing, integrating and drawing inferences from data are essential (Sadler, 2002). These chapters should assist you with the methods and tasks associated with key approaches to data collection and analysis.

Chapter 6 introduces discourse analysis. Discourse is particularly powerful as it can inform how social reality is created and maintained. It can also be used to explore how individuals use language to make sense of their reality. Fanny Salignac gives examples of the methods utilised in discourse analysis, and provides clear examples relevant for researchers exploring the context of social entrepreneurship. Salignac details a constructivist approach to discourse (this is not to understate the power of critical discourse analysis and critical linguistic analysis as research tools). Readers particularly interested in critical perspectives should read much broader than this overview. The chapter will be of particular interest to those scholars with a particular focus on the narrative (detailed in Part II of the *Handbook*).

Chapter 7 takes another approach to gathering data and insight, and focuses on social network analysis. Cynthia Webster and Jennifer Ruskin have written an informative chapter that will, I hope, generate interest in social network analysis by making the methods much more accessible for social entrepreneurship researchers. Webster and Ruskin introduce the social network approach, and then explore network data collection, representations and measures. The authors bring clarity with a data set associated with two leading organisations. The chapter concludes with a review of network theories and their interest to social entrepreneurship researchers. Pay particular attention to the theories and methods introduced, as they provide the vehicles for a rich research pipeline.

Chapter 8 explores the methods and issues associated with large data sets and quantitative analysis. Steven D'Alessandro and Hume Winzar have written a very practical chapter that sets out the basis of how to conduct survey research and interpret the large data sets resulting. D'Alessandro and Winzar also provide a review of the nature of surveys and their design, and give advice on how to construct surveys including measurement, questionnaire design, sampling and analysis.

A short Chapter 9 has been included to look specifically at the logic of developing insights. It will be of interest whether you are conducting quantitative or qualitative research, and will be of particular note to clarify the differences between statistical generalisation, analytical generalisation and abductive conclusion. The second half of the chapter will be of interest to researchers utilising qualitative methods, as it 'translates' terminologies utilised primarily by positivist methodologies. The chapter should be read in conjunction with Part IV of the *Handbook*.

Part III concerns gathering data and insight, and I hope that the following chapters will form a platform for a wide variety of interesting and valuable research projects.

6 Discourse analysis

Fanny Salignac

A discursive approach can inform a researcher interested in social entrepreneurship through the study of how individuals use language to make sense of their reality (Dick, 2004). This focus also offers significant insights into the creations of social realities: 'Discourse analysts explore how the socially produced ideas and objects that comprise . . . the social world in general are created and maintained through the relationship among discourse, text, and action' (Phillips et al., 2004, p. 637).

This chapter aims to provide you with the basic foundations for conducting discourse analysis in the field of social entrepreneurship. It first presents an overview of the discourse literature and insights from specialists in the field. This is followed by a brief look at its relevance for social entrepreneurship researchers. The main part of the chapter focuses on the provision of a set of guidelines for researchers, drawing on examples in the context of social entrepreneurship research.

6.1 WHAT IS DISCOURSE ANALYSIS?

In its most general sense, discourse analysis is concerned with how language is used in specific social contexts (Dick, 2004); it is a tool to understand how a piece of text is constructed. Texts refer to a variety of forms such as, but not limited to, written documents, transcribed interviews, verbal reports and also spoken words and dialogues, art work, symbols and pictures (Fairclaugh, 2003; Phillips et al., 2004). In choosing a discursive approach, discourse analysts explore 'how structured sets of texts come to function as "reality constructors", which help constitute the social phenomena in question' (De Cock et al., 2005, p. 38; see also Marshak and Grant, 2008).

Discourse, however, is more than just language use: Fairclough (1992) argues that it is a type of social practice. It is not just that language is social; rather it constitutes the social (Fairclaugh and Wodak, 1997). In other words, language is not seen as just reflecting the nature of the social but as actively constructing it (Dick, 2004; Fairclough, 1992), which Phillips and Hardy (2002) argue is the most important contribution of discourse analysis. Discourse analysis is not only a method enabling the examination of language use to produce explanations of the world we live in, of how individuals use language to make sense of their reality (Dick, 2004), but it also fills an epistemological function by informing us on how social reality is created (Phillips and Hardy, 2002).

While definitions of discourse are manifold, this chapter draws on Parker's definition of discourse as 'a system of statements which constructs an object' (Parker, 1992, p. 5). Discourse is concerned with the interrelatedness of a textual corpus (also referred to as bodies of text). The way in which texts are produced, but also disseminated and received, informs the researcher on how the object under scrutiny has come into being (see Parker, 1992; Maguire and Hardy, 2009; Hardy et al., 2005; Phillips et al., 2004; Phillips and Hardy, 2002; Fairclough, 1992). As discourses cannot be found in their entirety, bodies of text and their interrelatedness must be examined as opposed to isolated individual texts. This means that discourses can only be studied by looking at the texts that constitute them (Phillips and Hardy, 2002; Marshak and Grant, 2008; Phillips et al., 2004; Maguire and Hardy, 2009; Hardy et al., 2005). To make sense of the social reality and meaning created, it is critical to take into account the context in which the texts are produced and collected. The extent to which the local, social or broader context needs to be taken into account is informed by the theoretical underpinnings of the approach to discourse analysis chosen for the project. An overview of available approaches will be discussed in a later section.

6.1.1 The Value of Discourse Analysis in the Context of Social Entrepreneurship

While discursive methods enable significant insights into social entrepreneurship projects through the analysis of the construction of new social realities, discourse analysis also presents several shortcomings. In this section I propose a brief review of the main methodological strengths and weaknesses of discourse analysis.

There are a few obvious, although general, reasons why the researcher might consider not adopting a discursive approach. First of all, as with any inquiry into new methods of analysis, newcomers to the field of discourse might find it time-consuming to master such a method. Phillips and Hardy (2002) argue that this is even more so due to the relatively low availability of methodological writings and exemplars in the field. Secondly, discourse analysis is a relatively lengthy and labour-intensive method of analysis compared to quantitative methods; discourse analysis requires the analysis of bodies of text and can therefore be a slow process. Thirdly, with regard to a subjective versus objective approach to social sciences, a discursive approach to data analysis typically conveys results of a subjectivist nature (ontological underpinnings to discourse analysis assume reality as a social construction, as opposed to a concrete structure in the positivist tradition) (Morgan and Smircich, 1980). While this point will also be argued as one of the method's strengths, it is here presented as a weakness, considering the claim that qualitative research or research of a subjectivist nature is typically more difficult to publish than its more positivistic counterpart in the business field.

On the other hand, several positive reasons for adopting discourse analysis can be identified, and outweigh the method's weaknesses. First of all, Phillips and Hardy (2002, p. 12) argue that: 'the idea that language is much more than a simple reflection of reality – that, in fact, it is constitutive of social reality – has become commonly accepted'. Alvesson and Karreman (2000, p. 1126) argue that the study of language use is increasingly considered as the most appropriate method for empirical investigation in social research. Discourse analysis is, therefore, a timely method of analysis specifically well suited to social entrepreneurship as it aims to investigate the construction of new social phenomena through the analysis of bodies of text. Secondly, the entrepreneurial nature of social entrepreneurship projects, and therefore the investigation of social value creation through innovation, seem particularly well suited to a discursive approach as significant insights will be gained on the construction of new social realities.

6.2 HOW TO UNDERTAKE DISCOURSE ANALYSIS

This section aims to equip the researcher with the necessary know-how for conducting discourse analysis in the context of social entrepreneurship projects. The presented guidelines emanate from the author's experience with discourse analysis and will be supplemented by drawing on examples in the context of social entrepreneurship research. The study that will be used as an example throughout this section is a discourse analysis of the Fairtrade movement in the UK and France. Briefly, the purpose of the study is to gain insights into the construction of national Fairtrade identities.

6.2.1 The Diversity of Approaches to Discourse

This section aims at equipping the researcher with a clear understanding of the main approaches available. The first step to starting your analysis is to decide which approach to discourse to follow. For newcomers to the field this might involve conducting a brief literature review of the different

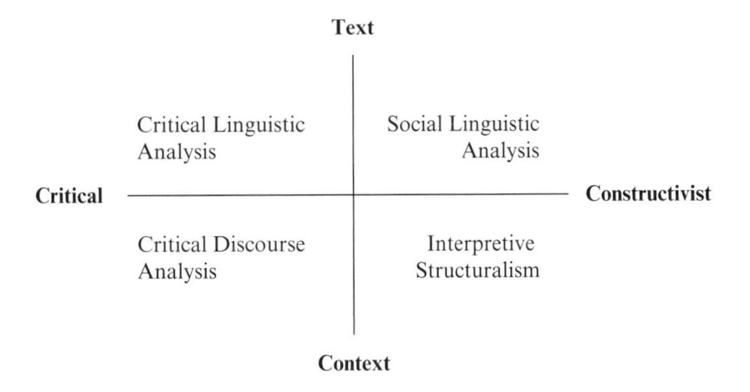

Source: Adapted from Philips and Hardy (2002, p. 20).

Figure 6.1 Different approaches to discourse analysis

writings and exemplars available in order to understand better the various choices available. Approaches range from 'micro', such as linguistics analysis, to 'macro', associated with broader contextual approaches (Phillips et al., 2004). For a complete and comprehensive categorisation of the various approaches to discourse analysis, refer to Phillips and Hardy (2002) as well as Jaworski and Coupland (1999) and Grant et al. (2004).

Philips and Hardy (2002) propose a valuable framework to understand better the diversity in the field (see Figure 6.1). Typically, two elements will influence your choice. First, the focus given to individual texts as opposed to bodies of text (represented by the 'Text' and 'Context' continuum on the vertical axis). The extent to which the context of the research should be taken into account (whether the local, social or broader context) depends on the specificities of the study under investigation. Interpretive structuralism, for example, helps in making sense of how social realities are constructed through the analysis of bodies of text, their interrelatedness and the context in which they are produced and consumed. Social linguistic analysis, on the other hand, while also focusing on social constructions, does so at a micro-textual level.

Second, the focus given to dynamics of power and relations of ideologies as opposed to social constructions (represented by the 'Constructivist' and 'Critical' continuum on the horizontal axis). Anchored in notions of critical theory, critical discourse analysis (CDA) is concerned with 'the way discourse (re)produces social domination, that is, the power abuse of one group over others, and how dominated groups may discursively resist such abuse' (Wodak and Meyer, 2009, p. 9). CDA therefore focuses on the dynamics of power by taking into account the broader social context, as opposed to the textually based approach taken by critical linguistic analysis.

It is important to note that the theoretical underpinnings of the researcher's empirical work will significantly influence the research style outcome. Different approaches lead to different focuses and therefore different results; the researcher's theoretical inclinations are bound to influence this choice.

Example

In the Fairtrade project, I was particularly interested in investigating how a new social reality had been constructed around the idea that a special kind of trade responding to specific requirements could help to benefit producers of the South. I wanted to investigate how the new social order of Fairtrade had emerged and whether it had developed homogenously in various national contexts. In order to do so, it seemed crucial to take the context of the research into account. I needed to be able to investigate not only the direct development of Fairtrade but also the context in which it had developed. Therefore, I chose to write my research in the tradition of interpretive structuralism.

Now, imagine that the specific focus of my study had been the power certain Fairtrade organisations have in developing the Fairtrade identity, and whether national Fairtrade organisations cooperate or compete against each other in the construction of a Fairtrade discourse. According to the continuum introduced by Phillips and Hardy (2002), the appropriate choice would then have moved from a constructivist focus to a critical one. The focus of the study is, therefore, an important indicator of which discourse approach to follow.

The multimodal aspect of discourse

Whether to take the position of textual elements and their relation to potential pictorial elements into account is concerned with the multimodal aspect of the text under analysis. Several authors argue that all texts are multimodal: 'language always has to be realized through, and comes in the company of, other semiotic modes' (Kress and van Leeuwen, 1998, p. 187; see also Lemke, 2002; Salway, 2010; O'Halloran, 2008; van Leeuwen, 2005; Martinec and Salway, 2005). The importance of textual–pictorial elements relations for sense making was originally mentioned by Halliday (1978) who argues for the constant interrelatedness of the pictorial and verbal modes or 'inter-semiotic layering' (Eckkrammer, 2004) for sense making.

Two frameworks enabling analysis of image–text interactions are reviewed in turn: (1) Kress and van Leeuwen (1998); (2) Martinec and

Salway (2005). See O'Halloran (2008) for a comprehensive review of existing frameworks.

In their framework, Kress and van Leeuwen (1998) emphasize the importance of page layout and text structure in sense making: 'written text is no longer structured by linguistic means . . . but visually through layout, through the spatial arrangement of blocks of text, of pictures and other graphic elements on the page' (Kress and van Leeuwen, 1998, p. 187). Their framework, originally developed in the context of newspaper layouts, involves three 'signifying systems' bringing the various elements of the text into a coherent whole: information value, salience and framing.

By 'information value', Kress and van Leeuwen (1998) refer to the placement of elements in a layout. Text can be either polarized or centred. Polarization happens along a horizontal/vertical axis. Horizontal polarization to the left is referred to as 'Given' – known to the reader, also seen as common sense. Horizontal polarization to the right is referred to as 'New' – not yet known to the reader, also seen as problematic. Vertical polarization to the top is referred to as 'Ideal' – general information. Vertical polarization to the bottom is referred to as 'Real' – specific information. Layouts can also be organized around a centre – representing the nucleus of information to which marginal elements are subordinated.

The second signifying system Kress and van Leeuwen (1998) refer to is the 'salience' of the elements, text or image, present in the layout and the degree to which these elements draw the reader's attention – not only because of its visual function but because of its role in structuring meaning. A certain number of factors are identified as informing the salience of elements: size, amount of detail, colour contrast and intensity, visual placement. 'Framing' is the last signifying system: elements can be strongly or weakly framed, respectively presenting disconnected or connected 'units of information' (Kress and van Leeuwen, 1998).

Let us now turn to the second framework. Martinec and Salway (2005) argue that the key to understanding image–text combinations resides in the way that these elements relate to each other. Drawing on the idea of Barthes (1977) and Halliday (1978), Martinec and Salway (2005) developed a framework for classifying image–text relations across all kinds of multimodal discourse. They identify two types of relations: (1) 'status relations' – concerned with the relative importance of the text and the image; and (2) 'logico-semantic relations' – concerned with the way they function to convey meaning.

With regards to their status relations, Martinec and Salway (2005) consider the relation between an image and a text to be 'equal' when either: (1) both elements are required for successful sense making – they are in this case said to be 'equal-complementary'; or (2) both elements can be understood individually – they are in this case said to be 'equal-independent'. The relation between an image and a text is 'unequal' when the pictorial or textual element can be understood individually; the one that cannot be understood individually is said to be subordinate to the other. The relative status of textual and pictorial elements is best classified by looking at two kinds of features: page layout – as mentioned by Kress and van Leeuwen (1998) – and lexical references. Martinec and Salway (2005) argue that the particularity of the English language, read and written from left to right and top to bottom, implies that the page layout will be organized so that important information is given most space and positioned to be read first: 'the subordinate media type [therefore] should appear to the right, below, and take less space' (Martinec and Salway, 2005, p. 9).

With regards to logico-semantic relations Martinec and Salway (2005) identify three types: elaboration, extension and enhancement. A text and an image can be said to elaborate each other by further detailing, specifying one another; they can be said to extend each other's meaning by adding information; or enhance each other by qualifying each other in reference to time and place, for example. Classifying logico-semantic relations requires comparisons between the text and the image.

Example

To illustrate the use and meaningfulness of such frameworks, I present below the multimodal analysis of Alter Eco's website (a French Fairtrade licensee selected for the study). The analysis is conducted on Alter Eco's first two web-pages.

Alter Eco makes extensive use of images throughout its website. According to Martinec and Salway (2005), it is suggested that their relationship to the textual elements is equal-independent, implying that both the textual and pictorial elements can be understood independently, but that for successful communication to occur both elements need to be taken into account in combination. Pictures appear most often strongly framed, disconnecting the featured units of information from each other (Kress and van Leeuwen, 1998). In terms of logico-semantics, text is used to inform the pictures, as such they can be said to extend each other. An analysis of the page layout and textual elements using Kress and van Leeuwen's (1998) framework for text organization will deepen the analysis.

Alter Eco's home page (see Figure 6.2) is organized around a strongly framed centre. A short margin is featured to the top and the bottom, a larger margin to the left, but none to the right, allowing the rest of the page to be occupied by the centre: nucleus of information. The salience of this page is complex, every element seems to attract the readers' attention. The

Figure 6.2 Alter Eco's home page

overall background of the page is red; the upper margin features the main menu and sub-menu illustrated with several photos representing the producers, Fairtrade products and Alter Eco's logo. Below, acting as a header to the centre, is featured a slideshow: photos of farmers and Fairtrade products. The centre's title speaks for itself and gives the tone of Alter Eco's commitment to the Fairtrade movement: 'It's so good to change the world', strongly positioning and affirming its position. The information supplied at the centre is weakly framed, suggesting a divide among new information given as well as a certain connection among them to keep the centre as a whole. The centre appears strongly framed against the left margin through the use of a different background colour, orange, while the margin appears on the overall page's background, red. The left margin is strongly framed, implying a divide between each given unit of information. To the left is presented a series of 'information boxes' – strongly framed units of information, featuring an image and salient caption acting also as an electronic link to further information on the stipulated theme. Each box is related to Alter Eco and therefore to Fairtrade in some way. By virtue of its centre versus margin position as well as the amount of space allocated, it is suggested that the nucleus presents a higher level of salience than that of the rest.

The second available link on the main menu opens a page entitled: 'Our Products' (see Figure 6.3). The layout is very similar: upper and lower margins featuring the exact same information and details as the home page; left margins featuring the same 'information boxes', except that fewer have been included (three as opposed to nine); the centre layout now features only one unit of information (textual element – black font on white background); the page background colour has changed, it is now pink. The salience of the centre is increased by the slideshow at the top featuring photos of Alter Eco's Fairtrade products. The textual element is relatively short and clearly emphasises Alter Eco's willingness to act for changing the rules of international trade not only in regard to the nature of commercial exchanges but also in regard to the environment: 'Alter Eco's products are committed and militant for a different vision of exchanges and our relation to the earth'. The relationship between the retailer and its producers is emphasised. When describing some of its products, Alter Eco stipulates: 'an organic rooibos militant for the autonomy of smallholder producers of South Africa and the preservation of biodiversity', emphasising the power that Fairtrade products have to benefit producers and bring about some changes. Lastly, on the left-hand side of the centre, where the background colour is visible, has been included a search engine to find Alter Eco's Fairtrade products according to several categories (products, countries, label).

Figure 6.3 Alter Eco's products page

In this example I demonstrate the appropriateness of multimodal discourse analysis (MDA) in hypertextual environments. MDA allows the researcher to draw meaningful conclusions from textual–pictorial interaction specifically prominent in hypermedia. Such analysis is particularly relevant to research with a high contextual level. Your data source as well as the purpose of your study will help guide your choice of whether to consider MDA or another type of discourse analysis for your study.

6.2.2 Topic and Case Selection

Depending on the focus of your study you can either choose to select specific case(s) or go straight to data collection. If for example the aim of your study was to investigate the effects of the financial crisis in Australia for the year 2009, you could start collecting data straight away by doing a newspaper article search all around the country for the selected sample year and therefore study this phenomenon at the national level. Or, in order to get specific results, you could select several financial institutions around the country and study the financial crisis at the organizational level. While there is no right or wrong answer, your research question and the focus of your study will influence your choice. Note that rightly justifying your selection is crucial to the success of your study.

Example

The context is examined by contrasting actors participating in the Fairtrade market in the United Kingdom (UK) (as a nation leading the Fairtrade movement, *Grocer*, 2005); and France (similar to the UK in terms of level of economic development, and market size, OECD, 2009, and yet lagging behind in terms of Fairtrade development, Lecomte, 2006). The selection of these case studies is further justified by the lead author's fluency in both English and French.

Contrasting cases of retailers from the UK and France were selected. Retailers were chosen both for their significant involvement in their respective Fairtrade market, as well as for their opposing retailing philosophies. In the UK, Tesco plc (hereafter referred to as Tesco), Marks & Spencer Group plc (hereafter referred to as M&S), Traidcraft plc (hereafter Traidcraft), and Oxfam Activities Ltd (the trading arm of Oxfam, hereafter Oxfam) were selected. For France: Groupe Carrefour SAS (hereafter Carrefour), Groupe Leclerc SC (hereafter Leclerc), Alter Eco SA (hereafter Alter Eco), and Fédération Artisans du Monde (hereafter ADM) were selected.

Tesco and Carrefour are considered to be traditional mass retailers that have not developed a strong positioning with Fairtrade (that is, leading mass retailers, supplying Fairtrade products, but with little active advocacy of the Fairtrade philosophy). Similarly, M&S and Leclerc were selected for demonstrating characteristics of being leading 'green' mass retailers in their respective national markets. In this chapter I use the terms 'traditional retailers', 'mass retailers' and 'supermarkets' interchangeably. Traidcraft and Alter Eco were selected for being legally structured as for-profit Fairtrade licensees with similar retailing philosophies. Finally, Oxfam and ADM, also Fairtrade licensees, were selected for their main activities being carried out as not-for-profit charities.

6.2.3 Data Collection

Deciding on the data source is an important step in collecting data. The researcher has to keep in mind that different data sources call for different types of discourse analysis, and vice versa. While 'all texts are multimodal' (Kress and van Leeuwen, 1998, p. 187), certain media will more likely necessitate the use of multimodal discourse analysis than others. It is argued, for example, that multimodality is specifically prominent in hypermedia:

> Hypertext favours non-linear structures in text and, through its computational medium, enables the use of more than one mode and overlapping semiotic codes. Multimodality is fostered by hypertextual environments just as much as the chunking and interconnection of texts through visible electronic relations (links). (Eckkrammer, 2004, p. 215)

If choosing websites as the project's data source, it is most likely that multimodality will need to be taken into account in order to conduct a sound analysis. It is worthwhile noting however that disregarding the multimodality of a specific textual corpus can also be done, but needs to be properly justified. To illustrate, it was argued in the Fairtrade project that the study was concerned with actions that are more likely to produce texts, as well as texts that are consumed and disseminated to influence discourse. In light of this, it was argued that newspaper articles would be used as the data source in an attempt to gain insights into the general status and understanding of Fairtrade in the respective societal contexts. The multimodality of the newspaper articles was not taken into account as it was not the focus of the study.

6.2.4 Corpus of Analysis

When collecting data, it is important to delimit the textual corpus for analysis: no discourse analyst can analyse everything. A certain number of elements need to be taken into consideration in regard to the method. To begin with, it is essential that a sample period be specified; of course justification needs to be given as to why this particular period is of interest, as well as its specific relevance to the project. If using newspapers as your data source, characteristics such as region, political stance, circulation and readership, will also need to be considered in regard to the focus the researcher wants to give the data set; clear justification will need to be given. To a certain extent the researcher should also aim at automatically eliminating certain articles by setting specific requirements that the articles will need to fulfil, in order to keep control over the data set.

According to the extent to which the context is taken into consideration, and the different levels of sampling, the discourse analyst might go through a large number of texts. In order to keep track of the number of texts gathered according to the different level of sampling, I find it useful to organize the data collected into a table (see Table 6.1). One of the major critiques regarding the method of discourse analysis is its potential subjectivity; it is therefore important to be able to show what you have done and the various stages you have gone through to collect and analyze your data in order to counter these sorts of criticisms.

Example

Data were collected over a three-year period: 2005–2007. In both countries, there was a spike in interest in Fairtrade in 2006: M&S announced that all its tea and coffee would be Fairtrade, propelling it at once 'from a Fairtrade laggard to a Fairtrade leader' (Lamb, 2008, p. 73). The shift was 'part of a wider trend by supermarkets to position themselves as greener or more ethical than their rivals – rather than just cheaper' (Lamb, 2008, p. 73). In France, Carrefour introduced a variety of Fairtrade products in late 2005 under their own label: Carrefour Agir Solidaire ('Carrefour Solidarity Act'), which slowly developed to include teas, coffees and fruit juices. The period 2005–2007 allows comparison of the period before and after events of 2006. A search on Factiva was conducted for Tesco, M&S, Traidcraft, Oxfam, Carrefour, Leclerc, Alter Eco, ADM and Coles. Articles containing respective company names and the word 'Fairtrade' (or for the French context 'Commerce Equitable') were collected.

6.2.5 Data Analysis

It is possible for the researcher to use qualitative software enabling the organisation of content-rich data text and therefore facilitating the analysis. NVivo was used throughout the Fairtrade project and was demonstrated to be extremely valuable in helping to organise elements of the data

Table 6.1 Data collection – UK

Date Range	Search 1 Fairtrade and Tesco			Search 2 Fairtrade and Traidcraft			Search 3 Fairtrade and Marks & Spencer***			Search 4 Fairtrade and Oxfam		
	Search 1	Sample*	Refined**	Search 2	Sample*	Refined**	Search 3	Sample*	Refined**	Search 4	Sample*	Refined**
01/01/1992 31/12/1992	0			2			0			2		
01/01/1993 31/12/1993	1			4			0			9		
01/01/1994 31/12/1994	4			8			2			14		
01/01/1995 31/12/1995	2			4			0			10		
01/01/1996 31/12/1996	6			3			7			14		
01/01/1997 31/12/1997	5			4			2			7		
01/01/1998 31/12/1998	7			4			1			10		
01/01/1999 31/12/1999	9			5			4			23		
01/01/2000 31/12/2000	20			13			7			28		
01/01/2001 31/12/2001	11			15			7			50		

01/01/2002 31/12/2002	29			31			12			78		
01/01/2003 31/12/2003	39			27			12			88		
01/01/2004 31/12/2004	73			54			31			126		
01/01/2005 31/12/2005	100	13	8	80	13	7	74	2	1	185	9	5
01/01/2006 31/12/2006	278	20	10	110	11	5	369	19	16	187	1	0
01/01/2007 31/12/2007	441	42	12	116	4	3	479	10	8	192	9	6
01/01/2008 31/12/2008	337			147			285			208		
01/01/2009 31/12/2009	242			90			166			112		

Notes:

* Represents stage one of data collection: Articles manually selected from the search on Factiva;

** Represents stage two of data collection: A deeper level of selection using a text search in Nvivo to refine the samples (producer(s) or farmer(s) or grower(s));

*** Throughout the British press, Marks and Spencer is also referred to as: Marks & Spencer or M&S. The search on Factiva accounted for each of these.

set as well as structuring the analysis. It is not, however, a requirement for the researcher to use such types of qualitative software, and analysis can be conducted 'by hand'. Most of the time, researchers who are not using qualitative software resort to the use of commonly available spreadsheet or database programs (for example Excel) to facilitate the organisation and recording of data.

Example

The analysis of the data comprises three main stages. In the first stage, articles related to the topic of interest were selected. The following articles were eliminated: (1) those less than 100 words as they were not context-rich; (2) those in which there was an accumulation of only very short daily news items; (3) those in which only the name of the retailer was mentioned, without any link to Fairtrade; (4) those in which Fairtrade was mentioned without any link to the retailer; and (5) 'op-ed' pieces.

In the second stage, the selected newspaper articles were imported into NVivo (a qualitative software enabling the organization of content-rich data text) to facilitate the organization of texts. The research argues that the presence of the producers in the retailers' discourse is a significant indicator of their involvement into the market. The body of texts is therefore limited to texts mentioning the words 'producer(s)', 'grower(s)' or 'farmer(s)' respectively '*producteur*(*s*)', '*paysan*(*s*)' and '*artisan*(*s*)' for our French sample. A text-search using NVivo was then carried out; articles containing such text were selected for analysis.

In the third stage, the selected articles were coded for reference to their respective national Fairtrade identities as identified by the results of the exploratory research: UK (mainstreaming), France (militant) and Australia (infantile awareness). Complementary coding was conducted with reference to: (1) supermarkets' involvement; and (2) producers and competition, to inform further the development of Fairtrade in the respective national contexts.

6.2.6 Writing Up the Analysis

Conducting the analysis, depending more or less on the size of your sample, can be a time-consuming activity. The discourse analyst will need to go through each and every textual element to identify references to the topic of interest, record these references and interpret them. This stage requires an intensive amount of work; I find it useful to organize occurrences to a specific theme into a table (see for example Table 6.2), as well as some notes on their significance (see for example Table 6.3). This helps to organize the analysis as well as to interprete the results. Sequential

Table 6.2 Word count for 'farmer(s)', 'producer(s)' or 'grower(s)' in UK

	Tesco	M&S	Oxfam	Traidcraft
Number of articles in sample	30	25	11	15
Frequency word count	93	74	36	42
Coverage – Frequency index	3.1	3	3.3	2.8

steps to discourse analysis are presented in the 'Researcher's toolbox', section 6.3.

Example – UK: producers and competition

Running a frequency search using the words producer(s), farmer(s) or grower(s) for Tesco, Traidcraft, M&S and Oxfam carries approximately the same results in terms of frequency word use (see Table 6.2); this does not, however, take the context into account. A deeper analysis suggests different discourse produced by the selected UK retailers (see Table 6.3 for a summary of references to 'producers').

In articles referring to Tesco, the word 'producer(s)' is usually mentioned very briefly. Illustrating our point are sentences such as: 'helping five million people across 49 developing countries' (underlined text is the result of the author's discourse analysis). The data collected throughout the 2005–2007 sample period did not suggest any noticeable improvements: the discourse Tesco utilises to refer to its Fairtrade producers has remained unchanged through the years. Any links between the retailer and benefits of the Fairtrade market to the producers are voiced by Fairtrade organizations' representatives, such as Harriet Lamb.

M&S makes different use of the word 'producer(s)', reconciling profit and producers' benefit. The following sentences best illustrate our point: 'Last year we also converted all the tea and coffee we sell to Fairtrade, which meant more than GBP340 000 in Fairtrade premium went directly back to our farmers to invest in their communities'. While the reference to producers is tied to market growth and profit, the sentence nonetheless links profit and producers' well-being, as well as containing the word 'communities' – vocabulary very specific to the Fairtrade discourse. Even more interestingly, the use of the possessive pronoun 'our' suggest a recognition of genuine corporate responsibility from M&S.

British Fairtrade licensees Oxfam GB and Traidcraft both make a clear link between profit and producers; their focus, however, clearly is the mainstreaming of Fairtrade. It is interesting to note that subtle references to changing international trade policies are recorded for Oxfam GB: 'let

Table 6.3 Reference to 'producers' in the UK sample (underlined text is the result of the author's discourse analysis)

Source	Quotes	Significance
Tesco 14/05/05	'Fairtrade is a fantastic way for the consumer to do something simple that will have a direct impact' (Fairtrade Foundation Executive Director).	The positive impacts of Fairtrade on producers are very briefly and indirectly mentioned by Harriet Lamb.
M&S 30/07/05	'Our customers have told us they not only want products which taste great but also ensure the farmers get a fair price for their crops. We're delighted that we can now offer our customers even more Fairtrade options, which is great news for both our customers and our producers' (M&S representative).	M&S here, with a direct quote, shows some genuine interest in the Fairtrade market and make an important link between Fairtrade's two most important actors: the producers and the consumers.
Traidcraft 02/12/05	'Buying Fairtrade products makes a huge difference. Fairtrade sees more money reach the communities the product comes from, which means more children can go to school, eat adequately and live in decent homes' (Traidcraft spokeswoman).	Quote very representative of a Fairtrade discourse – close to Fairtrade's original aims and definition.
M&S 30/01/06	'The new M&S clothing range would create a "brighter future" for Indian cotton farmers. Under the Fairtrade system, farmers get a fair price for their product, with a Fairtrade premium that is invested in their community' (Fairtrade Foundation Executive Director).	M&S's move into the Fairtrade market is strongly supported by Fairtrade advocate Harriet Lamb.
Traidcraft 09/03/06	'And once people become more aware of Fairtrade fashion, they will start to look around for more. In our case, we don't exist to sell, we exist to drive people out of poverty' (Traidcraft's representative).	Traidcraft's business objectives are clearly stipulated: profit is not its goal but poverty relief is.
Tesco 24/02/07	'Tesco extended its fair trade nut offer in December last year. It claimed more than 13 000 farmers in Malawi, Mozambique and India will benefit from the decision to launch a 200g Fairtrade peanut and raisin mix and Fairtrade natural cashews in 150g packs' (*The Journalist*).	Here again, as in 2005, producers are succinctly mentioned among Tesco's Fairtrade supply range.
M&S 01/03/07	'Last year we also converted all the tea and coffee we sell to Fairtrade, which meant more than GBP340 000 in Fairtrade premium went directly back to our farmers to invest in their communities' (M&S representative).	M&S again shows its commitment to the Fairtrade retailing philosophy, using the possessive pronoun 'our' suggesting its engagement to its farmers.

us be clear. The biggest problem facing farmers in the developing world [are] the subsidies the west provides to its own farmers. These are deeply unfair, if the west is truly serious about making poverty history, then agricultural subsidies must be abolished' (Oxfam spokeswoman). The data suggest Oxfam is working towards bringing changes to international trading practices. Traidcraft's motives are best summarized by this sentence: 'We shall carry on doing what we do best: gently trying to persuade folk that it really is a good thing to help the poorer producers overseas, that Traidcraft is one of the best ways of achieving this and, at the same time, giving folk the opportunity to taste very high-quality produce'. Here, helping producers is cast at the forefront, although while not losing the sight of consumers and supplying quality products. But here it is also worth noting that Traidcraft is positioning itself against competition, as judged by words such as 'what we do best', 'persuade' and 'one of the best ways of achieving this'.

This oblique reference to competition is, however, the only one for Traidcraft, while 19 references to competition were recorded for Tesco. In 2006, M&S switched entirely to Fairtrade tea and coffee and introduced a new range of clothing made of Fairtrade cotton, dramatically raising the bar of mass retailers' involvement in the Fairtrade market and increasing competition, thereby gaining the support of Fairtrade Foundation Executive Director Harriet Lamb, who in 2007 stated: 'The growth of the Fairtrade product range in M&S over the past year has been truly remarkable. We're delighted that M&S has shown real leadership'.

While the data suggest that competition has dramatically increased through the years in the British market for Fairtrade, it has been possible to appreciate the diverging approaches that selected retailers – Tesco, M&S, Traidcraft and Oxfam GB – have taken. All, however, converge towards the need for the mainstreaming of Fairtrade.

6.3 SUMMARY: THE RESEARCHER'S TOOLBOX

While the sequential steps to discourse analysis presented below are reiterated in most discourse projects, the researcher will find that certain steps might need to be either added to or cancelled from the list to suit a particular project. For further reference, it is worthwhile noting Jäger and Maier's (2009) structural analysis of the discourse strand from which these sequential steps are inspired, as well as Philips and Hardy's (2002) chapter on 'The challenges of discourse analysis'.

Steps are presented in a sequential order that appear logical to the author. The specific sequence of these steps, however, do not need to be strictly followed; rather, the analysis will emerge from the steps being analysed, combined and interpreted together.

1. Choosing your approach to discourse
   Before collecting or analysing your data, it is important that you position yourself within the different approaches to discourse analysis. Remember that the purpose of your research and theoretical underpinnings (whether you anchor your study within a constructivist or critical tradition), and the extent of contextual details, will hint at which approach to follow.
2. Choosing to take multimodality into account or not
   If the positioning of the texts you have chosen is of importance for your study (whether you have chosen media text or hypertext), you will need to use a multimodal approach to discourse analysis. Several details regarding the layout of the text as well as its relation to potential pictorial elements will need to be accounted for. See Kress and van Leeuwen (1998) and Martinec and Salway (2005) for further details. If, on the other hand, you are using media texts but choose for a specific reason not to use multimodal discourse analysis, you need to make sure that you are giving a strong and rational justification for your choice.
3. Selecting your topic and case(s)
   Your topic and cases for the study must be chosen according to what you are trying to achieve and approach to discourse chosen.
4. Collecting your data
   Deciding on the data source of your study is important as it will contribute to influencing your choice of discourse approach as well as whether or not to use multimodal discourse analysis.
5. Selecting texts for analysis
   A corpus of textual elements relevant to the discursive approach of the project is compiled. Note that in discursive terms 'text' here refers to a variety of forms such as: written documents, transcribed interviews and verbal reports, but also spoken words and dialogues, artwork, symbols, pictures and so on. You will need to keep as much information as possible about collected texts (for example, where were they produced? By whom? In what context?), as this will most likely significantly inform the analysis.
6. Analysing your data
   Particular topics of interest (themes), as well as subtopics, as formulated per the research project, need to be identified throughout the elements of the bodies of text. Occurrence of themes as well as their absence will inform the analysis. It is worthwhile noting that while

a specific topic of interest might be known to the researcher prior to conducting the analysis, several topics might also emerge as being particularly relevant as the analysis is carried out. If using qualitative software such as NVivo, theme identification will be carried out when coding the textual elements.

While discourse analysis is a qualitative approach to research and therefore context-rich conclusions are favoured, frequencies and word count can also prove valuable. In this step the researcher will need to look at the frequency of the identified topics of interest throughout the data set. The researcher here needs to draw conclusions from the frequency of appearance – occurrence or absence – of specifically identified topics, subtopics or words.

7. Writing up your analysis
   It is important in writing up your analysis to organize your thoughts around the broad themes of the research and to keep your analysis flowing logically. Think about using tables, as this will help in organizing your data and analysis.

6.4 CONCLUSION

This chapter concludes on the particular relevance of discourse analysis to the field of social entrepreneurship. The method is specifically useful for social entrepreneurship as it allows for examining how language constructs new phenomena, and therefore enables meaningful conclusions to be drawn regarding the social construction of new realities.

A word of advice regarding the conduct of discourse analysis, however, seems worthwhile to newcomers. Discourse analysis is a time-consuming and labour-intensive method; it requires rigorousness to be applied throughout the project as the bodies of text under analysis can potentially be made of a large amount of textual elements. The researcher also needs to be aware that discourse analysis is generally criticised for its impreciseness; it is therefore crucial that the discourse analyst keeps meticulous records of the various steps undertaken during analysis.

Discourse is, nonetheless, an exciting method of analysis leading to an amazing richness of conclusions and allowing the researcher to understand the construction of social realities through the use of language. It also allows the researcher to conduct analysis in different languages and therefore enlarge even further the array of fruitful findings. As such, it provides a powerful approach for the context of social entrepreneurship research.

REFERENCES

Alvesson, M. and D. Karreman (2000). Varieties of discourse: on the study of organizations through discourse analysis. *Human Relations* **53**, 1125.

Barthes, R. (1977). Introduction to the structural analysis of narratives. In R. Barthes (ed.), *Image Music Text*. New York: Hill & Wang, pp. 79–124.

De Cock, C., J. Fitchett and C. Volkmann (2005). Constructing the new economy: a discursive perspective. *British Journal of Management* **16**, 37–49.

Dick, P. (2004). Discourse analysis. In C. Cassell and G. Symon (eds), *Essential Guide to Qualitative Methods in Organizational Research*. London, UK; Thousand Oaks, CA, New Delhi, India: Sage Publications, pp. 203–212.

Eckkrammer, E.M. (2004). Drawing on theories of inter-semiotic layering to analyse multimodality in medical self-counselling texts and hypertexts. In E. Ventola, C. Charles and M. Kaltenbacher (eds), *Perspectives on Multimodality*. Amsterdam, Netherlands; Philadelphia, PA: John Benjamins Publishing Company, pp. 211–226.

Fairclough, N. (1992). *Discourse and Social Change*. Cambridge: Polity Press.

Fairclaugh, N. (2003). *Analysing Discourse: Textual Analysis for Social Research*. London, UK and New York, USA: Routledge.

Fairclaugh, N. and R. Wodak (1997). Critical Discourse Analysis. In T.A. Van Dijk (ed.), *Discourse as Social Interaction*. London: Sage, pp. 258–284.

Grant, D., C. Hardy, C. Oswick and L. Putman (eds) (2004). *The Sage Handbook of Organizational Discourse*. Los Angeles, CA; London, UK; New Delhi, India; Singapore: Sage.

Grocer (2005). Traidcraft in Tesco attack. 19 February.

Halliday, M.A.K. (1978). *Language as Social Semiotic: The Social Interpretation of Language and Meaning*. London: Arnold.

Hardy, C., L. Thomas and D. Grant (2005). Discourse and Collaboration: The Role of Conversations and Collective Identity. *Academy of Management Review* **30**, 59–77.

Jäger, S. and F. Maier (2009). Theoretical and methodological aspects of Foucauldian critical discourse analysis and dispositive analysis. In R. Wodak and M. Meyer (eds), *Methods of Critical Discourse Analysis*. London, UK; Thousand Oaks, CA, USA; New Delhi, India; Singapore: Sage, pp. 34–61.

Jaworski, A. and N. Coupland (1999). Perspectives on discourse analysis. In A. Jaworski and N. Coupland (eds), *The Discourse Reader*. London, UK and New York, USA: Routledge, pp. 1–44.

Kress, G. and T. Van Leeuwen (1998). Front pages: (the critical) analysis of newspaper layout. In A. Bell and P. Garrett (eds), *Approaches to Media Discourse*. Oxford and Malden: Blackwell Publishers, pp. 186–219.

Lamb, H. (2008). *Fighting the Banana Wars and Other Fairtrade Battles*, London, UK; Sydney, Australia; Auckland, NZ; Johannesburg, South Africa: Rider.

Lecomte, T. (2006). *Commerce et Développement Durable, Comment Passer de la Niche 'Éthique' Au Marché?* http://tristanlecomte.altereco.com/tristan/2006/05/de_la_niche_thi.html (accessed 30 July 2010).

Lemke, J.L. (2002). Travels in hypermodality. *Visual Communication* **1**, 299–325.

Maguire, S. and C. Hardy (2009). Discourse and deinstitutionalization: the decline of ddt. *Academy of Management Journal* **52**, 148–178.

Marshak, R.J. and D. Grant (2008). Organizational discourse and new organization development practices. *British Journal of Management* **19**, S7–S19.

Martinec, R. and A. Salway (2005). A system for image–text relations in new (old) media. *Visual Communication* **4**, 337–371.

Morgan, G. and L. Smircich (1980). The case for qualitative research. *Academy of Management Review* **5**, 491–500.

O'Halloran, K.L. (2008). Multimodal analysis and digital technology. In A. Baldry and E. Montagna (eds), *Interdisciplinary Perspectives on Multimodality: Theory and Practice. Proceedings of the Third International Conference on Multimodality*. Campobasso: Palladino.

OECD (2009). *OECD Statextracts: National Accounts at a Glance – 2009 Edition*. http://stats.oecd.org/Index.aspx?DataSetCode=NAG (accessed 8 March 2010).
Parker, I. (1992). *Discourse Dynamics: Critical Analysis for Social and Individual Psychology*. London: Routledge.
Phillips, N. and C. Hardy (2002). *Discourse Analysis: Investigating Process of Social Construction*. Thousand Oaks, CA, USA; London, UK; New Delhi, India: Sage Publications.
Phillips, N., T.B. Lawrence and C. Hardy (2004). Discourse and institutions. *Academy of Management Review* **29**, 635–652.
Salway, A. (2010). The computer-based analysis of narrative and multimodality. In R. Page (ed.), *New Perspectives on Narrative and Multimodality*. New York, USA and Abingdon, Oxon: Routledge, pp. 50–64.
Van Leeuwen, T. (2005). *Introducing Social Semiotics*. New York: Routledge.
Wodak, R. and M. Meyer (2009). Critical discourse analysis: history, agenda, theory and methodology. In R. Wodak and M. Meyer (eds), *Methods of Critical Discourse Analysis*. London, UK; Thousand Oaks, CA; New Delhi, India; Singapore: Sage Publications.

7 Social network analysis

Cynthia Webster and Jennifer Ruskin

Networks are fundamental to social entrepreneurship. Access to knowledge and resources; opportunities for collaboration; issues of trust, power and choice – all these involve more than simple dyadic relationships; most are embedded in networks of relationships. So realising when and to what extent to make use of personal and professional networks can be the decisive factor in success for many social ventures.

Accordingly, more and more academic research is being directed towards understanding the value of networks to entrepreneurship. For example, Jack (2010) recently reviewed the entrepreneurial literature and identified 71 articles on networks published from 1995 to 2005. Many of the early studies focus on:

- evolution, growth and performance (Donckels and Lambrecht, 1995; Hite and Hesterly, 2001; Larson, 1991; Larson and Starr, 1993; Lee and Tsang, 2001);
- network characteristics (Birley, 1985; Chell and Baines, 2000; Özcan, 1995); and
- social capital (Cooke and Wills, 1999; Davidsson and Honig, 2003; Honig, 1998).

Not surprisingly, these areas continue to be of research interest today (Milanov and Fernhaber, 2009; Pirolo and Presutti, 2010; Wu et al., 2008; De Carolis et al., 2009; Kor and Sundaramurthy, 2009; Molina-Morales and Martãnez-Fernãndez, 2010).

The real explosion of network research in entrepreneurship during the five years since 2006 has been in three key areas:

- Opportunity identification and innovation (Bhagavatula et al., 2010; Gellynck et al., 2007; Hingley et al., 2010; Ozgen and Baron, 2007).
- Internationalization and collaboration (Al-Laham and Souitaris, 2008; Belso-Martínez, 2006; Gellynck et al., 2007; Kariv et al., 2009; Marino et al., 2008; Patzelt et al., 2008; Sorenson et al., 2008).
- Network structure and embeddedness (Aldrich and Kim, 2007; Le Breton-Miller and Miller, 2009; Hallen, 2008; Kloosterman, 2010; Morse et al., 2007; Steier et al., 2009).

Work explicitly within social entrepreneurship has drawn attention to the importance of embeddedness within strategic entrepreneurial networks (Austin et al., 2006; Haugh, 2007; Kistruck and Beamish, 2010; Mair and Marti, 2006; Peredo and McLean, 2006).

Although there now is a substantial literature on networks and theoretical discussions of such structural issues as embeddedness, few studies in entrepreneurship have made use of the formal network quantitative techniques. Notable exceptions include, but are not limited to: Krackhardt's (1995) study on entrepreneurial opportunities and Aldrich and Kim's (2007) work on small-world versus scale-free networks. Even though texts have been written (Hannenman and Riddle, 2005; Scott, 1991; Wasserman and Faust, 1994; Wellman and Berkowitz, 1997) and many analytical techniques exist with user-friendly computer software available (Borgatti et al., 2002; Boer et al., 2001), few researchers in entrepreneurship have used them. The general avoidance of social network analytical techniques is most likely due to two factors: (1) the special data requirements needed to perform network analysis; and (2) familiarity with the basic network analytic models on hand.

Our aim here is to generate interest in social network analysis and make it more accessible to the field of social entrepreneurship. We include an illustrative network of organisations involved in social entrepreneurship utilising data accessed from the internet. Information from the webpages of two well-known foundations supporting social entrepreneurial activities, the Schwab Foundation (www.schwabfound.org) and the Skoll Foundation (www.skollfoundation.org), form the basis of the network example used in this chapter. While our network example draws on actual data, it is far from complete and is for instructive purposes only.

This chapter is organised as follows. To start, we give a brief introduction to social network analysis and discuss the data formats available. We then introduce an illustrative network example of organisations involved in social entrepreneurship and use one of the most accepted computer programs to calculate some common measures of network structure. Finally, we review selected network theories discussed widely in entrepreneurship to show the benefits of applying a structural analysis. Overall, we hope to stimulate new directions for research in entrepreneurship in terms of structural comparisons.

7.1 THE SOCIAL NETWORK APPROACH

Social network analysis is all about understanding structure (Wellman, 1983; Wellman and Berkowitz, 1997). From a network perspective, it is the structure of the network derived from the regularities in the patterning of relationships among network members that is informative, not simply member characteristics. Some studies in social entrepreneurship interested in network relationships gather information on network characteristics, for example network size (for example, number of strategic partners) and relationship type (for example, strong versus weak tie). Such information is useful but limited in revealing how structural properties of a network affect social entrepreneurship processes and outcomes.

Structural questions focus on such issues as: the ease of resource mobilization within dense versus sparse networks; or the success of social entrepreneurs who make use of their embedded local networks of relationships compared to those who act as brokers creating connections among otherwise disconnected firms and individuals; or the extent to which social value is more swiftly created within highly centralised versus decentralised networks. To examine these types of structural issues, a relational database is required with detailed information on the interrelationships among network members (Marsden, 1990).

7.1.1 Basic Network Elements and Types of Networks

All networks consist of two basic elements: actors and relationships. Actors are the distinct members of the network. Network actors can be individuals (for example, executive directors, chief executive officers – CEOs, investors, social entrepreneurs) or collective units (for example, foundations, venture capital firms, advisory boards, not-for-profit institutions). Relationships connect actors within a network. These relational ties can be formal (for example, whether one organisation funds another) or informal (for example, whether entrepreneurs know one another). Ties also differ in direction (for example, whether an organisation gives or receives funding support), strength (for example, weak, moderate, strong) and content (for example, advice, trust, communication).

Distinct types of networks exist. Socio-centric or complete networks consist of direct relationships among all members of a single, bounded community. An example would be information exchange relationships among all social entrepreneurs interacting via the online forum Social Edge (www.socialedge.org). In socio-centric studies, relevant relational data are obtained for each actor in the network, allowing for a complete analysis of the overall network structure as well as a positional analysis for each actor in the network. Typically, socio-centric networks are referred to as one-mode networks since the relationships are among the same set of actors. It is also possible to study socio-centric networks that are two-mode, where relationships are measured between two different sets of actors. An example would be the Kiva organisation, which provides a network platform for private donors seeking to provide financial support to social entrepreneurs.

Affiliation or co-membership networks are another type of two-mode network that involves a single, bounded community. The main point of difference is that relationships among the actors are not direct but instead are inferred. Individuals who attend the same forums, graduate from the same universities and support the same social ventures have multiple opportunities to become associated. Yet there is no guarantee that direct relationships are formed simply because actors attend the same events or are involved in the same forums. A study of interlocking directorates is a prime example of an affiliation network, as it is highly likely that members who are on the same boards have relationships with one another (Galaskiewicz et al., 1985; Mizruchi, 1996).

Ego-centric or personal networks are based on a focal actor ('ego'). Personal networks identify ego's direct relationships to a set of other actors ('ego's alters'). Additional information is then collected to identify the relationships among ego's alters. Without data on the inter-relationships among all actors within ego's network, not much structural analysis can be done. With only ego's direct ties identified and no others, the resulting network structure necessarily is a star with ego in the center. As such, it is critical to collect the inter-relationships among ego's alters (McCarty, 2002). Examining personal networks is useful if the research interest is to compare networks among similar kinds of focal actors involved in separate networks. For example, social entrepreneurs do not necessarily have connections to one another, though a study may investigate the extent to which the structure of social entrepreneurs' personal networks influences their decisions to enter international markets.

7.2 NETWORK DATA COLLECTION

Network data can be collected using any of the standard data collection techniques, including surveys, interviews, observations, experiments, documentary analysis and diaries. Typically, the network studies in entrepreneurship ask informants to report on the types of actors with whom they have relationships (for example, 'when searching for information, which of the following sources do you use: friends, family, colleagues, professional agencies?'). The data are then analysed, with assumptions made about family and friends being 'strong' ties, with the others being 'weak', and the findings reported (for example, more social entrepreneurs use strong tie sources, family and friends, for information than weak ties).

The key to conducting a network study is to elicit information regarding specific actors and relations (for example, 'List the initials or first names of all the people you would go to for advice. Who do you go to for financial support? Who do you trust?'). Once network actors and relationships are identified, then additional information regarding tie strength (for example, 'How often do you seek advice from each? How close are you to each network member on a scale from 1 'not at all close' to 5 'very close'?') and actor attributes should be collected (for example, 'Which actors are charities? How large is the organisation? In how many countries does it operate?').

By far the most common way to collect network data for small (50 actors or less) socio-centric studies is through a saturation survey. All actors within the network are asked to name their relational ties to all others in the network. Typically, some type of recognition task is used in which informants are asked to identify those with whom a particular relation exists (see Weller and Romney, 1988 for types of techniques). One simple recognition task is to give informants a roster of names of all actors in the network. Each informant then identifies their relationships, resulting in a single, binary vector of network data for each actor. These vectors are then joined to form a one-mode, actor-by-actor relational matrix. To collect valued data indicating relationship strength, some type of ranking or rating scale must be used (for example full rank order, paired comparisons, triads or Likert scales). With the roster method, informants report their ties without considering how other network members are interconnected. Other data collection techniques such as pile sort tasks (Webster, 1994) or the cognitive social structure method (Krackhardt, 1987) can be used to obtain informants' perspectives of the overall network.

For fairly large networks (Burt and Ronchi, 1994) and for ego-centric networks, recognition tasks are not feasible, as typically there are too many actors in the network to list. Instead, informants are asked to recall their network ties. Name generators and position generators are used to assist informant recall (see Burt, 1984; Killworth et al., 2003; McCallister and Fischer, 1978; van der Poel, 1993 for types of questions and procedures). Name generators ask informants to recall the names of others with whom they have a particular relationship, such as 'discusses important issues'. Names also can be used as probes. A name is stated (Bill or Sue or Klaus . . .) and informants are asked whether they have any relationship with an actor of that name. Position generators use specific roles or positions as stimuli (for example, venture capitalist or a charity or a financial institution) and informants are asked to name any individuals or organisations in those roles with which they have connections.

7.3 RELATIONAL DATA MATRIX

Once network data are collected, they are recorded in a matrix. Like a standard dataset, a relational dataset used in network analysis includes a set of informants as the rows of the matrix, and their responses to a set of questions as the columns of the matrix. The main difference is that with standard datasets the questions are about informants' attributes concerning specific issues, resulting in an actor-by-attribute matrix. With network data, the questions are about informants' relationships to specific actors, resulting in an actor-by actor matrix.

A binary adjacency matrix only records whether a tie exists between two actors. The data matrix shows 1 in the cell between two actors if the tie is present, or 0 if absent. If valued information has been obtained (frequency of interaction, strength, duration, intimacy) a real number is entered in the data matrix. Valued data may be entered as either distance data, which is like a road map where smaller numbers indicate closeness or stronger ties (for example, rank order from 1, most important, to 5, least important); or similarity data, where larger numbers in the cells of the matrix represent stronger ties (for example, duration of the relationship).

7.3.1 Adjacency Data Matrix Example

Table 7.1 is an example of an adjacency data matrix showing relationships among some organisations and foundations supporting social entrepreneurship. Note that actual names or code numbers can be used for actor labels. Reading across the rows shows that the Schwab Foundation, actor 1, has direct connections to actors 7, 10, 12, 14, 16, 17 and 19, whereas the Skoll Foundation, actor 2, has direct connections to actors 3, 4, 5, 6, 8, 9, 15, 16 and 19. Interestingly, the Schwab and Skoll Foundations do not have a direct relationship with one another, yet both have relationships with actors 16 and 19. Remember that the relational data matrix does not contain any attribute information regarding the actors. Attribute information is stored in a separate data set with the same actors as the rows and their attribute information recorded in the columns.

7.4 VISUAL REPRESENTATIONS: GRAPHS

The use of graph theory is among the major advantages of network analysis. Graphs provide a visual representation of the overall network structure and specific relational positions of actors (Freeman, 1984; Hage and Harary, 1983; Moreno, 1953). In a graph network actors are shown

Table 7.1 Social entrepreneur network data matrix for 19 organisations

Actor labels	1	2	3	4	5	6	7	8	9	10	11	12	13	14	15	16	17	18	19
1 Schwab	0	0	0	0	0	0	1	0	0	1	0	1	0	1	0	1	1	0	1
2 Skoll	0	0	1	1	1	1	0	1	1	0	0	0	0	0	1	1	0	0	1
3	0	1	0	1	0	0	0	1	0	1	0	0	0	0	1	1	0	0	0
4	0	1	1	0	1	1	0	0	1	0	1	0	1	0	0	0	0	1	0
5	0	1	0	1	0	0	0	0	0	0	0	1	1	0	0	1	0	0	0
6	0	1	0	1	0	0	0	0	0	0	0	0	0	0	0	0	0	0	0
7	1	0	0	0	0	0	0	0	0	0	0	0	0	0	0	0	0	0	0
8	0	1	1	0	0	0	0	0	0	0	0	0	0	0	0	0	0	0	0
9	0	1	0	1	0	0	0	0	0	0	0	0	0	0	0	0	0	0	0
10	1	0	1	0	0	0	0	0	0	0	0	0	1	0	1	0	0	0	0
11	0	0	0	1	0	0	0	0	0	0	0	0	0	0	0	0	0	0	0
12	1	0	0	0	1	0	0	0	0	0	0	0	0	0	0	0	0	0	0
13	0	0	0	1	1	0	0	0	0	1	0	0	0	0	1	0	0	0	0
14	1	0	0	0	0	0	0	0	0	0	0	0	0	0	0	0	0	0	0
15	0	1	1	0	0	0	0	0	0	1	0	0	1	0	0	1	0	0	1
16	1	1	1	0	1	0	0	0	0	0	0	0	0	0	1	0	1	1	0
17	1	0	0	0	0	0	0	0	0	0	0	0	0	0	0	1	0	0	0
18	0	0	0	1	0	0	0	0	0	0	0	0	0	0	0	1	0	0	1
19	1	1	0	0	0	0	0	0	0	0	0	0	0	0	1	0	0	1	0

as points, called nodes, and the relationships between actors as lines connecting the nodes. For mutual relations, such as communication, the ties between actors are shown with arrows headed at both ends or as a simple line with no arrows. For directed relations, such as financial support, the line is headed by a single arrow indicating a tie leading from one actor to another. Relationship strength can be shown with colour or line thickness. Actor attribute information also is easily incorporated using different node shapes and colours.

7.4.1 Graph of Network Actors Example

Figure 7.1 is a graph of the social entrepreneur support network for the 19 organisations in Table 7.1. In the figure Schwab and Skoll are in circles with other foundations, in diamonds and for-profit organisations in squares. A visual exploration of the network structure reveals differences between Skoll and Schwab. Many of Schwab's ties are to organisations like Boston Consulting Group and Goldman Sachs, actors 7 and 12 respectively, while Skoll's ties seem to be to non-profits like Global Giving, actor 4. In this example, there appears to be somewhat of a core–periphery structure with the Skoll Foundation plus a few other actors making up the core members.

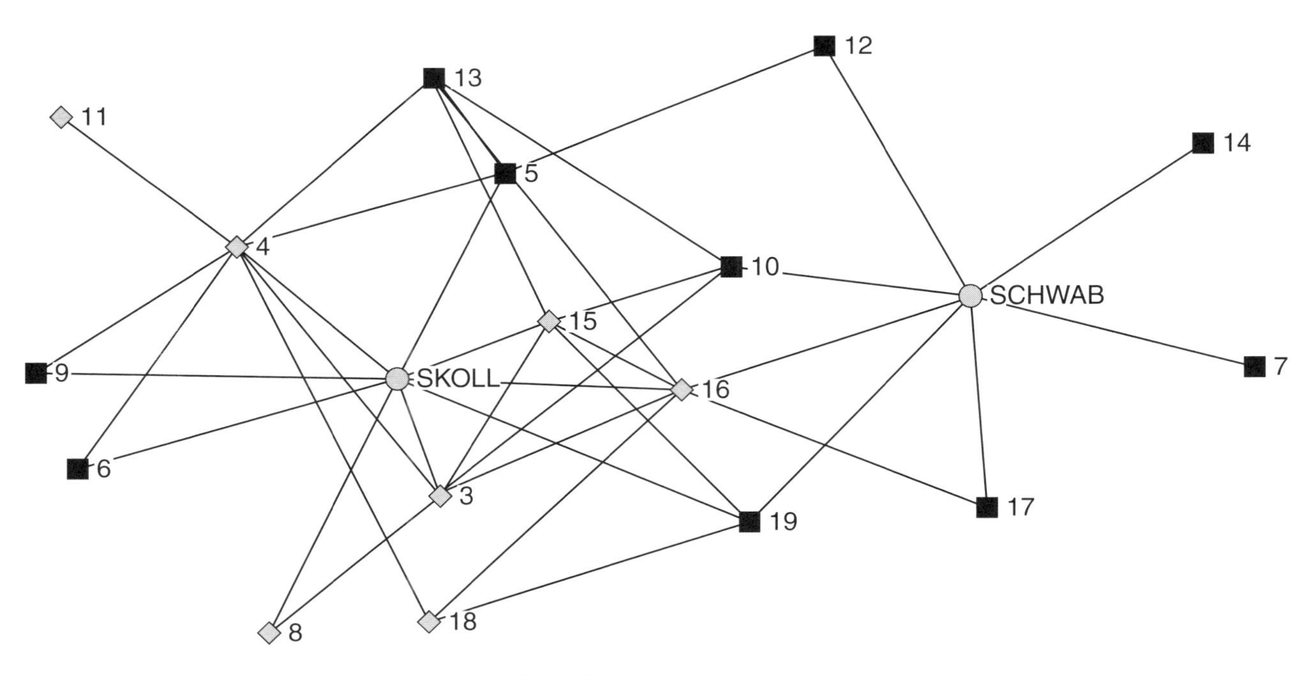

Figure 7.1 Social entrepreneur support network for 19 organisations

Of course, visually scanning a graph can provide some useful insights but the advantages of social network analysis lie in the precise calculations of network structure.

7.5 NETWORK MEASURES

As the size of the network increases, it becomes difficult to analyse the network visually. Quantification of the network structure is needed. Many network measures deal with one of two basic structural issues: cohesive subgroups and actor positions. Since over 50 network measures exist, we review the main ones of interest discussed in the social entrepreneur literature. All of the network calculations and visual displays have been produced using the network software program Ucinet 6 (Borgatti et al., 2002) and Netdraw (Borgatti, 2002).

7.5.1 Cohesion and Clustering

Cohesion is about the interconnectedness of actors in a network, whereas clustering is about partitioning actors into subgroups. We consider two measures of cohesion: reachability and density; and one measure, clique, to detect subgroups.

Reachability concerns whether actors can get to others within the network, either directly or indirectly (Doreian, 1974). Reachability is essential for diffusion of information, resources and innovation (Rogers, 1995). Actors directly connected to one another are only one step away, or a distance of one. Actors not connected to other network members are 'isolates' and, predictably, are at a greater disadvantage. In the social entrepreneur network example even the most peripheral network members (actors 7, 11 and 14) can get to one another within five steps.

Density measures the extent to which all possible ties are present within a network. Dense networks are thought to encourage cooperation, trust and coordination of activity among the actors involved, because everyone is directly invested in each other's business (Coleman, 1988). The downside of dense networks is the pressure to conform to established systems and norms. As such, loose-knit networks tend to benefit actors that wish to operate differently. Figure 7.1 shows 76 ties present out of a possible 342, giving a network density of 22.22 per cent. Density also can be calculated for each actor's personal network by examining the interconnectedness among an actor's direct ties. For example, Skoll's network, consisting of nine direct ties, has a substantially higher density at 27.78 per cent than does Schwab, whose density is only 4.76 per cent. Of Schwab's seven direct ties, only actors 16 and 17 have ties to one another; all of the other possible ties among the others are missing.

Clique analysis is a robust technique used to identify network subgroups (Luce and Perry, 1949). A clique is a maximally complete subgraph, meaning that a clique is the largest subset of actors which all are directly connected to one another. Accordingly, all cliques have a density of 100 per cent. Due to the strict definition of a clique, most networks have many cliques that are small in size with many of the same actors.

For the 19 actors in the social entrepreneurship network example, there are 12 cliques with all but one having only three members. Of the 12 cliques, Skoll is a member of eight cliques and actors 3 and 4 are in four cliques each. Clearly, there are too many cliques with too much overlap. To uncover the overall subgroup structure for a network, a hierarchical clustering of the clique co-membership matrix is recommended (Freeman, 1996). Figure 7.2 shows the hierarchical clustering of the 12 cliques. Basically, two subgroups are present. There is a small group consisting of Schwab and actors 16 and 17; and a larger clustering with two subgroups, one with Skoll and actors 4, 5 and 13, and the other with actors 3, 15 and 10. The clique analysis also identifies five actors – 7, 11, 12, 14 and 18 – as not belonging to any clique.

7.5.2 Centrality and Role Equivalence

The structural position of actors – where and how actors are located in a network – can seriously influence performance for individual actors and the network as a whole. We look at three measures of centrality: degree, closeness and betweenness; followed by measures of role: equivalence, structural and regular.

Measures of centrality

Centrality has to do with popularity, prominence and power (Bonnacich, 1987; Freeman, 1979; Katz, 1953; Taylor, 1969). Actors in central network positions are 'key' players because they typically have the connections that provide them with access to more resources and allow them to control the flow of resources throughout the network. Actors in peripheral positions are vulnerable since they rely on fewer network ties.

Degree is the most basic measure of centrality. An actor's degree centrality is simply the total number of direct ties. It can be calculated separately for ties sent and ties received for relationships that are not mutual, such as donations. Degree centrality is a local measure of an actor's activity or popularity, as the entire network of connections is not considered. In Figure 7.1, Skoll has the highest degree centrality with 13 direct ties;

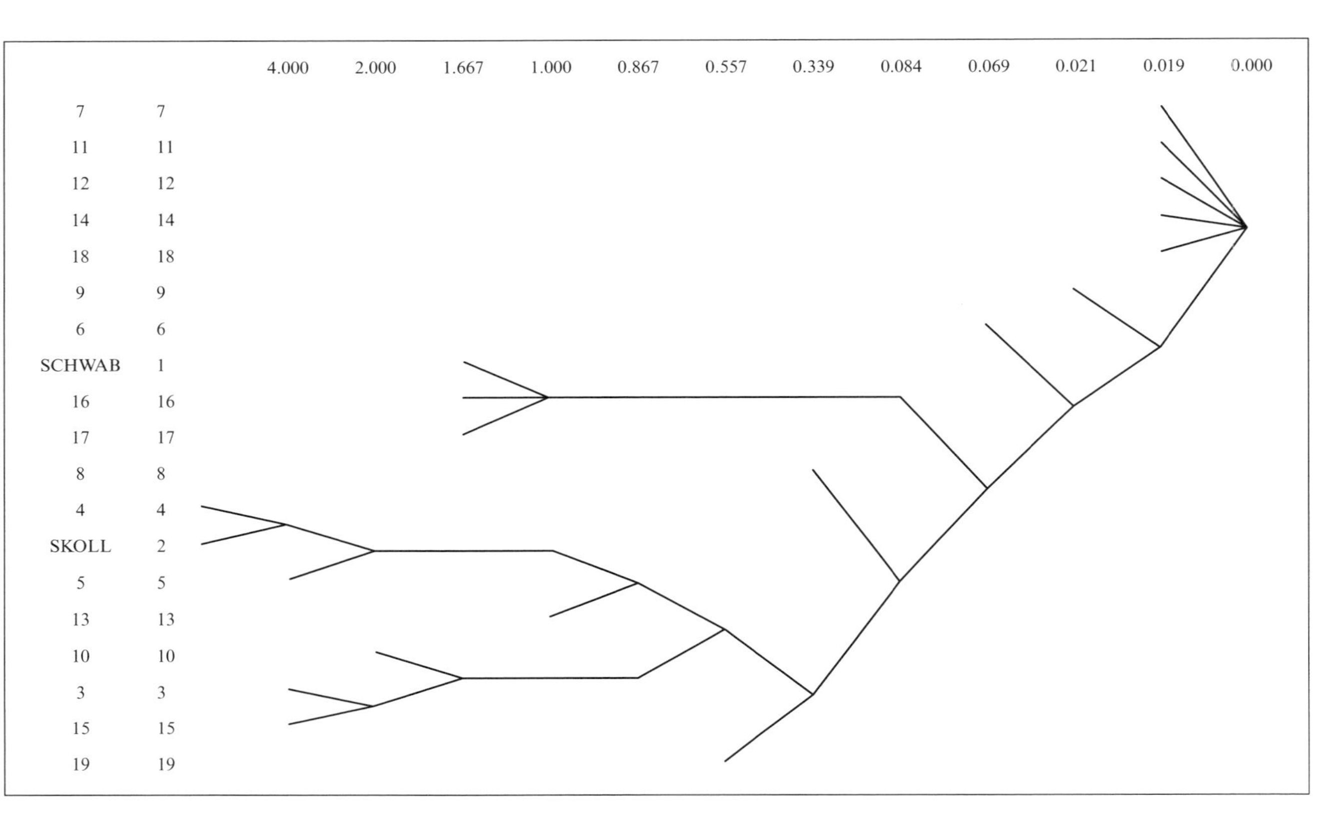

Figure 7.2 Hierarchical clustering for clique co-membership matrix

followed closely by actor 4, Global Giving, with 12 direct ties. Schwab is the eighth most central actor, with nine direct ties.

Closeness is based on distance and takes into account direct and indirect ties. An actor which is close to all others in the network, either directly connected or only a few links away, is not dependent on any other to reach everyone in the network. Closeness is a measure of independence or efficiency. In Figure 7.1, Skoll again is the most central, but followed this time by actor 16, the Lemelsen Foundation. Actors 7 and 14 are the farthest from all others and thus the least central.

Betweenness is the number of times an actor lies in the path between pairs of other actors. It is a measure of power, since an actor high in 'betweenness' is a type of gatekeeper positioned to control the flow of resources between network members. Interestingly, Skoll is not the most central actor in betweenness centrality. Instead, Schwab turns out to be the most powerful actor in Figure 7.1. This is mainly because actors 7 and 14 must go through Schwab to reach any of the others in the network, whereas all of Skoll's connections also have direct ties to other actors.

Remember, these measures of centrality are structural measures of popularity, independence and power. Some network actors may be on the periphery structurally but still exert substantial power over the network due to their size or reputation, or through their power to enforce sanctions. Such actors typically have considerable resources, status or authority in their own right.

Measures of role equivalence

Role equivalence measures identify actors whose network ties are similarly structured. Actors occupy the same structural role in the network not because they are connected to one another directly, but because they have similar relations to others. Role equivalence is important in competitive situations (Burt, 1987). For example, when businesses want information about their competitors, they do not go to their competitors directly but instead get the information by going to the same third parties.

Structural equivalence finds actors in a network whose relations are structured identically. Structurally equivalent actors are substitutable in that they have exactly the same connections to others (Lorrain and White, 1971). In the social entrepreneur network example, the only actors that are structurally equivalent are actors 7 and 14 – both are tied to Schwab and no others; and actors 6 and 9 – both are connected to Skoll and actor 4.

Regular equivalence is a relaxation of the strict definition of structural equivalence (White and Reitz, 1983). Actors regularly equivalent have similar ties to comparable others, not necessarily identical others. For example, two venture capitalist firms that provide funding to different social ventures are 'regularly equivalent' but not 'structurally equivalent' since they are not funding exactly the same ventures.

Hierarchical clustering for regular equivalence example

Figure 7.3 presents a hierarchical clustering of the regular equivalence results for the social entrepreneur network. In stark contrast to the clique results, where Skoll and actor 4 (Global Giving) are in the same clique, here Schwab and actor 4 are placed in the same equivalence class. They share none of the same connections, but both Schwab and Global Giving have ties to actors with only two ties and to actors that are not connected to any others.

Notice that even though network actors may perform the same functional services and have similar business strategies, structurally they may be noticeably different. For example, both Skoll and Schwab seek to build strong global networks of social entrepreneurs through sponsoring world forums and social entrepreneur awards, yet they do not appear to be substitutable in a structural sense. Rich opportunities for research exist in investigating the extent to which individual and business outcomes relate to actors occupying similar positions or roles.

7.6 NETWORK THEORIES IN SOCIAL ENTREPRENEURSHIP RESEARCH

We now turn to discuss three highly regarded network theories in social entrepreneurship: strength of weak ties, small world and embeddedness. After we briefly outline the theories, we then focus on a few recent studies to show how network research has developed in the field of entrepreneurship.

7.6.1 Strength of Weak Ties

Granovetter's (1973, 1983) strength-of-weak-ties theory suggests that novel information is gained from less intimate relationships rather than from close ties. The logic behind this argument is that individuals in strongly connected networks tend to share their information, resulting in a limited, homogeneous knowledge base. New information, therefore, tends to come from external connections which are likely to be weak. The strength-of-weak-ties theory has been investigated within entrepreneurship for over 20 years (Birley, 1985; Larson and Starr, 1991). Research continues today with substantial new findings. For example, Lechner and Dowling (2003) in Munich's information technology (IT)

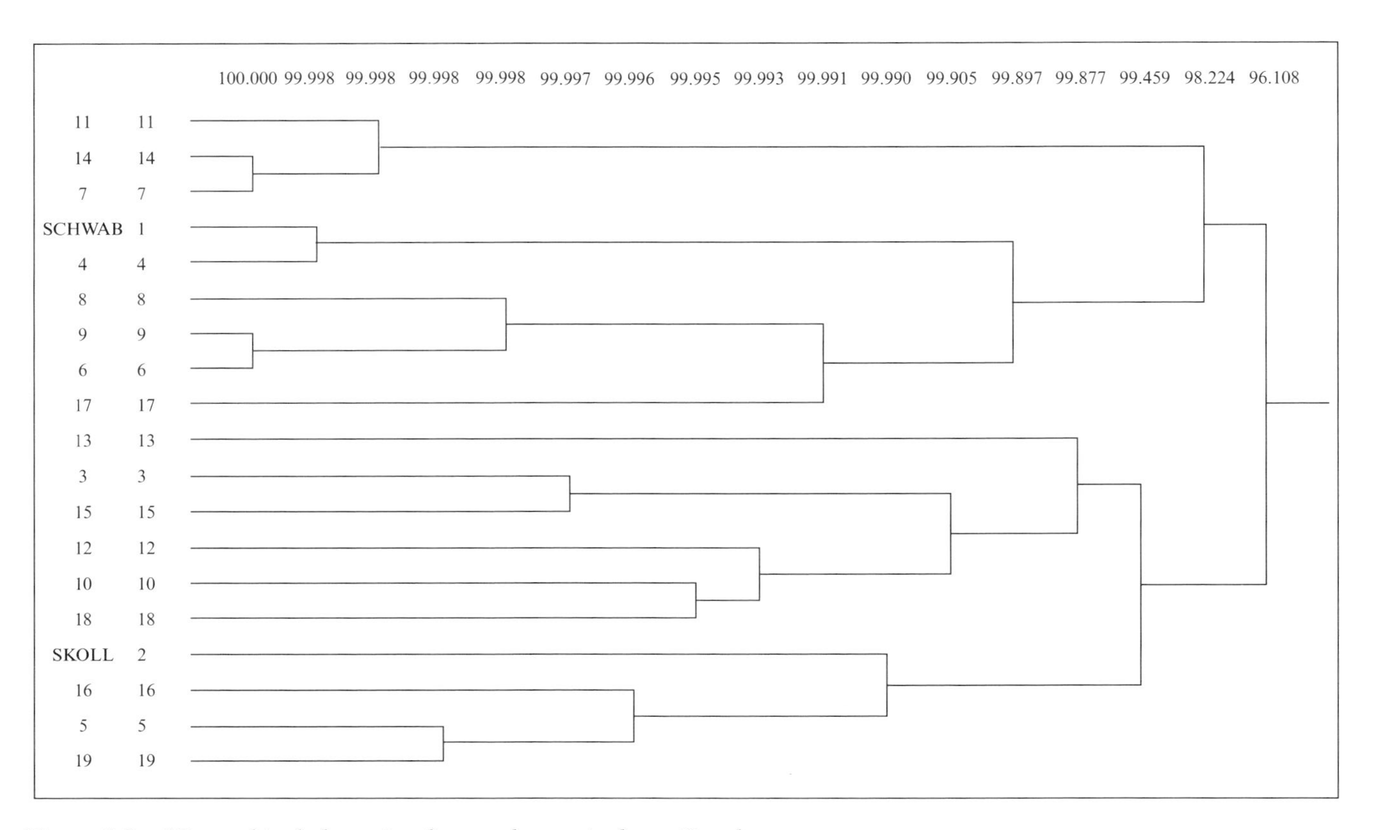

Figure 7.3 Hierarchical clustering for regular equivalence Results

industry find that both strong and weak ties are important for innovation and growth. Increasingly, entrepreneurial firms are creating 'knowledge-sharing' forums bringing together weak ties that are based on referrals from trusted relationships. They also caution that entrepreneurial firms that do not bring in weak ties face potential growth barriers. Recent work by Mort and Weerawardena (2006) further suggests that 'network rigidity' can restrict actors from pursuing external opportunities, which results in greater homogeneity and a less competitive network environment.

7.6.2 Small-World Phenomenon

The small-world phenomenon (Milgram, 1967; Watts, 1999) is one of the most well-known network theories. It is the frequently stated experience that everyone in the world is able to reach one another by going through only a few others. Small-world networks combine the structural features of local cohesive network clustering with a small number of bridging ties linking the clusters to arrive at global reachability. Many actors in the network would have similar degree centrality scores with a few actors, the 'bridges', quite high in betweenness centrality. Aldrich and Kim (2007) compare small-world with truncated-scale free networks to examine nascent entrepreneurial teams. Unlike small-world networks, truncated scale-free networks are characterised by many sparsely connected actors linked to a few well-known 'popular' actors. These 'popular' actors high in degree centrality are in a position to recognise the diverse talents of others and are thus able to build teams quickly. In their work Aldrich and Kim argue that the more standard entrepreneurial ventures tend to form in small-world contexts where founders utilise their dense networks to start the venture, with growth occurring via bridging ties to other densely knit networks. Conversely, high-growth ventures in competitive fields requiring highly competent diverse teams with recognised standards, as in the creative industries, do better in truncated scale-free environments.

7.6.3 Embeddedness

The importance of embeddedness is a given within the field of entrepreneurship (Hite, 2005; Jack and Anderson, 2002; Uzzi and Gillespie, 2002). Simply put, embeddedness is the understanding that social relationships influence behaviour and that economic activities cannot be separated from the social environments in which they occur (Granovetter, 1985; Polanyi, 1944). Zukin and DiMaggio (1990) identify four types of embeddedness: structural, cognitive, political and cultural. Social network analysis is concerned with structural embeddedness, which primarily focuses on how the composition and patterning of social relationships influences behaviour. Uzzi's (1997) qualitative work on structural embeddedness reveals the paradox of embeddedness. He warns that social relationships can both facilitate business opportunities, creating competitive advantages for firms; and at times constrain firm performance, impeding their ability to respond to change. Krackhardt (1999) formalises embeddedness in network analytic terms with his 'Simmelian ties', which are essentially dyads embedded in a three-actor clique. In formal terms a 'Simmelian tie' is a reciprocal pair of actors with mutual ties to a third actor. Krackhardt and Kilduff (2002) apply this definition of embeddedness to examine organisational culture in three entrepreneurial firms, and find that high levels of embeddedness lead to greater agreement concerning organisational culture. More recently embeddedness has been the focus of research in social entrepreneurship (Kistruck and Beamish, 2010). Mair and Martí (2006) specifically stress the need for research on the role of embeddedness. They suggest that high levels of embeddedness may inhibit social change and may negatively affect those social entrepreneurs who wish to start ventures that challenge societal norms.

7.7 CONCLUSION

Network theories have been widely used in entrepreneurship. Although network measures are non-standard and the collection of network data is demanding, researchers have found network analysis to complement and extend traditional methods. We have reviewed only a few of the available network analytical techniques and theories. Many more exist that have yet to be applied to social entrepreneurship research. The review also has pointed to the limitations in taking a purely structural approach. Characteristics of the actors, of the relationships and of the situation, should all be regarded to ensure that a comprehensive investigation is performed.

REFERENCES

Al-Laham, A. and V. Souitaris (2008). Network embeddedness and new-venture internationalization: Analyzing international linkages in the German biotech industry. *Journal of Business Venturing* **23**, 567–586.

Aldrich, H. and P. Kim (2007). Small worlds, infinite possibilities? How social networks affect entrepreneurial team formation and search. *Strategic Entrepreneurship Journal* **1–2**, 147–166.

Austin, J.E., H. Stevenson and J. Wei-Skillern (2006). Social and commercial entrepreneurship: same, different, or both? *Entrepreneurship: Theory and Practice* **30**, 1–22.

Belso-Martínez, J.A. (2006). Why are some Spanish manufacturing firms internationalizing rapidly? The role of business and institutional international networks. *Entrepreneurship and Regional Development* **18**, 207–226.
Bhagavatula, S., T. Elfring, A. Van Tilburg and G.G. Van de Bunt (2010). How social and human capital influence opportunity recognition and resource mobilization in India's handloom industry. *Journal of Business Venturing* **25**, 245–260.
Birley, S. (1985). The role of networks in the entrepreneurial process. *Journal of Business Venturing* **1**, 107–117.
Boer, P., M. Huisman, T.A.B. Snijders and E.P.H. Zeggelink (2001). StOCNET: an open software system for the advanced statistical analysis of social networks. Groningen: ProGAMMA / ICS.
Bonnacich, P. (1987). Power and centrality: a family of measures. *American Journal of Sociology* **92**, 1170–1182.
Borgatti, S.P. (2002). *Netdraw 2.097 Visualization Software*. Harvard, MA: Analytic Technologies.
Borgatti, S.P., M.G. Everett and L.C. Freeman (2002). *Ucinet for Windows: Software for Social Network Analysis*. Harvard, MA: Analytic Technologies.
Burt, R.S. (1984). Network items and the general social science survey. *Social Networks* **6**, 293–339.
Burt, R.S. (1987). Social cohesion and innovation: cohesion versus social equivalence. *American Journal of Sociology* **92**, 1287–1335.
Burt, R.S. and D. Ronchi (1994). Measuring a large network quickly. *Social Networks* **16**, 91–135.
Chell, E. and S. Baines (2000). Networking, entrepreneurship and microbusiness behaviour. *Entrepreneurship and Regional Development* **12**, 195–215.
Coleman, J.S. (1988). Social capital in the creation of human capital. *American Journal of Sociology* **94**, 95–120.
Cooke, P. and D. Wills (1999). Small firms, social capital and the enhancement of business performance through innovation programmes. *Small Business Economics* **13**, 219–234.
Davidsson, P. and B. Honig (2003). The role of social and human capital among nascent entrepreneurs. *Journal of Business Venturing* **18**, 301–331.
De Carolis, D.M., B.E. Litzky and K.A. Eddleston (2009). Why networks enhance the progress of new venture creation: the influence of social capital and cognition. *Entrepreneurship: Theory and Practice* **33**, 527–545.
Donckels, R. and J. Lambrecht (1995). Networks and small business growth: an explanatory model. *Small Business Economics* **7**, 273–289.
Doreian, P. (1974). On the connectivity of social networks. *Journal of Mathematical Sociology* **3**, 245–258.
Freeman, L.C. (1979). Centrality in social networks: conceptual clarification. *Social Networks* **1**, 215–239.
Freeman, L.C. (1984). Turning a profit from mathematics: the case of social networks. *Journal of Mathematical Sociology* **10**, 343–360.
Freeman, L.C. (1996). Cliques, gallois lattices and the structure of human social groups. *Social Networks* **18**, 173–187.
Galaskiewicz, J., S. Wasserman, B. Rauschenbach, W. Bielefeld and P. Mullaney (1985). The influence of corporate power, social status, and market position on corporate interlocks in a regional market. *Social Forces* **64**, 403–431.
Gellynck, X., B. Vermeire and J. Viaene (2007). Innovation in food firms: contribution of regional networks within the international business context. *Entrepreneurship and Regional Development* **19**, 209–226.
Granovetter, M.S. (1973). The strength of weak ties. *American Journal of Sociology* **78**(6), 1360–1380.
Granovetter, M.S. (1983). The strength of weak ties: a network theory revisited. *Sociological Theory* **1**, 201–233.

Granovetter, M. (1985). Economic action and social structure: the problem of embeddedness. *American Journal of Sociology* **91**, 481–510.
Hage, P. and F. Harary (1983). *Structural Models in Anthropology*. Cambridge: Cambridge University Press.
Hallen, B.L. (2008). The causes and consequences of the network positions of new organizations: from whom do entrepreneurs receive investments? *Administrative Science Quarterly* **53**, 685–718.
Hanneman, R. and M. Riddle (2005). *Introduction to Social Network Methods*. Riverside, CA: University of California, Riverside.
Haugh, H. (2007). Community-led social venture creation. *Entrepreneurship: Theory and Practice* **31**, 161–182.
Hingley, M.K., A. Lindgreen and M.B. Beverland (2010). Barriers to network innovation in UK ethnic fresh produce supply. *Entrepreneurship and Regional Development* **22**, 77–96.
Hite, J.M. (2005). Evolutionary processes and paths of relationally embedded network ties in emerging entrepreneurial firms. *Entrepreneurship Theory and Practice* **29**, 113–144.
Hite, J.M. and W.S. Hesterly (2001). The evolution of firm networks: from emergence to early growth of the firm. *Strategic Management Journal* **22**, 275–286.
Honig, B. (1998). What determines success? Examining the human, financial, and social capital of Jamaican microentrepreneurs. *Journal of Business Venturing* **13**, 371–394.
Jack, S.L. (2010). Approaches to studying networks: implications and outcomes. *Journal of Business Venturing* **25**, 120–137.
Jack, S. and A. Anderson (2002). The effects of embeddedness on the entrepreneurial process. *Journal of Business Venturing* **17**(5), 467–487.
Kariv, D., T.V. Menzies, G.A. Brenner and L.J. Filion (2009). Transnational networking and business performance: ethnic entrepreneurs in Canada. *Entrepreneurship and Regional Development* **21**, 239–264.
Katz, L. (1953). A new status index derived from sociometric analysis. *Psychometrika* **18**, 39–43.
Killworth, P.D., C. McCarty, H.R. Bernard, E.C. Johnsen, J. Domini and G.A. Shelley (2003). Two interpretations of reports of knowledge of subpopulation sizes. *Social Networks* **25**, 141–160.
Kistruck, G.M. and P.W. Beamish (2010). The interplay of form, structure, and embeddedness in social intrapreneurship. *Entrepreneurship: Theory and Practice* **34**, 735–761.
Kloosterman, R.C. (2010). Matching opportunities with resources: a framework for analysing (migrant) entrepreneurship from a mixed embeddedness perspective. *Entrepreneurship and Regional Development* **22**, 25–45.
Kor, Y.Y. and C. Sundaramurthy (2009). Experience-based human capital and social capital of outside directors. *Journal of Management* **35**, 981–1006.
Krackhardt, D. (1987). Cognitive social structures. *Social Networks* **9**, 109–134.
Krackhardt, D. (1995). Entrepreneurial opportunities in an entrepreneurial firm: a structural approach. *Entrepreneurship: Theory and Practice* **19**, 53–70.
Krackhardt, D. (1999). The ties that torture: Simmelian tie analysis in organizations. *Research in the Sociology of Organizations* **16**, 183–210.
Krackhardt, D. and M. Kilduff (2002). Structure, culture and Simmelian ties in entrepreneurial firms. *Social Networks* **24**, 279–290.
Larson, A. (1991). Partner networks: leveraging external ties to improve entrepreneurial performance. *Journal of Business Venturing* **6**, 173–188.
Larson, A. and J.A. Starr (1993). A network model of organization formation. *Entrepreneurship: Theory and Practice* **17**, 5–15.
Le Breton-Miller, I. and D. Miller (2009). Agency vs. stewardship in public family firms: a social embeddedness reconciliation. *Entrepreneurship: Theory and Practice* **33**, 1169–1191.
Lechner, C. and M. Dowling (2003). Firm networks: external relationships as sources for the growth and competitiveness of entrepreneurial firms. *Entrepreneurship and Regional Development* **15**, 1–26.

Lee, D. and E. Tsang (2001). The effects of entrepreneurial personality, background and network activities on venture growth. *Journal of Management Studies* **38**, 584–602.
Lorrain, F. and H.C. White (1971). Structural equivalence of individuals in social networks. *Journal of Mathematical Sociology* **1**, 49–80.
Luce, R.D. and A.D. Perry (1949). A method of matrix analysis of group structure. *Psychometrika* **14**, 95–116.
Mair, J. and I. Martí (2006). Social entrepreneurship research: a source of explanation, prediction, and delight. *Journal of World Business* **41**, 36–44.
Marino, L.D., F.T. Lohrke, J.S. Hill, K.M. Weaver and T. Tambunan (2008). Environmental shocks and SME alliance formation intentions in an emerging economy: Evidence from the Asian financial crisis in Indonesia. *Entrepreneurship: Theory and Practice* **32**, 157–183.
Marsden, P.V. (1990). Network data and measurement. *Annual Review of Sociology* **16**, 435–463.
McCallister, L. and C. Fischer (1978). A procedure for surveying personal networks. *Sociological Methods and Research* **7**, 131–148.
McCarty, C. (2002). Structure in personal networks. *Journal of Social Structure* **3**(1), available at http://zeeb.library.cmu.edu:7850/JoSS/McCarty.htm.
Milanov, H. and S.A. Fernhaber (2009). The impact of early imprinting on the evolution of new venture networks. *Journal of Business Venturing* **24**, 46–61.
Milgram, S. (1967). The small-world problem. *Psychology Today* **1**, 62–67.
Mizruchi, Mark S. (1996). What do interlocks do? An analysis, critique, and assessment of research on interlocking directorates. *Annual Review of Sociology* **22**, 271–298.
Molina-Morales, F.X. and M.A.T. Martínez-Fernández (2010). Social networks: effects of social capital on firm innovation. *Journal of Small Business Management* **48**, 258–279.
Moreno, J.L. (1953). *Who Shall Survive? Foundations of Sociometry, Group Psychotherapy and Sociodrama*. New York: Beacon House.
Morse, E.A., S.W. Fowler and T.B. Lawrence (2007). The impact of virtual embeddedness on new venture survival: Overcoming the liabilities of newness. *Entrepreneurship: Theory and Practice* **31**, 139–159.
Mort, G.S. and J. Weerawardena (2006). Network capability and international entrepreneurship. How networks function in Australian born global firms. *International Marketing Review* **23**, 549–572.
Özcan, G.B. (1995). Small business networks and local ties in Turkey. *Entrepreneurship and Regional Development* **7**, 265–282.
Ozgen, E. and R.A. Baron (2007). Social sources of information in opportunity recognition: Effects of mentors, industry networks, and professional forums. *Journal of Business Venturing* **22**, 174–192.
Patzelt, H., D.A. Shepherd, D. Deeds and S.W. Bradley (2008). Financial slack and venture managers' decisions to seek a new alliance. *Journal of Business Venturing* **23**, 465–481.
Peredo, A.M. and M. McLean (2006). Social entrepreneurship: a critical review of the concept. *Journal of World Business* **41**, 56–65.
Pirolo, L. and M. Presutti (2010). The impact of social capital on the start-ups' performance growth. *Journal of Small Business Management* **48**, 197–227.
Polanyi, K. (1944). *The Great Transformation*. New York: Farrar & Rinehart.
Rogers, E.M. (1995). *Diffusion of Innovations*, 4th edn. New York: Free Press.
Scott, J. (1991). *Social Network Analysis: A Handbook*. Newbury Park, CA: Sage Publications.
Sorenson, R.L., C.A. Folker and K.H. Brigham (2008). The collaborative network orientation: Achieving business success through collaborative relationships. *Entrepreneurship: Theory and Practice* **32**, 615–634.
Steier, L.P., J.H. Chua and J.J. Chrisman (2009). Embeddedness perspectives of economic action within family firms. *Entrepreneurship: Theory and Practice* **33**, 1157–1167.
Taylor, M. (1969). Influence structures. *Sociometry* **32**, 490–502.
Uzzi, B. (1997). Social structure and competition in interfirm networks: the paradox of embeddedness. *Administrative Science Quarterly* **42**, 35–67.
Uzzi, B. and J.J. Gillespie (2002). Knowledge spillover in corporate financing networks:

embeddedness and the firm's debt performance. *Strategic Management Journal* **23**(7), 595–618.
van der Poel, M.G.M. (1993). Delineating personal support networks. *Social Networks* **15**, 49–70.
Wasserman, S. and K. Faust (1994). *Social Network Analysis: Methods and Applications*. Cambridge: Cambridge University Press.
Watts, D.J. (1999). *Small Worlds: The Dynamics of Networks between Order and Randomness*. Princeton, NJ: Princeton University Press.
Webster, C.M. (1994). A comparison of observational and cognitive measures. *Quantitative Anthropology* **4**, 313–328.
Weller, S.C. and A.K. Romney (1988). *Systematic Data Collection*. Newbury Park: Sage.
Wellman, B. (1983). Network analysis: some basic principles. In R. Collins (ed.), *Sociological Theory*. San Francisco, CA: Jossey-Bass, pp. 155–199.
Wellman, B. and S.D. Berkowitz (1997). *Social Structures: A Network Approach*. Greenwich, CT: JAI Press.
White, D.R. and K.P. Reitz (1983). Graph and semigroup homomorphisms on networks of relations. *Social Networks* **5**, 193–234.
Wu, L.-Y., C.-J. Wang, C.-P. Chen and L.-Y. Pan (2008). Internal resources, external network, and competitiveness during the growth stage: a study of Taiwanese high-tech ventures. *Entrepreneurship: Theory and Practice* **32**, 529–549.
Zukin, S. and P. DiMaggio (1990). *Structures of Capital: The Social Organization of the Economy*. Cambridge: Cambridge University Press.

8 Surveys and data sets

Steven D'Alessandro and Hume Winzar

Surveys and large data sets are an important aspect of social entrepreneurship research and practice. Surveys and large data sets are usually an important aspect of program evaluation as well as opportunity analysis for social entrepreneurship undertakings. Large-scale surveys and data sets may also show a need for a social intervention or provide support for external funding of social entrepreneurship. Examples include the evaluation of HIV/AIDS campaigns in health (Lombardo and Leger, 2007), other health policies, promoting social development and protection of the environment (Andreasen, 1995).

It is important, therefore, that researchers in social entrepreneurship have an understanding of how to conduct survey research, and how to interpret results from large data sets. This chapter provides a brief outline of survey research in the context of social entrepreneurship, along with a guide to how to conduct it. The chapter is organised as follows: it introduces the nature of surveys and their design, reviews the nature of errors in survey research and presents the different ways to conduct surveys. The chapter then details the six steps of measurement, and the nine steps of survey design. Sampling, fieldwork and editing are then introduced. Finally, the chapter gives overviews of some of the key tools of data analysis. Examples are provided throughout.

8.1 THE NATURE OF SURVEYS AND THEIR DESIGN

A survey can be defined as an ordered attempt to collect information, using structured and semi-structured questions, from a representative cross-section of a particular target population. Surveys are popular in social science research, since (if they are constructed and administered correctly) they provide a relatively quick, inexpensive and accurate overview or description of phenomena.

8.1.1 Survey Design

Qualitative designs are favoured when theory development and initial understanding of the research phenomena are required; for example, the processes of new product development of not-for-profit organisations (Barczac et al., 2006) have been studied by use of qualitative interviews. Social entrepreneurship research may also favour the use qualitative research approaches over surveys as: 'Direct and active engagement with participants provides opportunities for those actively engaged in the change process to explain expressions used, clarify issues as they emerge, or illuminate researchers' concerns' (Douglas, 2008).

Note, however, that surveys should not be used when the research issue or problem is not well defined, or when the researcher wishes to discover new and innovative ways in which to conduct a social entrepreneurship. Such issues are better addressed by qualitative and observational research. Typically, such research will be followed by a qualitative study; for example, survey research will follow a study that has identified the key research or policy issues for a population.

8.1.2 The Nature of Surveys

Surveys can be categorised by their degree of structure and degree of disguise of the purpose of the study. For example, interviews in qualitative research might use unstructured-disguised surveys, or in any other combination: structured-undisguised, unstructured-undisguised and structured-disguised. Note, however, that such classifications have two limitations. First, the degree of structure and the degree of disguise vary; they are not clear-cut categories. Second, most surveys are hybrids, asking both structured and unstructured questions. Recognising the degrees of structure and disguise necessary to meet survey objectives will help in the selection of the appropriate communication medium for conducting the survey.

Cross-sectional studies

Most social research surveys are cross-sectional studies, and aim to find out descriptive information about a group of people at a moment in time. The typical method of analysing a cross-sectional survey is to divide the sample into appropriate subgroups. For example, if a charity expects income levels to influence attitudes towards donations, the data are broken down into subgroups based on income and analysed to reveal similarities or differences among the income subgroups. Cross-sectional surveys are also frequently used as the results are quickly obtained and they cost less than other designs (discussed next). The disadvantage with cross-sectional designs is that they measure behaviour and attitudes at a point in time, so the predictability of findings is questionable. Findings on what drives the adoption of social entrepreneurship policies by local government, by use of a survey (Leroux, 2005), for example, can only apply to past recollections of policymakers at a point in time; they do not provide the researcher with the means to project these results into the future.

Longitudinal studies

In a longitudinal study respondents are questioned at two or more different times. The purpose of longitudinal studies is to examine the continuity of responses and to observe changes that occur over time. Examples of such longitudinal research in the context of social entrepreneurship include projects exploring the success of social entrepreneurship start-ups (Cieslik and Eugene, 2009), the impact of micro-credit in poverty reduction (Mohan and Devendra, 2010) and the development of regional social capital (Lee et al., 2004).

Longitudinal studies can also track successive cross-sectional samples (known as tracking studies). Successive waves are designed to compare conditions and identify changes in variables such as changes in social behaviour, or the reported use of recycling. These studies are useful for assessing aggregate trends, but do not allow for tracking changes in individuals over time. An example of this type of research is a series of surveys on the use of African-American social household human capital in the development of self-employment (Smith, 2005).

While the choice of survey design is somewhat straightforward, limiting biases and errors from survey research is problematic at best. This is because of the degree of interaction between respondents and interviewers and the use of samples to generalise results to the wider population. All errors in survey research have to be dealt with within a limited budget. We now turn our attention to some of these errors.

8.2 ERRORS IN SURVEY RESEARCH

It is often said that all surveys are pretty good, but some are better than others. How good a survey is, depends on how well errors associated with this research method are addressed by the researcher. The two major sources of survey error are random sampling error and systematic error. This section introduces the two errors, and then presents ways that these errors can be avoided and managed.

8.2.1 Random Sampling Error

Most surveys try to portray a representative cross-section of a particular target population. Even with technically proper random probability samples, however, statistical errors will occur because of chance variation in the elements selected for the sample. Without increasing sample size, these statistical problems are unavoidable.

8.2.2 Systematic Error

Systematic error results from some faulty aspect of the research design or from a gaffe in the execution of the research. Because all sources of error rather than those introduced by the random sampling procedure are included, these errors or biases are also called non-sampling errors. The many sources of error that in some way systematically influence answers can be divided into two general categories: respondent error and administrative error. These are now discussed.

Respondent error

Surveys ask people for answers. If people oblige and give honest answers, a survey will likely accomplish its goal. If these conditions are not met, non-response error or response bias, will occur.

Non-response error Few surveys have 100 percent response rates. A researcher who obtains a 10 percent response to a five-page questionnaire concerning the use of a needle exchange has a real problem in claiming the results are indicative of the population of intravenous drug users. To use the results, the researcher must be sure that those who did respond to the questionnaire were representative of those who did not.

The statistical differences between a survey that includes only those who responded and a perfect survey that would also include those who failed to respond, are referred to as non-response error. This problem is especially acute in mail, email, fax and Internet surveys, but it also threatens telephone and face-to-face interviews.

People who are not contacted or who refuse to cooperate are called non-respondents. A non-response occurs if someone is not at home at the time of both the initial call and a subsequent callback. The number of no contacts in survey research has been increasing because of the proliferation of answering machines and growing use of caller ID to screen telephone calls (Tuckel and O'Neill, 2001). A parent who must juggle the telephone and a baby and refuses to participate in the survey because he or she is too busy is also a non-response. Refusals occur when people are unwilling to participate in the research. No contacts and refusals can seriously bias survey data.

After receiving a refusal from a potential respondent, an interviewer can do nothing other than be polite. The respondent who is not at home when called or visited should be scheduled to be interviewed at a different time of day or on a different day of the week.

With a mail survey the researcher never really knows whether a non-respondent has refused to participate or is just indifferent. Researchers know that those who are most involved in an issue are more likely to respond to a mail survey. Self-selection bias is a problem that frequently plagues self-administered questionnaires. On controversial issues such as immigration, working for unemployment benefits and capital punishment, respondents who have extreme positions on these issues are more likely to complete a self-administered questionnaire online than individuals who are indifferent about these issues. Self-selection biases distort surveys because they over-represent extreme positions while under-representing responses from those who are indifferent. Several techniques will be discussed later for encouraging respondents to reply to mail and internet surveys.

Non-response error can be high when conducting international social research. In China, citizens are reluctant to provide information over the phone to strangers. In many Islamic countries in Asia, such as Malaysia and Indonesia, some women may refuse to be interviewed by a male interviewer.

A response bias occurs when respondents tend to answer questions with a certain slant. People may consciously or unconsciously misrepresent the truth. If a distortion of measurement occurs because respondents' answers are falsified or misrepresented, either intentionally or inadvertently, the resulting sample bias will be a response bias. A response bias may occur because it is deliberate (the respondent intended to provide incorrect or the best information they could, which may not be accurate) or unconscious (the respondent did not consciously intend to deceive the interviewer or provide the wrong information).

Deliberate falsification Sporadically, people deliberately give false answers. It is difficult to assess why people knowingly misrepresent answers. A response bias may occur when people misrepresent answers to appear intelligent, to conceal personal information, to avoid embarrassment, and so on. For example, respondents may be able to remember to whom they donated money, but they may forget the exact social programmes that the donated money was for. Rather than appear ignorant or unconcerned about social programmes, they may provide their best estimate and not tell the truth – namely, that they cannot remember. Sometimes respondents become fed up with the interview and provide answers just to get rid of the interviewer. At other times respondents provide the answers they think are expected of them to appear well informed. On still other occasions, they give answers simply to please the interviewer.

One explanation for conscious and deliberate misrepresentation of facts is the so-called 'average man' hypothesis. Individuals may prefer to be viewed as average and they alter their responses to conform more closely to their perception of the average person. Average man effects have been found to exist in response to questions about such topics as donation amounts, alcohol consumption, sexual practices, voting behaviour and hospital stays.

Unconscious misrepresentation Even when a respondent is consciously trying to be truthful and cooperative, response bias can arise from the question format, the question content or some other stimulus. For example, bias can be introduced by the situation in which the survey is administered.

Respondents who misunderstand questions may unconsciously provide biased answers. Or they may be willing to answer but unable to do so because they have forgotten the exact details. Asking, 'When was the last time you helped out a community function?' may result in a best-guess estimate because the respondent has forgotten the exact date.

A bias may also occur when a respondent has not thought about an unexpected question. Many respondents will answer questions even though they have given them little thought. For example, in most investigations of respondents' intentions, the predictability of the intention scales depends on how close the subject is to making a decision with respect to their behaviour. Asking respondents how fair trade is, is unlikely to produce well-articulated answers. In many cases consumers cannot adequately express their feelings in words; there is an unconscious communication breakdown. As the time between a donation or a community event and the survey contact increases, the tendency for under-reporting information about that event increases. Time lapse influences people's ability to remember precisely and communicate specific factors. Unconscious misrepresentation bias may also occur because consumers unconsciously avoid facing the realities of a future buying situation.

Types of response bias There are five specific categories of response bias: acquiescence bias, extremity bias, interviewer bias, auspices bias and social desirability bias. These categories overlap and are not mutually exclusive. A single biased answer may be distorted for many complex reasons, some distortions being deliberate and some being unconscious misrepresentations.

Acquiescence bias: some respondents are very agreeable; these yeasayers accept all statements they are asked about. This tendency to agree with all or most questions is known as acquiescence bias, and it is particularly prominent in new policy research. Questions about a new policy idea generally elicit some acquiescence bias because respondents give positive connotations to most new ideas. Another form of acquiescence is evident in some people's tendency to disagree with all questions. Thus, acquiescence bias is a response bias due to the respondents' tendency to concur with a particular position (Arndt and Crane, 1975).

Extremity bias: some individuals tend to use extremes when responding to questions; others always avoid extreme positions and tend to respond more neutrally. Response styles vary from person to person, and extreme responses may cause an extremity bias in the data (for an interesting study of extremity bias, see Baumgartner and Steenkamp, 2001). Another form of extremity bias is the tendency of respondents who do not want to be seen as controversial or do not want to offend the interviewer to use the mid-point to indicate a neutral view on an issue (Roberts, 2005a). This may be particularly so in Asian cultures which include Confucian philosophy (for example, China/Hong Kong, Singapore and South Korea), which teaches moderation and avoids extremes. Respondents from such cultures may not wish to stand out in the crowd and may seek a non-offensive middle way when answering direct questions. A means of reducing such a bias may be to include a calibration question, which will assess the degree of mid-point bias (Roberts, 2005b). The response to this question can then be used to weight further questions to take into account any mid-point or other response bias issues.

Interviewer bias: response bias may arise from the interplay between interviewer and respondent. If the interviewer's presence influences respondents to give untrue or modified answers, the survey will be marred by interviewer bias. Many homemakers and retired people welcome an interviewer's visit as a break in routine activities. Other respondents may give answers they believe will please the interviewer rather than the truthful responses. Respondents may wish to appear intelligent and wealthy – of course they read *Time* rather than *Playboy*.

The interviewer's age, sex, style of dress, tone of voice, facial expressions or other non-verbal characteristics may also have some influence on a respondent's answers. For example, if an interviewer smiles and makes a positive statement after a respondent's answers, the respondent will be more likely to give similar responses. In a research study on sexual harassment against saleswomen, male interviewers might not yield as candid responses as female interviewers would. Also, if interviews go on too long, respondents may feel that time is being wasted and may answer as abruptly as possible with little forethought.

Also note that many interviewers, contrary to instructions, shorten or rephrase questions to suit their needs. This potential influence on responses can be avoided to some extent if interviewers receive training and supervision that emphasise the necessity of appearing neutral.

Auspices bias: when respondents are interviewed by people or by organisations that they hold in high esteem (the United Nations, Organisation for Economic Co-operation and Development – OECD, Greenpeace, Red Cross, Salvation Army, a local church), their answers to the survey may be deliberately or subconsciously misrepresented because respondents wish to assist the organisation or individual conducting the study. This is known as auspices bias.

Note that there can also be culture-bound sources of response bias. For example, in Asia, cultural values about survey research differ from those in Australia and New Zealand. Asians have less patience with the abstract and rational question wording commonly used in Australia and New Zealand. Researchers must be alert for culture-bound sources of response bias in international marketing research. For example, the Japanese do not wish to contradict others, leading to a bias toward acquiescence and yea-saying.

Social desirability bias: a social desirability bias (SDB) may occur either consciously or unconsciously because the respondent wishes to create a favourable impression or save face in the presence of an interviewer. Incomes may be exaggerated, education overstated or perceived respectable answers given to gain prestige. In contrast, answers to questions that seek factual information or responses about matters of public knowledge (postcode, number of children and so on) usually are quite accurate. An interviewer's presence may increase a respondent's tendency to give inaccurate answers to sensitive questions such as, 'Did you vote for the Conservatives in the last election?' 'Do you recycle your rubbish?' or 'Do you wear a wig?' Social desirability bias appears to be influenced by the degree of development and culture. Research suggests that respondents from Asian countries such as Malaysia exhibit higher social desirability bias than Western countries such as the US and France (Kellior et al., 2001). It appears that social desirability bias in this study in Malaysia was influenced by reactions of family and friends, while in the US it appeared to be influenced by society and the media. The French respondents, on the other hand, were not influenced greatly by other factors in terms of social desirability bias, other than the overall reaction from society. Therefore research in international contexts needs to take into account not only the degree but also causes of social desirability bias.

Administrative error

The results of improper administration or execution of the research task are administrative errors. They are caused by carelessness, confusion, neglect, omission or some other blunder. Four types of administrative error are data-processing error, sample-selection error, interviewer error and interviewer cheating.

Data-processing error Processing data by computer, like any arithmetic or procedural process, is subject to error because data must be edited, coded and entered into the computer by people. The accuracy of data processed by computer depends on correct data entry and programming. Data-processing errors can be minimised by establishing careful procedures for verifying each step in the data-processing stage.

Sample-selection error Sample-selection error is systematic error that results in an unrepresentative sample because of an error in either the sample design or the execution of the sampling procedure. Executing a sampling plan free of procedural error is difficult. A firm that selects its sample from the phone book will have some systematic error, because unlisted numbers are not included. Stopping female respondents during daytime hours in shopping centres excludes working people who shop by mail, internet or telephone. In other cases, the wrong person may be interviewed. Consider a social entrepreneurship study that interviews farmers in Africa who are male: in some countries in Africa it may be the women who are the farmers or contribute to farming.

Interviewer error Interviewers' abilities vary considerably. Interviewer error is introduced when interviewers record answers but tick the wrong response or are unable to write fast enough to record answers verbatim. Or, selective perception may cause interviewers to mis-record data that do not support their own attitudes and opinions.

Interviewer cheating Interviewer cheating occurs when an interviewer falsifies entire questionnaires or fills in answers to questions that have been intentionally skipped. Some interviewers cheat to finish an interview as quickly as possible or to avoid questions about sensitive topics.

If interviewers are suspected of faking questionnaires, they should be told that a small percentage of respondents will be called back to confirm whether the initial interview was actually conducted. This should discourage interviewers from cheating.

8.2.3 Reducing Survey Error

It is impossible to remove all errors from a survey. While random sampling error can be estimated by the use of statistical confidence intervals, non-sampling or systematic error cannot and a conservative 'rule of thumb' may need to be used. Estimates vary, but some commercial studies suggest that error rates as much as 50 per cent need to be included when estimating the likelihood of future behaviour.[1] Some suggested tips for reducing survey error are as follows:

- Have good clear, well-worded measurements and questions (these are discussed later in the chapter).
- Avoid sensitive issues and questions whenever possible.
- Have well-trained and supervised interviewers. Make sure you check a sample of interviews collected.
- Use sample procedures, which will best allow you to sample the people you want to get the information from.
- Always pilot – test your survey on a small sample of respondents – so that any major problems are identified before you go into the field.

8.3 DIFFERENT WAYS TO CONDUCT SURVEYS

There is no single 'correct' method in which to conduct a survey. There are, however, several approaches that will be appropriate, depending on the research objectives, nature of the study, the type of respondents and the available budget.

In designing a questionnaire (or an interview schedule), the researcher must decide: (1) how much structure or standardisation is needed; (2) whether to utilise disguised or undisguised questions; and (3) how to communicate with the respondent.

8.3.1 (Un)Structured and (Un)Disguised Questions

A structured question limits the number of allowable responses. For example, respondents may be instructed to choose one alternative response such as 'under 18', '18 to 35', or 'over 35' to indicate his or her age. Unstructured questions do not restrict the respondent's answers. For example, an open-ended, unstructured question such as, 'What do you think about fair trade?' allows the respondent considerable freedom in response.

The researcher must also decide whether to use undisguised questions or disguised questions (introduced above). A straightforward, or undisguised, question such as, 'Do you have sexual problems?' assumes that the respondent is willing to reveal the information. However, researchers know that some questions are threatening to a person's ego, prestige or self-concept. It may, therefore, be more appropriate to utilise indirect techniques of questioning to disguise the purpose of the study.

8.3.2 How to Communicate with Respondents

A researcher has a number of options with regards to communication; the appropriate choice will depend on the type of research, speed of data collection required and budget limitations.

Personal interviews

Personal interviews are the most expensive way to conduct research but provide the lowest chance of misinterpretation of questions because the interviewer can clarify any questions respondents have regarding the instruction or questions. Circumstances may dictate that at the conclusion of the interview, the respondent be given additional information concerning the purpose of the study. This is easily accomplished with the personal interview.

An important characteristic of personal interviews is the opportunity to follow up by probing. If a respondent's answer is too brief or unclear, the researcher may probe for a more comprehensive or clearer explanation. In probing, the interviewer asks for clarification of answers to standardised questions such as, 'Can you tell me more about what you had in mind?' The personal interview is especially useful for obtaining unstructured information. Skilled interviewers can handle complex questions that cannot easily be asked in telephone or mail surveys.

If the research objective requires an extremely lengthy questionnaire, personal interviews may be the only option. The social interaction between a well-trained interviewer and a respondent in a personal interview increases the likelihood that the respondent will answer all the items on the questionnaire. Interviewing respondents face to face allows the investigator to show visual aids. Although some people are reluctant to participate in a survey, the presence of an interviewer generally increases the percentage of people willing to complete the interview. Respondents typically are required to do no reading or writing – all they have to do is talk. For this reason personal interviews are best used in countries with low literacy rates. Personal interviews also have some disadvantages. Respondents are not anonymous and therefore may be reluctant to provide confidential information to another person.

Telephone interviews

Telephone interviews are quick, relatively inexpensive when compared to personal interviews, and have the best means of interviewer control. They do suffer from sample biases and are only useful for short surveys.

Whereas data collection with mail or personal interviews can take several weeks, hundreds of telephone interviews can be conducted literally overnight. When the interviewer enters the respondents' answers directly into a computerised system, the data processing speeds up even more. Telephone interviews can provide representative samples. However, willingness to cooperate with telephone surveys has declined in recent years. In addition, the widespread use of answering machines and caller ID systems makes it increasingly difficult to contact individuals.

As the cost of personal interviews continues to increase, telephone interviews are becoming relatively inexpensive. It is estimated that the cost of telephone interviews is less than 25 per cent of the cost of door-to-door personal interviews. Travel time and costs are eliminated. However, the typical internet survey is less expensive than a telephone survey.

Telephone interviews are more impersonal than face-to-face interviews. Respondents may answer embarrassing or confidential questions more willingly in a telephone interview than in a personal interview.

Although telephone calls may be less threatening because the interviewer is not physically present, the absence of face-to-face contact can also be a liability. The respondent cannot see that the interviewer is still writing down the previous comment and may continue to elaborate on an answer. If the respondent pauses to think about an answer, the interviewer may not realise this and may go on to the next question. Hence, there is a greater tendency for interviewers to record no answers and incomplete answers in telephone interviews than in personal interviews.

In some countries and localities, people are reluctant to allow a stranger to come inside the house or even stop on the doorstep. The same people, however, may be perfectly willing to cooperate with a telephone survey request. Telephone interviewing avoids these problems.

One trend is very clear. In the decade to 2000, telephone response rates have dropped from 40 per cent to as low as 15 per cent (Rubin, 2000). It is estimated that the average response rate in Australia is 27 per cent (Australian Market and Social Research Society, 2003) and that response rates are declining at about 3 per cent per year. In addition, it is increasingly difficult to establish contact with potential respondents for three major reasons: (1) the proliferation of telephone numbers dedicated exclusively to fax machines and/or computers; (2) the widespread use of a non-dedicated phone line to access the internet; and (3) the use of call-screening devices to avoid unwanted calls (Tuckel and O'Neill, 2001). We can add to that the increasing number of people who have no landline, and use only mobile phones.

Refusal to cooperate with interviews is directly related to interview length. A good rule of thumb is to keep telephone interviews approximately

10 to 15 minutes long. In general, 30 minutes is the maximum amount of time most respondents will spend unless they are highly interested in the survey subject.

Practical difficulties complicate obtaining representative samples based on listings in the telephone book. Around 99 per cent of households in Australia have fixed-line telephones. Unlisted phone numbers and numbers too new to be printed in the directory are a greater problem. The unlisted group tends to be younger, more urban, and less likely to own a single-family dwelling. Households that maintain unlisted phone numbers by choice tend to have higher incomes. It is also possible that some low-income households may be unlisted by circumstance. In Australia it is estimated that around 15 per cent of phone numbers are unlisted (Hughes and Stone, 2002). Complicating matters is that around 72 per cent of Australian households have a mobile phone (ABS, 2003), and that the number of telephone lines and mobile phones per 100 people in Australia (in 2002) is 118 (ABS, 2004). The increasing use by households of multiple telephone numbers for mobiles and possibly internet connections means that obtaining a representative sample in telephone interviewing is much more difficult than it used to be.

The problem of unlisted phone numbers can be partially resolved through the use of random-digit dialling. Random-digit dialling also helps to overcome the problem of new listings and recent changes in numbers. Unfortunately, the refusal rate in commercial random-digit dialling studies (approximately 40 per cent) is higher than the 25 per cent refusal rate for telephone surveys that use only listed telephone numbers.

Because visual aids cannot be used in telephone interviews, copy testing of television and print advertising, and concept tests that require visual materials, cannot be conducted by phone. Certain attitude scales and measuring instruments, such as the semantic differential, cannot be used easily because they require the respondent to see a graphic scale.

Self-administered surveys or questionnaires

The absence of an interviewer greatly reduces costs and is useful when collecting information about sensitive information, since respondents are not directly identified from the research. Self-administered questionnaires include mail, fax, email and internet surveys. Of these, internet surveys are proving now the most popular, given the advantages of lower costs and speed of data collection. There are two major issues of self-administered surveys: these are the low response rates, of around 5–10 per cent; and the self-selection bias – people who have more extreme positions are more likely to take part in online surveys, because they feel very strongly about the issues covered in the research.

Table 8.1 Internet penetration in the Asia-Pacific region

Nation	Population	Internet users	Internet penetration (%)
South Korea	48508972	35599000	73.39
Australia	21261641	15300000	71.96
Japan	127078679	88110000	69.34
New Zealand	4213418	3360000	79.74
Taiwan	22974347	14760000	64.24
Singapore	4657542	3105000	66.67
Malaysia	25715919	15868000	61.70
China	1338612968	235000000	17.55

Source: CIA (n.d.).

There is also not the control over sample selection that there is in personal and telephone interviews. The main advantage of self-administered surveys is that they can be used for longer questionnaires and that the respondent can answer the survey at a time convenient to them.

In terms of dealing with low response rates, a number of solutions are used. In mail surveys, the use of a cover letter which promises confidentiality and shows the sponsorship of the survey has been shown to increase response rates. Money helps: the respondent's motivation for returning a questionnaire may be increased by offering monetary incentives or premiums. Although pens, lottery tickets and a variety of premiums have been used, monetary incentives appear to be the most effective and least biasing incentive. Starting the questionnaire with interesting questions also helps respondent cooperation. Follow-ups, or reminders to complete the survey, also help to increase response rates.

Researchers who use self-administered questionnaires should recognise that conducting surveys in more than one country must recognise that postal services and cultural circumstances differ around the world. Care also needs to be taken with incentives, especially if they are sweepstakes or lottery tickets, which may be seen as gambling, particularly in Muslim countries. Literacy rates also vary across nations. For this reason, market researchers when conducting surveys in less-developed countries may rely on personal interviews rather than mail surveys. The use of internet and mail surveys is also limited when doing international research, as the internet penetration figures differ substantially. This is shown in Table 8.1.

In order to increase response rates in internet surveys, many researchers now use online panels, whereby a respondent becomes a member of a survey group and gets paid for the completion of surveys. While this may greatly increase response rates – up to 80 per cent is claimed in some cases

– there are concerns about response bias and whether people interviewed repeatedly by market research companies represent the views of the public (Australian Market and Social Research Society, 2004).

8.3.3 What is the Appropriate Survey Method?

To determine the appropriate method, the researcher must ask several questions: is the assistance of an interviewer necessary? Are respondents interested in the issues being investigated? Will cooperation be easily attained? How quickly is the information needed? Will the study require a long and complex questionnaire? How large is the budget? The criteria – cost, speed, anonymity and so forth – may differ for each project.

Table 8.2 summarises the major advantages and disadvantages of typical door-to-door, mall intercept (approaching people in a shopping mall or other public space), telephone, mail and internet surveys. It emphasises the typical types of surveys. For example, a creative researcher might be able to design highly versatile and flexible mail questionnaires, but most researchers use standardised questions. An elaborate mail survey may be far more expensive than a short personal interview, but generally this is not the case.

8.4 MEASUREMENT: THE SIX STEPS

In many social science research studies measurements are taken of key phenomena; the same applies to research on social entrepreneurship (Eikenberry and Kluver, 2004; Leroux, 2005). Many foci of social science research deal with measures of mental constructs such as attitudes, personalities, values and categories which cannot be directly measured in the same way that physical properties of elements can, like temperature and weight. It is recommended therefore that measurements are developed in a systematic fashion, which are objective as possible and free from errors in social sciences. The following steps need to be considered when developing a measure or set of measures:

- Step 1: Determine what is to be measured.
- Step 2: Determine how it is to be measured.
- Step 3: Apply a rule of measurement.
- Step 4: Determine whether the measure consists of a number of measures.
- Step 5: Determine the type of attitude and the scale to be used to measure it.
- Step 6: Evaluate the measure.

Table 8.2 Advantages and disadvantages of typical survey methods

	Door-to-door personal interview	Mall intercept personal interview	Telephone interview	Mail survey	Internet survey
Speed of data collection	Moderate to fast	Fast	Very fast	Slow; researcher has no control over return of questionnaire	Instantaneous; 24/7
Geographic flexibility	Limited to moderate	Confined, possible urban bias	High	High	High (worldwide)
Respondent cooperation	Excellent	Moderate to low	Good	Moderate; poorly designed questionnaire will have low response rate	Varies depending on website; high from consumer panels
Versatility of questioning	Quite versatile	Extremely versatile	Moderate	Not versatile; requires highly standardised format	Extremely versatile
Questionnaire length	Long	Moderate to long	Moderate	Varies depending on incentive	Moderate; length customised based on answers
Item non-response rate	Low	Medium	Medium	High	Software can assure none
Possibility for respondent misunderstanding	Low	Low	Average	High; no interviewer present for clarification	High

Table 8.2 (continued)

	Door-to-door personal interview	Mall intercept personal interview	Telephone interview	Mail survey	Internet survey
Degree of interviewer influence on answers	High	High	Moderate	None; interviewer absent	None
Supervision of interviewers	Moderate	Moderate to high	High, especially with central-location WATS* interviewing	Not applicable	Not applicable
Anonymity of respondent	Low	Low	Moderate	High	Respondent can be either anonymous or known
Ease of call-back or follow-up	Difficult	Difficult	Easy	Easy, but takes time	Difficult, unless email address is known
Cost	Highest	Moderate to high	Low to moderate	Lowest	Low
Special features	Visual materials may be shown or demonstrated; extended probing possible	Taste tests, viewing of TV commercials possible	Fieldwork and supervision of data collection are simplified; quite adaptable to computer technology	Respondent may answer questions at own convenience; has time to reflect on answers	Streaming media software allows use of graphics and animation

Note: * WATS = Wide-Area Telecommunications Service.

Source: Zikmund et al. (2010).

8.4.1 Step 1: Determine What is to be Measured

The first question the researcher must answer is, 'What is to be measured?' This is not as simple a question as it may at first seem. A precise definition of the concept may require a description of how it will be measured – and frequently there is more than one way to measure a particular concept.

Before the measurement process can occur, a marketing researcher must identify the concepts relevant to the problem. A concept (or construct) is a generalised idea about a class of objects, attributes, occurrences or processes. Concepts such as age, gender and the number of children are relatively concrete properties, and they present few problems in definition or measurement. Other characteristics of individuals or properties of objects may be more abstract. Take for example the measurement of social entrepreneurship; this is defined in some studies as: 'initiatives that are associated with aspects of innovation and modes of earned income generation by non-governmental organizations' (Leroux, 2005, p. 353).

A category on the other hand, such as social entrepreneurs, is defined more broadly, as: 'nonprofit executives who pay attention to market forces without losing sight of their organizations' underlying missions and seek to use the language and skills of the business world to advance the material wellbeing of their members or clients' (Eikenberry and Kluver, 2004).

As these definitions of constructs determine what is to be measured, the researcher must carefully consult the literature and find agreement where ever possible as to what is being measured. They may well have to justify the selection of their own definition of a construct if different definitions of the measure exist in the peer-reviewed literature.

8.4.2 Step 2: Determine How it is to be Measured

Concepts must be made operational in order to be measured. An operational definition gives meaning to a concept by specifying the activities or operations necessary to measure it. In Table 8.3 is an operational definition of social entrepreneurship that was used in research.

8.4.3 Step 3: Apply a Rule of Measurement

A rule is a guide that tells someone what to do. An example of a measurement rule might be: 'Assign the numerals 1 to 7 to individuals according to how concerned about climate change they are. If the individual is extremely concerned, assign a 7. If the individual is not at all concerned, assign the numeral 1.' The operational definition, as discussed previously in Table 8.3, shows the researcher the rules for assigning numbers.

Table 8.3 Social Entrepreneurship: an operational definition

Concept	Conceptual definition	Operational definition
Social Entrepreneurship	Initiatives that are associated with aspects of innovation and modes of earned income generation by non-governmental organizations.	Self report, open-ended questions. Non-profit organisations which asked if any changes to their budget in the past five years that reflected any of the below: The development of a new business enterprise, commercial sales activity, and charging fees for services. Social Entrepreneurship is measured as value of 1 if the respondent reported the adoption of one or more of these approaches and 0 if the respondent did not report undertaking any of these strategies in the 5-year time period.

Source: Leroux (2005, p. 356).

The values assigned in the measuring process can be manipulated according to certain mathematical rules. The properties of the scale of numbers may allow the researcher to add, subtract or multiply answers. In some cases there may be problems with the simple addition of the numbers, or other mathematical manipulations may not be permissible. Table 8.4 shows some of the common approaches used in assigning numbers for different types of measurements. It is important that these are identified in the questionnaire, as the type of analysis and conclusions drawn later in the research study depend on the level of measurement.

8.4.4 Step 4: Determine Whether the Measure Consists of a Number of Measures

In many instances, a measurement of a construct may require a collection of a number of measures. Research (Korosec and Berman, 2008) on local government support for social entrepreneurship found that there were three types of support: coordination and implementation; resource acquisition; and information and awareness. A number of items were used to assess support for resource acquisition, and respondents were asked:

Table 8.4 Levels of measurements used in social science research

Type of scale	Example	Numerical operation	Descriptive statistics
Nominal	Yes-no Female-Male Social Entrepreneur-Not a social Entrepreneur Postcode____	Counting	Frequencies Mode
Ordinal	Rankings Indicate your level of education: High school Some university University degree Graduate university degree	Counting and Rank ordering	Frequencies Mode Median Range
Interval	Most Attitude scales Agree-Disagree 5 point scale	Arithmetic operations that preserve order and relative magnitudes	Mean Median Standard deviation Variance
Ratio	Amount donated Probability of donation Time spent on a webpage Number of villages visited by doctor Webpage hits	All Arithmetic	Mean Median Standard deviation Variance

'We assist private organizations that work on important social issues or causes by . . .'

1. Contributing to grant proposals of private organizations by pledging support through city programs and resources
2. Helping private organizations to submit grant proposals on important issues
3. Participating with private organizations in grant proposals on important issues
4. Supporting the grant proposals of private organizations
5. Helping private organizations identify funding opportunities related to important social issues and problems

6. Providing program support for private organizations that address important social issues and problems
7. Helping private organizations to locate grant opportunities
8. Contributing start-up funding for private organizations that address important social issues and problems.

These were answered on a five-point attitude scale from 1 ('strongly disagree') to 5 ('strongly agree'). These responses were then summed to provide an overall score of local government support for resource acquisition, which can range from 8 to 40. Before summing items, the researcher would need to examine the internal consistency of the measure (often called the internal reliability).

8.4.5 Step 5: Determine the Type of Attitude and its Measurement Scale

A remarkable variety of techniques have been devised to measure attitudes. This variety stems in part from lack of consensus about the exact definition of the concept. Furthermore, the affective, cognitive and behavioural components of an attitude may be measured by different means. Direct verbal statements concerning affect, belief or behaviour are used to measure behavioural intent. However, attitudes may also be measured indirectly using the qualitative techniques. Obtaining verbal statements from respondents generally requires that the respondents perform a task such as ranking, rating, sorting or making choices.

A ranking task requires the respondent to rank order a small number of objects on the basis of overall preference or some characteristic of the stimulus. Rating asks the respondent to estimate the magnitude of a characteristic or quality that an object possesses. A quantitative score, along a continuum that has been supplied to the respondent, is used to estimate the strength of the person's attitude or belief; in other words, the respondent indicates the position on one or more scales at which he or she would rate the object. A sorting task might present the respondent with several product concepts printed on cards and require the respondent to arrange the cards into a number of piles or otherwise classify the product concepts. Choice between two or more alternatives is another type of attitude measurement. If a respondent chooses one object over another, the researcher can assume that the respondent prefers the chosen object over the other. The following sections describe the most popular techniques for measuring attitudes. Table 8.5 defines the types of choices of attitude scales that are used in research. The measurement of local government support discussed previously used a Likert rating scale.

Table 8.5 Common attitude scales

Rating measure	Subject must	Advantages	Disadvantages
Category scale	Indicate a response category	Flexible, easy to respond to	Items may be ambiguous; with few categories, only gross distinctions can be made
Likert scale	Evaluate statements on a scale of agreement	Easiest scale to construct	Hard to judge what a single score means
Semantic differential and numerical scales	Choose points between bipolar adjectives on relevant dimensions	Easy to construct; norms exist for comparison, such as profile analysis	Bipolar adjectives must be found; data may be ordinal, not interval
Stapel scale	Choose points on a scale with a single adjective in the centre	Easier to construct than semantic differential, easy to administer	Endpoints are numerical, not verbal, labels
Constant-sum scale	Divide a constant sum among response alternatives	Approximates an interval measure	Difficult for respondents with low education levels
Graphic scale	Choose a point on a continuum	Visual impact, unlimited scale points	No standard answers
Graphic scale with picture response categories	Choose a visual picture	Visual impact, easy for poor readers	Hard to attach a verbal explanation to a response

Source: Zikmund et al. (2010).

8.4.6 Step 6: Evaluate the Measure

There are three major criteria for evaluating measurements: reliability, validity and sensitivity.

Reliability

Reliability applies to a measure when similar results are obtained over time and across situations. Broadly defined, reliability is the degree to which measures are free from random error and therefore yield consistent results. For example, ordinal measures are reliable if they consistently rank order items in the same manner; reliable interval measures consistently rank order and maintain the same distance between items. Imperfections in the measuring process that affect the assignment of scores or numbers in different ways each time a measure is taken, such as when a respondent misunderstands a question, cause low reliability. The actual choice among plausible responses may be governed by such transitory factors as mood, whim or the context set by surrounding questions; measures are not always error-free and stable over time.

Reliability is a necessary condition for validity, but a reliable instrument may not be valid. For example, a purchase intention measurement technique may consistently indicate that 20 per cent of those sampled are willing to donate to Queensland flood relief. Whether the measure is valid depends on whether 20 per cent of the population indeed does donate money. A reliable but invalid instrument will yield consistently inaccurate results.

Validity

Validity can be defined as: the measure measures what it is supposed to measure. Validity is assessed in three ways, including: face or content validity, criterion validity and construct validity. Face, or content, validity refers to the subjective agreement among professionals, or in the research literature, that a scale logically appears to reflect accurately what it purports to measure.

Criterion validity is assessed by the degree of relationship between other measures of the same construct. In our local government support for social entrepreneurship example, the criterion validity of support resource acquisition is assessed by its relationship to other measures of local government support, which included coordination and implementation, and information and awareness.

Construct validity is established by the degree to which the measure confirms a network of related hypotheses generated from a theory based on the concepts. Construct validity implies that the empirical evidence generated by a measure is consistent with the theoretical logic behind the concepts. In its simplest form, if the measure behaves the way it is supposed to in a pattern of intercorrelation with a variety of other variables, there is evidence of construct validity.

Sensitivity

The sensitivity of a scale is an important measurement concept, particularly when changes in attitudes or other hypothetical constructs are under investigation. Sensitivity refers to an instrument's ability to measure accurately the variability in stimuli or responses. A dichotomous response category, such as 'agree or disagree', does not allow the recording of subtle attitude changes. A more sensitive measure with numerous categories on the scale may be needed. For example, adding 'strongly agree', 'mildly agree', 'neither agree nor disagree', 'mildly disagree' and 'strongly disagree' will increase the scale's sensitivity. The sensitivity of a scale based on a single question or single item can also be increased by adding questions or items. In other words, because index measures allow for a greater range of possible scores, they are more sensitive than single-item scales.

Lastly, measures must be practical. Practical measures are shorter (have less items), while still being sensitive, and are easy to administer, timely and simple enough for respondents to understand. Results from practical measures should be easy to interpret. Skill in designing practical measures is often due to questionnaire design, and this is discussed in the following section.

8.5 QUESTIONNAIRE DESIGN: THE NINE STEPS

Developing questionnaires is as much an art as it is a science. Like the previous discussion on surveys, it is important to minimise any potential errors and biases and ensure that the measures obtained represent the views of respondents. It is suggested that the development of questionnaires should follow nine steps:

- Step 1: Specify what information will be sought.
- Step 2: Determine the type of questionnaire and type of survey research methods.
- Step 3: Determine the content of individual questions.
- Step 4: Determine the form of response to each question.
- Step 5: Determine the wording of each question.
- Step 6: Determine question sequence.
- Step 7: Determine physical characteristics of the questionnaire.

- Step 8: Re-examine and revise Steps 1–7 if necessary.
- Step 9: Pre-test questionnaire.

8.5.1 Step 1: Specify what Information Will be Sought

A questionnaire is relevant if no unnecessary information is collected and only the information needed to meet the information objectives and/or hypotheses is obtained. Asking the wrong question or an irrelevant question is a common problem. To ensure information relevance, the researcher must be specific about data needs and have a rationale for each item of information (see the previous discussion on measurement). The researcher should first list in order of importance the specific research objectives and information required to meet those objectives before constructing a questionnaire.

8.5.2 Step 2: Determine the Type of Questionnaire and Type of Survey Research Methods

This depends on the types of respondents and nature of information needed. A small sample of experts on social entrepreneurship is best obtained by personal interview. Generally, as noted in the design of surveys, personal interviews are best for more open-ended and qualitative studies. Telephone interviews are good for short questionnaires; mail and online surveys are good for collecting information about sensitive issues such as health, criminal behaviour, drug taking or depression.

8.5.3 Step 3: Determine the Content of Individual Questions

It is a good idea at this stage of the process to consider the following:

1. Is the question necessary?
2. Are several questions needed instead of one?
3. Do the respondents have the necessary information to respond to the question?
4. Will respondents give the information freely and accurately?

Respondents' willingness to answer your questions will be determined by the work involved in producing an answer, their ability to articulate an answer, and the sensitivity of the issue. Respondents will find it difficult to answer questions which involve calculating a quantity, for example, body mass index (kg/m^2), amount of calories or standard drinks consumed in a week. Respondents sometimes may not be able to articulate an answer, due to their age, literacy level or lack of knowledge on a particular topic. In this case more simple and direct language relevant to the respondent should be used in framing questions.

Asking sensitive questions requires special consideration in questionnaire design. Sensitive questions can include topics such as age, marital status for women, income, sexual habits and health (exercise and alcohol consumption). Sensitive issues are also likely to be influenced by culture; this would be especially so for questions regarding sexual behaviour and gambling. In persuading respondents to provide information about sensitive issues, there are a number of approaches that can be used. The first is to 'hide' the question in a group of less sensitive questions. The second is to state that the behaviour or attitude is not that unusual before asking the question. For example:

> One out of four households have problems meeting their monthly financial obligations.
> Do you find that you have problems meeting your financial obligations at least once a month?

Another approach is to phrase the question in terms of others and how they might feel or act (in the third person). This usually elicits a response that is not threatening but still applies to the respondent:

> Do you think most people cheat on their income tax? Why?

Stating the responses in the form of categories that the respondent may simply check or tick, or as closed response questions, is also likely to yield information on sensitive issues; this is used especially when asking questions about income. Another way to deal with sensitive issues is to only ask them on a random basis. This is called the randomised-response model – paired sensitive and innocuous questions are drawn randomly (for example, red/black balls in turn).

8.5.4 Step 4: Determine the Form of Response to each Question

Two basic types of questions can be identified based on the amount of freedom respondents have in answering. Open-ended response questions pose some problem or topic and ask respondents to answer in their own words. If the question is asked in a personal interview, the interviewer may probe for more information. For example:

> What names of charities can you think of offhand?
> What comes to mind when you think about social responsibility?

In what way, if any, could this policy be changed or improved? I'd like you to tell me anything you can think of, no matter how minor it seems.
What things do you like most about Mission Australia's counselling service?
Why do you donate more money to the Salvation Army than other charities?
How can the local government serve your environmental needs?
Please tell me anything at all that you remember about the Body Shop commercial you saw last night.

Open-ended response questions are most beneficial when the researcher is conducting qualitative and exploratory research, especially when the range of responses is not known. Such questions can be used to learn which words and phrases people spontaneously give to the free-response question.

Major disadvantages of open-ended response questions include cost, which is higher than that of administering fixed-alternative questions because the job of editing, coding and analysing the data is quite extensive. Open-ended questions are more likely to be influenced by interviewer bias in the way the question is asked and the manner in which responses are recorded. Articulate individuals tend to give longer answers to open-ended response questions. Such respondents often are better educated and from higher-income groups and therefore may not be representative of the entire population, and yet they may give a large share of the responses.

Closed-ended questions give respondents specific limited-alternative responses and ask them to choose the one closest to their own viewpoints. For example:

Did you donate any free time to community organisations in 2010?
  Yes
  No
As compared with 10 years ago, would you say that the quality of solar panels is higher, about the same, or not as good?
  Higher
  About the same
  Not as good
Do you think the government's greenhouse gas legislation has affected your business?
  Yes, for the better
  Yes, for the worse
  Not especially
In which type of bookstore is it easier for you to shop – a regular bookstore or a bookstore on the Internet?
  Regular bookstore
  Internet bookstore
How much of your shopping for clothes and household items do you do in second-hand stores run by charities?
  All of it

Most of it
About one-half of it
About one-quarter of it
Less than one-quarter of it

Closed-ended questions require less interviewer skill, take less time and are easier for the respondent to answer. This is because answers to closed questions are classified into standardised groupings prior to data collection. Standardising alternative responses to a question provides comparability of answers, which facilitates coding, tabulating and ultimately interpreting the data. Where possible, use closed response questions as they require less interviewer skill and are easier to administer and code.

8.5.5 Step 5: Determine the Wording of each Question

No hard-and-fast rules determine how to develop a questionnaire. Fortunately, research experience has yielded some guidelines that help prevent the most common mistakes.

- Avoid complexity: use simple, conversational language.
- Avoid leading and loaded questions.
- Avoid ambiguity: be as specific as possible.
- Avoid double-barrelled questions (questions that ask two things).
- Avoid making assumptions.
- Avoid burdensome questions that tax the respondent's memory.

Avoid complexity: use simple, conversational language

Words used in questionnaires should be readily understandable to all respondents. The researcher usually has the difficult task of adopting the conversational language of people at the lower education levels without talking down to better-educated respondents. Remember, not all people have the vocabulary of a university student; a substantial number of Australians have never gone beyond high school.

Respondents can probably tell an interviewer whether they are married, single, divorced, separated or widowed, but providing their marital status may present a problem. The technical jargon of academics should be avoided when surveying respondents not from the same background. Some things to be avoided when phrasing questions include the following.

Avoid leading and loaded questions

> When effluents from a paper mill can be drunk and exhaust from factory smokestacks can be breathed, then humankind will have done a good job in

Table 8.6 Complex and simple words

Complex	Simple
Acquaint	Inform, or tell
Assist	Help
Consider	Think
Desire	Wish
Factor	Fact, consideration, circumstance, feature, element, constituent, cause
Function (verb)	Work, operate, act
Inform	Tell
Locate	Find
Practically	Virtually; almost, nearly; all but
Purchase	Buy
Require	Want, need
Residence	Home
State	Say
Sufficient	Enough
Terminate	End
Visualise	Imagine; picture

Source: Payne (1951, pp. 102–3).

> saving the environment . . . Don't you agree that what we want is zero toxicity: no effluents?

Besides being too long and confusing, this question is leading. Table 8.6 gives a list of complex words with their more simple equivalents. Note that some words have multiple meanings.

Leading and loaded questions are a major source of bias in question wording. Leading questions suggest or imply certain answers. A study of the dry-cleaning industry asked this question:

> Many people are using dry-cleaning less because of improved wash-and-wear clothes. How do you feel wash-and-wear clothes have affected your use of dry-cleaning facilities in the past four years?
> Use less   No change   Use more

The potential 'bandwagon effect' implied in this question threatens the study's validity. Partial mention of alternatives is a variation of this phenomenon:

> Do small imported cars, such as Toyotas get better economy than small Australian-built cars?

> How do you generally spend your free time, watching television or what?

Sometimes questions may be designed to get a particular response. Consider a recent online poll in the *Australian* newspaper.

> Do you think the Australian government is too soft in its immigration policy?

Most respondents would agree that the government is soft on a number of issues, including immigration. The question also does not ask which aspect of immigration policy or for particular aspects of agreement with that policy. One could also phrase another question as:

> Are you in favour of the Australian government's humane immigration policy which reunites families?

This would get a more sympathetic response than the previous question.

Loaded questions suggest a socially desirable answer, or are emotionally charged. Consider the following:

> In light of today's farm crisis in Queensland, it would be in the public's best interest to offer interest-free loans to businesses in Queensland?
> Strongly agree   Agree   Disagree   Strongly disagree

Answers might be different if the loaded portion of the statement, 'farm crisis', was worded to suggest a problem of less magnitude than a crisis.

Invoking the status quo is a form of loading resulting in bias because most people tend to resist change (Newspoll News, 2006). A Newspoll survey of 400 Sydneysiders found that support for a desalination plant was only 15 per cent, with 72 per cent preferring that the $1.3 billion to be spent on this project be allocated to recycling water. Respondents were not asked if they would accept drinking recycled water or water produced by desalination. Although 65 per cent had reservations about the price of desalinated water, 77 per cent expressed a concern about the impact of a desalination plant on greenhouse gases. The survey was sponsored by an alliance of local councils, scientists, engineering experts and environmental groups.

Asking respondents 'how often' they do something leads them to generalise about their habits, because there usually is some variance in their behaviour. In generalising, one is likely to portray one's ideal behaviour rather than one's average behaviour. For instance, brushing one's teeth after each meal may be ideal, but busy people may skip a brushing or two. An introductory counter-biasing statement or preamble to a question that reassures respondents that their 'embarrassing' behaviour is not abnormal may yield truthful responses:

> Some people have the time to brush three times daily; others do not. How often did you brush your teeth yesterday?

If a question embarrasses the respondent, it may elicit no answer or a biased response. This is particularly true with respect to personal or classification data such as income or education. The problem may be mitigated by introducing the section of the questionnaire with a statement such as:

> To help classify your answers, we'd like to ask you a few questions. Again, your answers will be kept in strict confidence.

A question statement may be leading because it is phrased to reflect either the negative or the positive aspects of an issue. To control for this bias, the wording of attitudinal questions may be reversed for 50 per cent of the sample.

Avoid ambiguity: be as specific as possible

Items on questionnaires often are ambiguous because they are too general. Consider such indefinite words as often, occasionally, regularly, frequently, many, good, fair and poor. Each of these words has many different meanings. For one person, frequent reading of *Fortune* magazine may be reading six or seven issues a year; for another it may be two issues a year. The word 'fair' has a great variety of meanings; the same is true for many other indefinite words.

Questions such as the following one, used in a study measuring the reactions of consumers to a television boycott, should be interpreted with care:

> Please indicate the statement that best describes your family's television viewing during the boycott of Channel 7.
> We did not watch any television programs on Channel 7.
> We watched hardly any television programs on Channel 7.
> We occasionally watched television programs on Channel 7.
> We frequently watched television programs on Channel 7.

A student research group asked this question:

> What media do you rely on most?
> Television
> Radio
> Internet
> Newspapers

This question is ambiguous because it does not ask about the content of the media. 'Rely on most' for what? News, sports, entertainment?

Avoid double-barrelled items

A question covering several issues at once is referred to as a double-barrelled question and should always be avoided. Making the mistake of asking two questions rather than one is easy; for example, 'Please indicate your degree of agreement with the following statement: "Wholesalers and retailers are responsible for the high cost of meat".' Which intermediaries are responsible, the wholesalers or the retailers? When multiple questions are asked in one question, the results may be exceedingly difficult to interpret. For example, consider the following question from a magazine's survey entitled 'How do you feel about being a woman?'

> Between you and your husband, who does the housework (cleaning, cooking, dishwashing, laundry) over and above that done by any hired help?
> I do all of it.
> I do almost all of it.
> I do over half of it.
> We split the work fifty–fifty.
> My husband does over half of it.

The answers to this question do not tell us if the wife cooks and the husband washes the dishes.

A survey by a consumer-oriented library asked:

> Are you satisfied with the present system of handling 'closed-reserve' and 'open-reserve' readings? (Are enough copies available? Are the required materials ordered promptly? Are the borrowing regulations adequate for students' use of materials?)
> Yes No

A respondent may feel torn between a 'yes' to one part of the question and a 'no' to another part. The answer to this question does not tell the researcher which problem or combination of problems concerns the library user.

Consider this comment about double-barrelled questions:

> Generally speaking, it is hard enough to get answers to one idea at a time without complicating the problem by asking what amounts to two questions at once. If two ideas are to be explored, they deserve at least two questions. Since question marks are not rationed, there is little excuse for the needless confusion that results [from] the double-barrelled question. (Payne, 1951)

Avoid making assumptions

Consider the following question:

> Should the Salvation Army continue its excellent crisis program?
> Yes No

This question has a built-in assumption: that people believe the crisis program is excellent. By answering 'yes', the respondent implies that the program is, in fact, excellent and that things are fine just as they are; by answering 'no', he or she implies that either the Salvation Army should not continue the program; or that the program is not excellent. The researchers should not place the respondent in that sort of bind by including an implicit assumption in the question.

Another frequent mistake is assuming that the respondent had previously thought about an issue. For example, the following question appeared in a survey concerning the Salvation Army: 'Do you think the Salvation Army should consider changing its name?' It is very unlikely that respondents had thought about this question before being asked it. Most respondents answered the question even though they had no prior opinion concerning the name change. Research that induces people to express attitudes on subjects they do not ordinarily think about is meaningless.

Avoid burdensome questions that may tax the respondent's memory
A simple fact of human life is that people forget. Researchers writing questions about past behaviour or events should recognise that certain questions may make serious demands on the respondent's memory. Writing questions about prior events requires a conscientious attempt to minimise the problems associated with forgetting.

Telescoping and squishing are two additional consequences of respondents forgetting the exact details of their behaviour. Telescoping occurs when respondents believe that past events happened more recently than they actually did. The opposite effect, squishing, occurs when respondents think that recent events took place longer ago than they really did. A solution to this problem may be to refer to a specific event that is memorable – for example, 'How often have you gone to a sporting event since the last Ashes series in Australia?' Because forgetting tends to increase over time, the question may concern a recent period: 'How often did you watch the History Channel on cable television last week?' (During the editing stage, the results can be transposed to the appropriate time period.)

In situations in which 'I don't know' or 'I can't recall' is a meaningful answer, simply including a 'don't know' response category may solve the question-writer's problem.

8.5.6 Step 6: Determine Question Sequence

The order of questions, or the question sequence, may serve several functions for the researcher. If the opening questions are interesting, simple to comprehend and easy to answer, respondents' cooperation and involvement can be maintained throughout the questionnaire. Asking easy-to-answer questions teaches respondents their role and builds their confidence; they know that this is a professional researcher. If respondents' curiosity is not aroused at the outset, they can become disinterested and terminate the interview.

Generally more sensitive and personal information, such as demographics, should be asked at the end of the questionnaire. Order bias can also distort survey results. For example, suppose a questionnaire's purpose is to measure levels of awareness of several charitable organisations. If Care Australia and the Salvation Army are always mentioned first, the Red Cross second, and Guide Dogs for the Blind third, Care Australia and the Salvation Army may receive an artificially high awareness rating because respondents are prone to yea-saying (by indicating awareness of the first item in the list).

It is advisable to ask general questions before specific questions to obtain the freest of open-ended responses. This procedure, known as the funnel technique, allows the researcher to understand the respondent's frame of reference before asking more specific questions about the level of the respondent's information and the intensity of his or her opinions.

8.5.7 Step 7: Determine Physical Characteristics of the Questionnaire

Good layout and physical attractiveness are crucial in mail, internet and other self-administered questionnaires. For different reasons it is also important to have a good layout in questionnaires designed for personal and telephone interviews.

Experienced researchers have found that it pays to phrase the title of a questionnaire carefully. In self-administered and mail questionnaires a carefully constructed title may capture the respondent's interest, underline the importance of the research ('Nationwide Study of Blood Donors'), emphasise the interesting nature of the study ('Study of Internet Usage'), appeal to the respondent's ego ('Survey among Top Executives'), or emphasise the confidential nature of the study ('A Confidential Survey among . . .'). The researcher should take steps to ensure that the wording of the title will not bias the respondent in the same way that a leading question might.

8.5.8 Step 8: Re-examine and Revise Steps 1–7 if Necessary

Many novelists write, rewrite, revise and rewrite again certain chapters, paragraphs or sentences. The researcher works in a similar world. Rarely does he or she write only a first draft of a questionnaire. Ideally, the draft questionnaire should be examined by other experts or researchers in the field. The language used in questionnaires should be understandable and familiar also to those from a non-technical background.

8.5.9 Step 9: Pre-test Questionnaire

Pretesting or piloting a survey is important, as how well the questionnaire works in the field is examined and feedback from interviews can be used to improve the questionnaire or address any faults in its construction.

International marketing researchers often have questionnaires back-translated. Back-translation is the process of taking a questionnaire that has previously been translated from one language to another, and having it translated back again by a second, independent translator. The back-translator is often a person whose native tongue is the language that will be used for the questionnaire. This process can reveal inconsistencies between the English version and the translation. For example, when a soft-drink company translated its slogan 'Baby, it's cold inside' into Cantonese for research in Hong Kong, the result read, 'Small mosquito, on the inside, it is very cold'. In Hong Kong, 'small mosquito' is a colloquial expression for a small child. Obviously the intended meaning of the advertising message had been lost in the translated questionnaire (Cateora, 1990, pp. 387–9). In another international marketing research project, 'out of sight, out of mind' was back-translated as 'invisible things are insane' (Jain, 1990, p. 338).

8.6 SAMPLING, FIELDWORK AND EDITING

A sampling frame is the method by which we actually make contact with our respondents. It is the specific definition of who is in our sample and who is not in our sample. An ideal sampling frame is a list of all members of the population of interest. This might be an email list of people who have subscribed to a non-profit organisation, or a list of those people who fulfil certain criteria in a metropolitan phonebook. It is from this list that the sample might be randomly selected. Most social research, however, does not have the advantage of a list and so samples must be drawn on a convenience basis or through making contacts with others who might then snowball their introductions on to others.

8.6.1 Sample Size

Much is made in the research methodology textbooks of calculations and interpretations of sample size. Typically, an entire chapter is devoted to the calculation and estimation of the necessary number of respondents to get valid research. The reason for this, while rarely stated, is that sample size is one of the few things that the researcher has any control over. We focus on sample size because we can. Ironically, the level of error associated with poor questionnaires and improper sampling frame is far greater than the level of error created from a small sample size. If the researcher must make a choice between spending more time verifying and refining the questionnaire, compared with having a questionnaire out in the field for a longer time, then we strongly recommend choosing the former.

With respect to specific sample size recommendations, all the textbooks and other sources will agree that the researcher will find convergence on a theme with sample sizes in excess of about 30, and that sample sizes of more than about 300 are unnecessary. We will see later in this chapter that quite useful comparisons can be made with subsamples of less than 30 subjects.

8.6.2 Fieldwork and Editing

Fieldwork is the dirty part of survey research. This is where the researchers and research assistants come into direct contact with their subjects and are confronted with the difficulties of asking questions and persuading people to respond to their survey questionnaires. This is where we learn that if there is any possible way that a question can be misinterpreted, then it will be; and any small variation in the way a question is asked can cause differences in response. Researchers in the field then need to ensure that they consistently ask questions in exactly the same way.

The researcher prefers to deal with questionnaires so that there is a minimum of additional work required by the researcher, and that all questions are answered, and answered correctly. Online questionnaires are ideal for this. If, however, a questionnaire is completed face to face, with the interviewer asking the questions and filling in responses, then it is important to ensure that all questions are answered, that the interpretations are the same and that respondents are consistent in their replies. A set of rules reinterpreting classifying and recording the data, a codebook, is necessary to any field interviewing process. This ensures that all other researchers have an agreed-upon system by which responses can be recorded.

8.7 DATA ANALYSIS

This section demonstrates basic analytical techniques to serve most survey analyses. Our purpose is to demonstrate the basic steps in a statistical analysis, highlighting that the type of data determines the type of analysis.

In this study, we have six variables drawn from a survey of city administrators in the USA: resource acquisition; assist coordination and implementation; information and awareness; perceived prevalence of social entrepreneurship; region; and form of government. These data are artificially created for the purposes of this demonstration, but the variables are suggested by Korosec and Berman (2008).

The first four variables refer to the policies and behaviours of municipal government. They are Likert-scale variables, created by averaging several 1–7 rating scale questions – for example, assist coordination and implementation is the average of the following 1–7 Agree–Disagree items:

Encouraging community organizations to work together
Conducting periodic meetings with city officials
Helping them deal with various government agencies
Providing them with counsel when they ask for it
Coordinating their efforts with others
Helping them with permit applications
Creating community coalitions to address common problems
Providing a structure for local coordination

Generally, we treat such variables as interval-scale variables.

The two variables region and form of government refer to the city's location in the USA, and whether the city is managed by an elected mayor or by an appointed municipal manager. These are categories, or nominal-scaled variables.

Data here are analysed using Minitab, but we would get the same results from SPSS, SAS, Systat or any other analysis package.

8.7.1 Univariate and Descriptive Analysis

Most data are presented as simple univariate tables and graphs – one variable at a time. Categories can only be presented as straightforward frequencies and percentages, which can be published either as tables or as graphs. Say we want to present summary information about the two categorical variables, form of government and region. Data can be presented in simple tabular form as below:

Table 8.7a Form of government

Government	Count	%
Manager	55	31
Mayor	125	69
N =	180	

Table 8.7b Region

Region	Count	%
Midwest	29	16
Northeast	74	41
South	32	18
West	45	25
N =	180	

Note that percentages have been rounded to the nearest full percentage figure. Most statistics packages will present summary results to two or more decimal places. This is rarely informative, and it suggests that your results are accurate to one in a thousand or better. Many statistical programmes include in the table, a column for cumulative percentage and valid percentage. These are only useful if we want to know the proportions of non-missing data, and where cumulative percentages are meaningful. If they are not needed then they should be removed from the table. Data can be presented in simple graphical form as in Figure 8.1.

Graphs are valuable tools for quickly showing differences amongst categories. Note that in the regions bar graph we have reordered the bars to show highest to lowest. The default was to present the categories either in alphabetical order or in order of occurrence in the original data. It is worth taking the trouble to order from largest to smallest for ease of reading. The pie chart in Figure 8.2 is less easy to read.

Pie charts are popular because they are visually attractive and often colourful. Unfortunately, they are usually not informative. Think about how you are processing and digesting the information contained. From which region did we get the more responses: the West or the South? You had to look at the labels, find the correct items, and then look at the numbers. Effectively you had to use the pie chart as a table. If you want to inform your readers rather than distract them with colours or occupy space, then avoid pie charts and use either tables or bar graphs for categorical data.

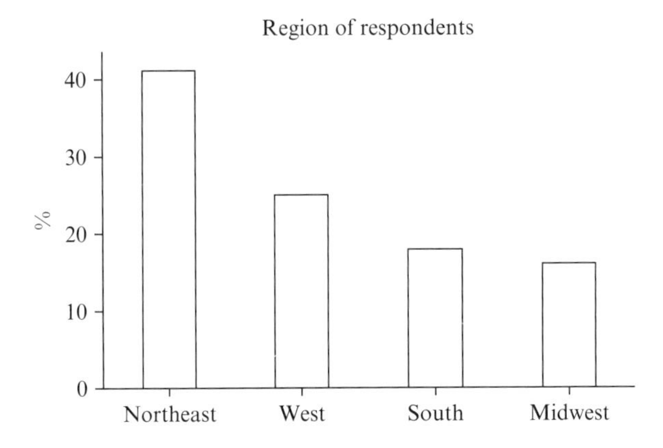

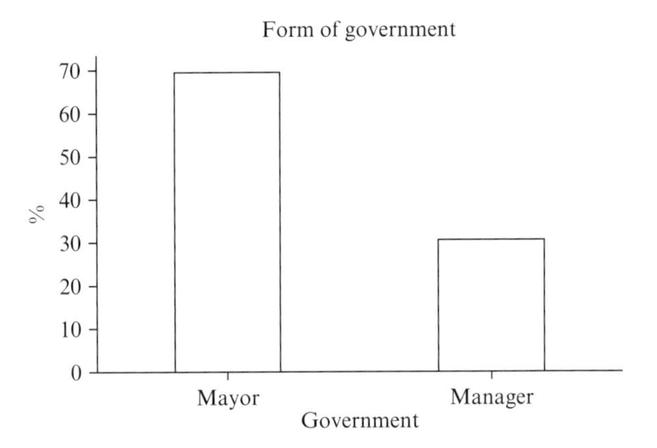

Figure 8.1 Examples of simple graphical presentations

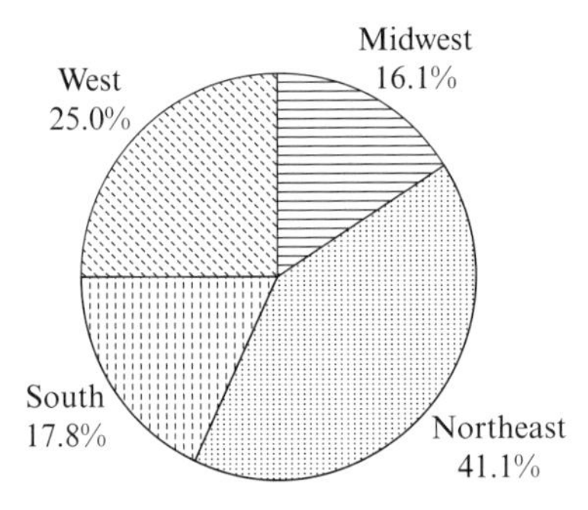

Figure 8.2 Region

Table 8.8 Descriptive statistics for sample interval-scale variables

Variable	Mean	StDev	Min	Q1	Median	Q3	Max
Resource Acquisition	3.22	0.75	1.1	2.8	3.3	3.7	5.4
Coordination and Implementation	4.02	0.85	1.4	3.5	4.0	4.6	6.1
Information and Awareness	5.07	0.86	2.7	4.5	5.1	5.7	6.8
Prevalence of Social Entrepreneurship	3.91	0.79	1.8	3.4	3.9	4.5	6.2

8.7.2 Interval-Scaled Data

The advantage of interval-scaled data is that we can legitimately calculate arithmetic means, standard deviations and other parametric statistics. Data can be summarised quickly with established measures; data also can be transformed into other scales, such as ordinal groups (high, medium and low) or categories.

As with nominal-scaled data, both tabular and graphical presentations of summary information are appropriate. Tables permit the presentation of large amounts of detailed information in a very small space (see Table 8.8).

Such information sometimes just merges into a 'sea of grey' for some readers, so it is often useful to show graphically the relative distributions of our data. There are a number of graphical presentations that assist with the presentation of data, for example histograms and boxplots (Figures 8.3 and 8.4).

Histograms show a great deal of information, but can be confusing when you want to get the overall picture. Boxplots, on the other hand, present graphically the mean, the interquartile range and the 90 per cent ranges for all variables. We can see very clearly and quickly which variable has the highest overall scores and which the lowest.

8.7.3 Bivariate Analysis of Difference

Univariate analysis of interval data usually is an examination of the averages and distributions of each variable. Often we want to know if the averages are different between groups. For example, are women better credit risks than men? This problem is usually expressed with the question: is the average for this group different from the average for this other group? If we are considering two groups then the technique is a two-sample t-test. If

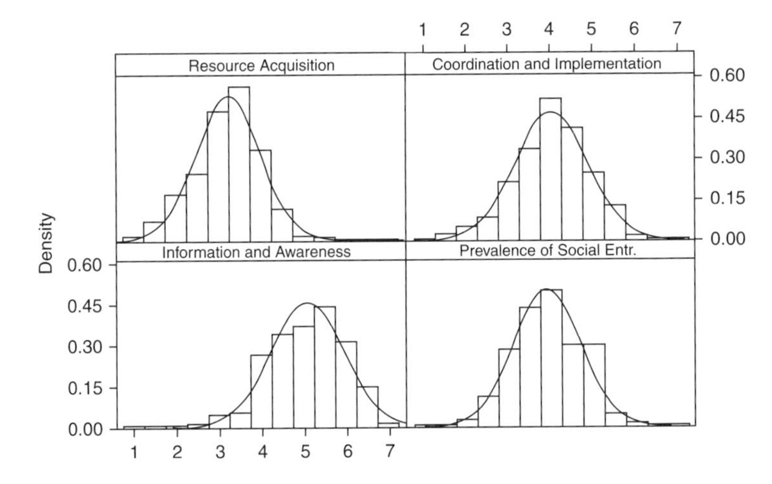

Figure 8.3 Histograms of policy and behaviour scales

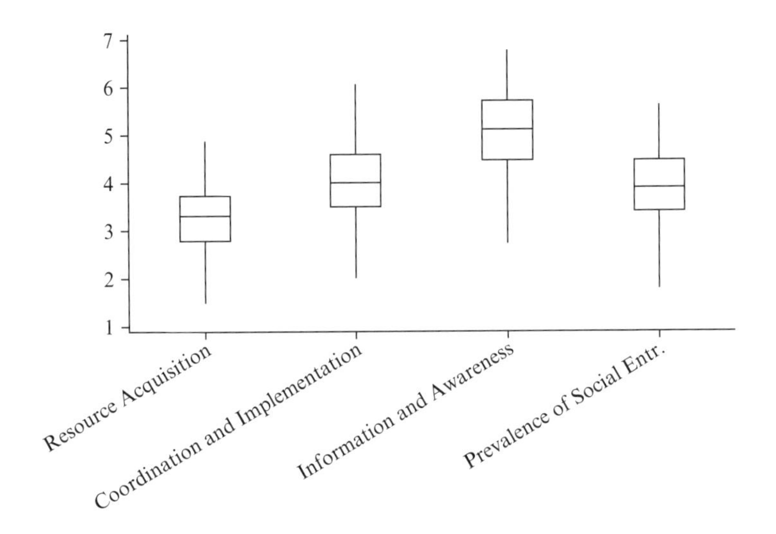

Figure 8.4 Boxplot of policy and behaviour scales

we are considering three or more groups then we use analysis of variance (ANOVA).

t-Test

A t-test is a test of whether an estimate differs from zero. In an 'independent samples' t-test, we ask if the difference between two means is different

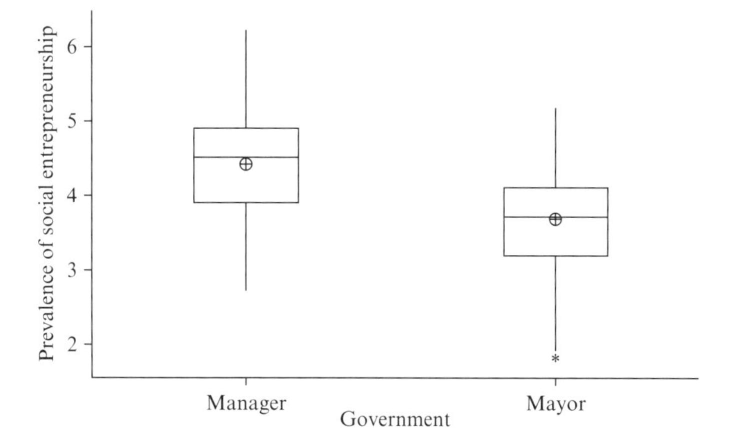

Figure 8.5 *Boxplot of prevalence of social entrepreneurship*

from zero. Let us say we are interested in learning whether the average prevalence of social entrepreneurship differs between two differently governed cities. A first step always should be to look at the data, as in the Figure 8.5 boxplot which shows the distributions of perceived prevalence of social entrepreneurship for two government forms. We can see that the two means do appear to be different, with a manager-based city seeing more entrepreneurs than do mayor-based cities, on average. A t-test formalises this observation and permits us to make generalisations about the nature of the population based on this sample.

The two-sample t-test asks the question, is the difference between the two means different from zero? In this case, the answer is yes: we can say with more than 99 per cent confidence (the significance or p-value is less than 0.01) that the two means are indeed different. The 95 per cent confidence interval suggests that the true difference between the two means within the population, not just in our sample, is between 0.503 and 0.955 – zero does not fit in this range so we can be confident that the true difference is not zero (Table 8.9).

Analysis of variance (ANOVA)

If we have two groups to compare, then a t-test is straightforward. However, what if there are three or more groups to be compared? We could run a series of t-tests, but there are theoretical and practical limitations to such an exercise. Generally, we should first check to see if any of the means in the groups are different from any of the others, and then conduct our t-tests to check which means are different. This is an analysis of variance.

Table 8.9 Examples of confidence intervals

Government	N	Mean		StDev	SE Mean
Manager	55	4.416		0.698	0.094
Mayor	125	3.687		0.721	0.065
Difference in means		0.729			
95% confidence interval		0.503		0.955	
	t = 6.39		p = 0.000	df = 106	

First, a graphical inspection of the data distributions gives a strong hint that the averages amongst the four groups are indeed different (Figure 8.6).

Analysis of variance is a test to check whether any of the means is different from any of the other means. The test is a ratio of the amount of variation that is found within each group and the variation between the groups. In this case (Table 8.10) we can see from the F-statistic that there is more than 62 times as much variation averaged within the regions as there is averaged between the regions. So we can conclude that at least one region is different from at least one of the others. The basic F-test in ANOVA, however does not tell us which means are different from each other.

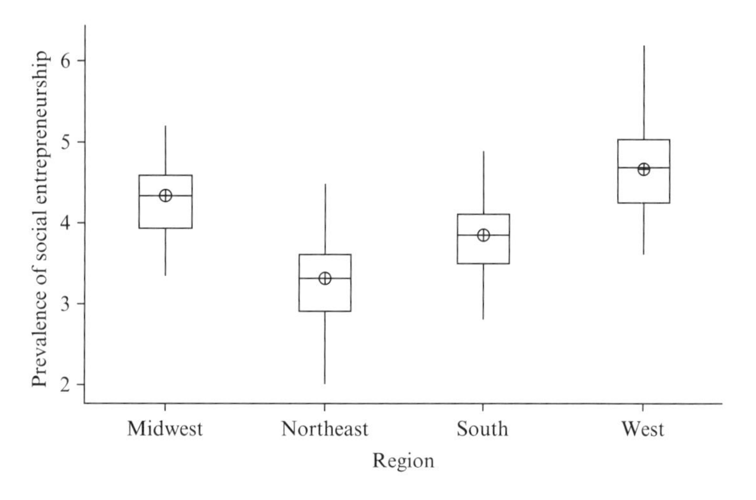

Figure 8.6 Boxplot of prevalence of social entrepreneurship

To learn which means are different from what other means, we run a series of post-hoc modified t-tests. These usually are an option within any ANOVA statistical routine. There are several different post-hoc tests that

Table 8.10 Basic F-test in ANOVA

Source	DF	SS	MS	F	P
Region	3	57.229	19.076	62.23	0.000
Error	176	53.953	0.307		
Total	179	111.182			

Table 8.11 Grouping information using Tukey method

Level	N	Mean	StDev	Grouping			
West	45	4.68	0.56	A			
Midwest	29	4.28	0.46		B		
South	32	3.89	0.53			C	
Northeast	74	3.31	0.59				D

Means that do not share a letter are significantly different

all give similar results. Your choice depends on the general practice within your discipline and your publication, and who is your statistics guru. In Table 8.11 we have used Tukey tests, which summarise results by nominating different groups for each set of data. In this example, each of the regions is different from each of the other regions in their levels of prevalence of social entrepreneurship.

8.7.4 Bivariate Analysis of Association

While t-tests and ANOVA address the question of differences in means between groups, often we are not interested in groups, but in the extent that some variables are related to each other.

Cross-tabulation and chi-square (are some categories related to other categories?)

Is there a relationship between the form of government in a city and the region where the city is located? In the univariate analyses, we created tables of frequencies for each of these two variables. We can combine these into a table of joint frequencies, or a cross-tabulation (Table 8.12).

While not strictly necessary, cross-tabulations usually are arranged in the direction of causality. Here it is more likely that the region would determine the form of government rather than the government affecting the region, so it makes sense to regard region as the independent variable

Table 8.12 Cross-tabulation: region by type of government

Government	Midwest	Northeast	South	West	All
Manager	11	14	9	21	55
	38%	19%	28%	47%	31%
Mayor	18	60	23	24	125
	62%	81%	72%	53%	69%
All	29	74	32	45	180
	100%	100%	100%	100%	100%

Pearson Chi-Square = 11.1, DF = 3, p-value = 0.01

and form of government as the dependent variable. A cross-tabulation is usually presented as simply as possible, with the raw frequency counts and column percentages. The column percentages thus give percentages in the direction of causality. We can see that overall about 70 per cent of principalities are managed by a mayor, compared with 30 per cent, managed by a professional manager. However, when we look at individual regions we see that cities in the West are less likely to have a mayor, and cities in the Northeast are more likely to have a mayor.

It would appear from these differences in percentages that there is a relationship between municipal region and form of government. The usual test of association in a cross-tabulation is the chi-square test (pronounced 'kai', as in sky). In this context, chi-square, like other tests, helps us infer whether an apparent relationship in our sample can be applied to the wider population. Here the chi-square is statistically significant at the 95 per cent confidence level, so we can infer that there is indeed a relationship between region and form of government.

Correlation (how much does this scale relate to another scale?)

Correlation using Pearson's r is used to check for association between two variables that are interval or ratio scaled (there are similar statistics for ordinal-scaled variables that are interpreted in the same way as Pearson's r). Let us say we want to check whether there is a relationship between the prevalence of social entrepreneurship and the extent to which a municipality provides coordination and implementation, and the relationship between prevalence of social entrepreneurship and the extent to which a municipality provides information and awareness. Again, a good first step is to visualise the data with a graph (Figure 8.7). Scatterplot is the appropriate tool in this case. Our scatterplot program includes an option for a line of best fit or regression line. To the extent that our observations are closely gathered around this line, we can say that there is a high correlation.

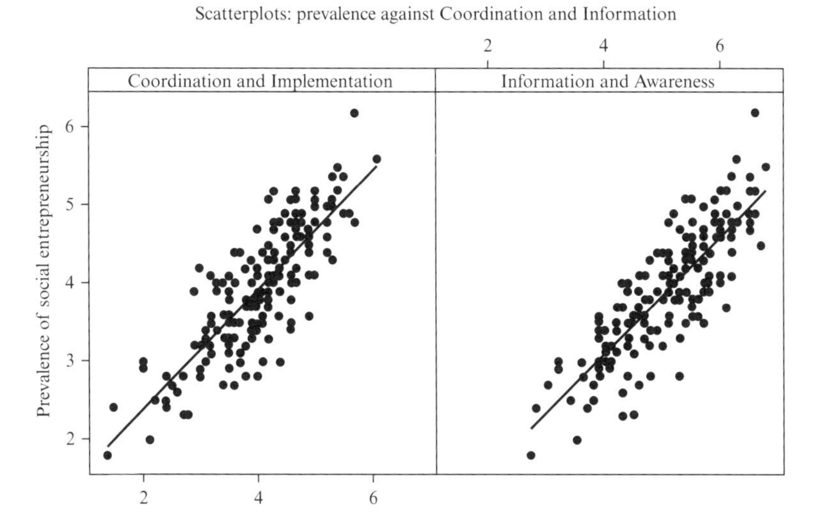

Figure 8.7 *Scatterplots: prevalence of social entrepreneurship against coordination and implementation, and information and awareness*

Table 8.13

	Resource	Coordination	Information
Resource acquisition			
Coordination and implementation	0.75		
Information and awareness	0.61	0.71	
Prevalence of social entrepreneurship	0.60	0.82	0.83
N = 180			
All correlations p < 0.01			

We formalise the apparent relationship by calculating Pearson's r and significance level for each correlation. In this case (Table 8.13), we can see that all four variables are moderately to highly correlated with one another. Moreover, in all cases, the correlations are statistically significant. That is, we can be confident that the true correlations in the population are not zero.

Most statistical analysis programmes present correlations and other tabular data to more than two decimal places. Note that here we have edited the data output so that just two decimal places are shown. In addition, significance levels for each correlation have been removed and the summary comment placed at the bottom of the table. This removes redundant information and makes the table easier to read.

8.8 CONCLUSIONS

As can be seen, the process of using survey designs in social science research is not a straightforward one. There is no such thing as a perfect survey research design, but some surveys are better than others to the extent that they minimise errors and biases. This chapter has outlined some important steps that can be taken by a researcher in design, implementing and analysing surveys. Of course, survey research is only one tool in the toolbox of methodologies that social entrepreneurship researchers can use. The reader is advised to consult further texts on survey design, and also to examine the various chapters outlining other methodologies in this *Handbook*.

NOTE

1. See Lavidge (1990, 1984). Lavidge says: 'Suppose a researcher asks purchasing intention questions for an inexpensive nondurable product using answer categories as follows: "Definitely will buy", "Probably will buy", "May or may not buy", "Probably will not buy" and "Definitely will not buy". Based on past experience the researchers may estimate that about 80 per cent of the "Definitely will buy" respondents plus 30 per cent of the "Probably will buy" category will actually buy the product if it becomes available on the market'.

REFERENCES

Andreasen, A.R. (1995). *Marketing Social Change: Changing Behavior to Promote Health, Social Development and the Environment*. San Francisco, CA: Jossey-Bass.

Arndt, Johan and Edgar Crane (1975). Response bias, yea-saying and the double negative. *Journal of Marketing Research*, **12**(May), 218–220.

Australian Bureau of Statistics (ABS) (2003). Measures of a knowledge based economy and society. Catalogue no. 1377.0.

Australian Bureau of Statistics (ABS) (2004). Measures of Australia's progress. Catalogue no. 1370.0.

Australian Market and Social Research Society (2000). 'Call for action on response rates', November, www.mrsa.com.au/index.cfm?a=detail&eid=33&id=152, accessed 20 December 2011.

Australian Market and Social Research Society (2003). 'Australia a "high cost" country in which to conduct research', *Research News*, April, www.mrsa.com.au/index.cfm?a=detail&eid=91&id=1209, accessed 20 December 2011.

Australian Market and Social Research Society (2004). Cash for comments. *Research News*, March, www.amsrs.com.au/index.cfm?a=detail&eid=98&id=1378, accessed 9 April 2006.

Barczak, G., K.B. Kahn and R. Moss (2006). An exploratory investigation of NPD practices in nonprofit organizations. *Journal of Product Innovation Management* **23**(6), 512–527.
Baumgartner, H. and J.E.M. Steenkamp (2001), Response styles in marketing research: a cross-national investigation, *Journal of Marketing Research* **38**(2), 143–56.
Cateora, Philip (1990). *International Marketing*, Homewood, IL: Richard D. Irwin.
CIA (Central Intelligence Agency) (n.d.). CIA *World Factbook*, https://www.cia.gov/library/publications/the-world-factbook/rankorder/2153rank.html, accessed 20 December 2011.
Cieslik, J. and K. Eugene (2009). The speed of internationalization of entrepreneurial start-ups in a transition environment. *Journal of Developmental Entrepreneurship* **14**(4), 375–392.
Douglas, Heather (2008). Creating knowledge: a review of research methods in three societal change processes. *Journal of Nonprofit and Public Sector Marketing* **20**(2), 141–163.
Eikenberry, Angela and Kluver Drapal (2004). The marketization of the nonprofit sector: civil society at risk? *Public Administration Review* **64**(2), 132–140.
Hughes, Jody and Wendy Stone (2002). Families, social capital and citizenship project: fieldwork report, May, Institute of Family Studies.
Jain, Subhash (1990). *International Marketing*, Boston, MA: PWS Kent, p. 338.
Kellior, Bruce, Deborah Owens and Charles Pettijohn (2001). A cross-cultural/cross national study of influencing factors and socially desirable response biases. *International Journal of Market Research* **43**(1), 63–84.
Korosec, Ronnie and Evan Berman (2008). Municipal support for social entrepreneurship. *Administration Review*, May–June, 449–462.
Lavidge, R. (1984). Seven tested ways to abuse and misuse strategic advertising research. *Marketing Research*, March, 43.
Lee, S., Richard Florida and Zoltan Acs (2004). Creativity and entrepreneurship: a regional analysis of new firm formation. *Regional Studies* **38**(8), 879–891.
Leroux, Kelly (2005). What social entrepreneurship? A look at budget trends of metro Detroit social service agencies. *American Review of Public Administration* **35**(4), 350–362.
Lewis, Michael (2000). The two-bucks-a-minute democracy. *New York Times Magazine*, 5 November, p. 65.
Lombardo, A.P. and Y.A. Leger (2007). Thinking about 'Think Again' in Canada: assessing a social marketing HIV/AIDS prevention campaign. *Journal of Health Communication* **12**(4), 377–397.
Mohan, L. and P. Devendra (2010). Catalytic innovation in microfinance for inclusive growth: insights from SKS microfinance. *Journal of Asia-Pacific Business* **11**(3), 218–239.
Newspoll News (2006). Support for desalination down the drain. **15**(1), 1.
Payne, Stanley (1951). *The Art of Asking Questions*, Princeton, NJ: Princeton University Press.
Roberts, Gerrie (2005a). 'Stats: not eight, I said eight', *Research News*, Australian Market and Social Research Society, June, www.amsrs.com.au/index.cfm?a=detail&id=1803&eid=112, accessed 3 April 2006.
Roberts, Gerrie (2005b). 'You say, potato'. (How to deal with mid-point bias). *Research News*, Australian Market and Social Research Society, October, p. 24.
Rubin, Jon (2000). Online marketing research comes of age. *BrandWeek*, 30 October, p. 28.
Smith, D. (2005). Developing self-employment among African Americans: the impact of household social resources on African American entrepreneurship. *Economic Development Quarterly* **19**(4), 346–355.
Tuckel, Peter and Harry O'Neill (2001). The vanishing respondent in telephone surveys. A paper presented at the 56th annual conference of the American Association of Public Opinion Research (AAPOR), Montreal, 17–20 May.
Zikmund, W.G., S. Ward, B. Lowe, H. Winzar and B. Babin (2010). *Marketing Research*, 2nd Asia Pacific edn. Cengage Australia.

9 Drawing and verifying conclusions

Richard G. Seymour

This short chapter introduces the logic of drawing and verifying conclusions. Drawing and verifying conclusions is the most significant yet misunderstood component of research, and it is for this reason that I have included a separate chapter in the *Handbook*.

9.1 LOGICAL PROCESSES OF DRAWING CONCLUSIONS

Inferences can be classified as deductive/analytic or synthetic (which in turn can be classified as induction or hypothesis) (Peirce, 1878/1992). There are a number of logical processes utilised by researchers to draw and verify these inferences: deduction, induction and hypothesis.[1] The three logical approaches to cases, rules and results (based on Eco and Sebeok, 1988; Fann, 1970; Holbrook and Hirschman, 1993; Peirce, 1878/1992, 1903/1992; Truzzi, 1988) are summarised in Table 9.1.

Referring to Table 9.1, note that the fact that the social entrepreneur was

Table 9.1 Logical approaches to cases, results and rules

Deduction	Induction	Hypothesis
Rule – all successful social entrepreneurs are visionaries	Case – this social entrepreneur was visionary	Result/observed-fact – this social entrepreneur was visionary (surprise)
Case – this social entrepreneur was visionary	Result/observed-fact – this social entrepreneur was successful	(abductive process begins now) Rule (if) – social entrepreneurs were visionary, success would be a matter of course
Therefore result/ observed-fact – therefore this social entrepreneur was successful	Therefore rule – therefore all successful social entrepreneurs are visionary	Therefore case/abductive conclusion – there is reason to suspect that this social entrepreneur is successful

Table 9.2 Means of drawing general inference

	Deduction	Induction	Abduction
Alternative description	Retroduction	Presumption	Originary argument
Definition	The inference of particular instances by reference to a general law or principle	The inference of a general law from particular instances	The first stage of any inquiry involving the creative generation of hypotheses
Purpose	To collect the consequents of an hypothesis (from the general to the particular)	To test an hypothesis (from the particular to the general)	To develop an hypothesis
Means of drawing general conclusions	Statistical generalisation	Analytical generalisation	Abductive conclusion

visionary cannot be abductively conjectured until the premiss is present: 'If social entrepreneurs are visionary, success would be a matter of course.'

Comparing the purposes of these three logical processes: the 'purpose' of deduction is to collect the consequents of a hypothesis (from the general to the particular); the purpose of induction is to test a hypothesis (from a number of particular cases to the general); whereas the purpose of abduction is to form hypotheses (Fann, 1970; Magnani, 2001; Peirce, c1870/1950):

> Hypothesis/Abduction is where we find some very curious circumstance which would be explained by the supposition that it was a case of a certain general rule, and thereupon adopt that supposition. Or, where we find that in certain respects two objects have a strong resemblance, and infer that they resemble one another strongly in other respects. (Peirce, 1878/1992, p. 189)

The 'means' of drawing general inferences are set out in Table 9.2, these being: statistical, theoretical and abduction. The issues associated with the verification of the resulting conclusions are now presented.

9.1.1 Statistical Generalisation

Statistical generalisation (also referred to as empirical inference and statistical inference) has been the primary rationale for many researchers to extrapolate from a sample to a parent universe. Statistical generalisation:

> involves drawing inferences about features of a larger but finite population of cases from the study of a sample drawn from that population. At its simplest, this amounts to reaching conclusions about the distribution of particular features within a population. (Gomm et al., 2000, p. 103)

Statistical inference makes a statement about the confidence we may have 'that the surface relationships observed in our sample will in fact occur in the parent population' (Mitchell, 2000, p. 183).

Questions are frequently raised about the generalisability and validity of locally constrained works (Maxwell, 2002; Shadish, 1995), with a trade-off being external validity and the strengths of the ethnography. Attempts have been made to apply the logic of sample surveys to case study research, known as case cluster method, to address these weaknesses in an organisational studies context (McClintock et al., 1979). Note, however, that Cronbach (amongst others) criticises the focus in the human sciences on statistical induction: 'The time has come to exorcise the null hypothesis . . . The canon of parsimony, misinterpreted, has led us into the habit of accepting Type II errors at every turn, for the sake of holding Type I errors in check' (Cronbach, 1975, p. 124).

For more information about the processes associated with these generalizations, see Chapter 8 in this *Handbook*.

9.1.2 Analytical Generalisation

Analytic generalisation (also referred to as logical or theoretical inference): 'involves reaching conclusions about what always happens, or what happens with a given degree of probability, in a certain type of theoretically defined situation' (Gomm et al., 2000, p. 103).

Analytical generalisation makes a statement about the confidence we may have that the theoretically necessary or logical connection among features observed in the research pertain also to the parent population (Mitchell, 2000). Analytical generalisations do not rely on the logic of representative sampling. Robinson (2000) examines the concept in three parts: as a research procedure, as a method of causal analysis, and as a method of proof, as summarised in Table 9.3.

9.1.3 Abductive Conclusion

Essentially, abduction is the process of forming or inventing an explanatory hypothesis to account for the facts (Fann, 1970). In the logic of abduction, the case is the equivalent of 'abductive conclusion' (Harrowitz, 1988): 'The surprising fact C, is observed; But if A were true, C would be

Table 9.3 Types of analytic induction

Type of analytic induction	Description
Analytic induction as a research procedure	'In terms of procedure, then, the method of analytic induction begins with an explanatory hypothesis and a provisional definition of something to be explained. The hypothesis is then compared with facts, and modifications are made in two ways: (1) the hypothesis itself is modified so that the new facts will fall under it, and/or (2) the phenomenon to be explained is redefined to exclude the cases which defy explanation by the hypothesis' (Robinson, 2000, p. 188)
Analytic induction as a method of causal analysis	Analytic induction is similar to enumerative induction, it however gives only a necessary and not the sufficient conditions for a phenomenon to be explained. It therefore cannot be used for causal prediction.
Analytic induction as a method of proof	The method does not lead to conclusion that particular characters are 'essential' conditions for the phenomenon, apart from the fact that they are necessary and sufficient as operationally defined. Once we have located the 'essential' characters for a phenomenon we may not be sure that those characters will appear in any future instance of the phenomenon.

Source: Robinson (2000).

a matter of course, Hence, there is reason to suspect that A is true' (Peirce, c1870/1950, p. 151).

It is essential to note in Table 9.1, the chronology of information-obtaining (Harrowitz, 1988): one observes a fact and, in order to explain and understand this, the process of abduction takes place between the result and the rule and concludes with the positing of a hopefully satisfactory hypothesis: 'Abduction is the step between a fact and its origin; the instinctive, perceptual jump which allows the subject to guess an origin which can then be tested out to prove or disprove the hypothesis' (Harrowitz, 1988, p. 182).

The logic of abduction is most commonly applied in criminal investigations (Eco and Sebeok, 1988). Abductions are 'ampliative' and are not logically self-contained. Peirce notes that though abduction's security is low, its uberty (value in productiveness) is high: if we are to have any knowledge at all we must make abductive inferences (Misak, 1988).

Abductive logic moves beyond the traditional (statistical and analytic) conception of generalizability. It is particularly relevant for case study research, as it requires focus on only particular case(s), with the researcher developing hypotheses or testing theory by illuminating and concluding from the particular. For more information on the case study, see Chapter 5 of this *Handbook*.

9.2 VERIFYING CONCLUSIONS

Chapter 8 sets out a detailed summary of issues associated with drawing conclusions from survey and large data sets (including issues typically associated with deductive research). This chapter presents additional insights of interest to scholars undertaking 'non-deductive' research. Such a process is primarily an inductive process; however it also requires the far less commonly understood and more controversial 'abductive reasoning' (Magnani, 2001). It is important to note that 'generalizing the results of case studies is not a simple function of the number or diversity of cases studied' (George and Bennett, 2004, p. 123). Strong theoretical foundations will ensure that analytical (or theoretical) generalisations can be made with care.

There are only general and imprecise strategies with which to judge the quality of interpretive research (McCracken, 1988), and validity is not able to be dismissed or readily configured by interpretive researchers (Lincoln and Guba, 2003). To complement the 'traditional' perspectives of validity (which focus on rigour in the application of methods), interpretive researchers have looked to research traditions of the humanities, which focus on rigour in interpretation:

> The language of this critical tradition is strange to positivist ears. This language asks how 'illuminating', 'encompassing', and 'elegant' an argument is. When the data are especially complex, contradictory, or unclear, the terms 'supple', 'adroit', and 'cunning' are also used. (McCracken, 1988, p. 50)

The two rigours are now presented.

9.2.1 Rigour in the Application of Method

Validity as rigour in the application of method is traditionally considered in terms of construct validity, internal validity, external validity (generalisability) and reliability. Such (positivist) conceptualisations have been applied (most notably by Yin, 1981, 2003a, 2003b) to case study research with impressive results.

Reflecting their alternative philosophies of science, interpretivist researchers have considered a number of 'unconventional' approaches to validity. For the interpretivist researcher, verifying conclusions involves the consideration of: (1) authenticity, seeking to ensure fairness for stakeholders, the critical intelligence and capacity to engage in moral critique, and 'actionable' outcomes and opportunities for research participants (Lincoln and Guba, 2003); (2) the crystal metaphor, proposing the crystal's growth and change, reflection of externalities and self-refraction as an appropriate metaphor as 'what we see depends upon our angle of repose. Not triangulation, crystallization' (Richardson, 2003, pp. 517–518); (3) an ethical relationship between the researcher and research participants (Lincoln and Guba, 2003); and (4) understanding (Lincoln and Guba, 2003).

These interpretivist conceptualisations have been applied most notably by Maxwell (2002) in the application of case study research. Qualitative researchers will often seek to follow Maxwell's (2002) directions, ensuring theoretical, descriptive, interpretive and evaluative validity, as well as recognising the limits of external generalisability. Conceptualisations of rigour in the application of method by Yin (1981, 2003a, 2003b) and Maxwell (2002) are roughly aligned, though are qualitatively different, as clarified in Table 9.4.

Examples of the associated procedures to ensure rigour in the application of (interpretive) method include the following:

- Theoretical validity can be addressed through the utilisation of both organizing frameworks (for example the systems view of creativity) and theoretical lenses (for example social exchange theory), ensuring that the concepts themselves and relationships amongst those concepts are valid.
- Descriptive validity can be addressed through the use of interview recordings and transcription, multiple interviews with all involved in the innovation process, use of the 'coding frame' to standardise terminology developed throughout the research project; the use of multiple researchers to code the transcripts, and the avoidance of quasi-statistics.
- Interpretive validity can be addressed with consistent research methodology, which ensures a clear framework for analysis of objects/equipment, work and social projects undertaken by participants.
- Particularly with respect to case study research projects: external validity (generalisability) can be addressed with appropriate data selected for their potential to yield theoretical insights, the use of multiple informants, multiple sources of data, and care to avoid specific calls for widespread generalisability to other contexts.
- Evaluative validity (reliability) can be addressed by avoidance throughout the research project of subjective 'value statements', except where subjective perceptions are required. For example, the subjective consideration of considerations of value and exchanges is considered to be validly included in this analysis, whereas the objective analysis of episodes of innovation is prioritised over the subjective perceptions of participants. The use of a coding frame and glossary are integral to this effort.

Table 9.4 Validity: rigour in application of method (the procedural view)

Type of validity	Traditional conceptualisation	Interpretive
Construct validity • the extent to which the constructs of theoretical interest are successfully operationalised in the research (Hoyle et al., 2002) • most problematic of the tests in case study research	Construct validity can be maximised by: using multiple sources of evidence in a manner that will encourage convergent lines of enquiry; establishing a chain of evidence; and having the draft case study reports reviewed by key informants (Yin, 2003b)	Theoretical validity – concern with an account's validity as a theory of some phenomenon – noting that any theory has two components: the concepts or categories that the theory employs, and the relationships that are thought to exist among these concepts (Maxwell, 2002)
Internal validity • the extent to which the research design permits us to reach causal conclusions about the effect of the independent variable on the dependent variable (Hoyle et al., 2002) • a key concern if the study proposed is a causal (or explanatory) case study, in which the research is attempting to determine whether event *x* led to event *y* (and potentially missing the impact of some third factor *z*), or if inferences must be made from interview or documentary evidence	To help ensure internal validity, a researcher should: conduct pattern-matching and explanation-building; address rival explanations; and use logic models (Yin, 2003b)	Descriptive validity – concern with the factual accuracy of a researcher's account – can be primary (what the researcher reports having seen or heard, etc.) or secondary (the accounts that were inferred from other data). Important considerations are: • terms of descriptions (meaning, interpretive and evaluative validity); • omission as well as commission; and • use of quasi-statistics (simple counts of things to support claims that are implicitly quantitative) (Maxwell, 2002) Interpretive validity – concern with what the physical objects, events and behaviours mean to the people engaged in and with them, including language and terms used (Maxwell, 2002)

External validity (generalisability) • the process of reducing to general laws, or inferring by induction. The extent to which a study's findings are generalisable beyond the immediate case studies (Hoyle et al., 2002) • This can be a major barrier for case studies.	Researchers advised to use replication logic (i.e. multiple cases) in the research design stage to improve reliability (Yin, 2003b)	Concern with the extent to which one can extend the account of a particular situation or population to other persons, times or settings. There are two issues (Maxwell, 2002): • internal generalisability within the community, group, or institution studied to settings that were not directly observed; • external generalisability to other communities, groups or institutions.
Reliability • The reliability of a study is defined as the extent to which it is free from random error (Hoyle et al., 2002). If a later investigator followed the same procedures and same case studies, they would arrive at the same findings and conclusions.	Documentation is important, and case study protocols should be applied (Yin, 2003b)	Evaluative validity – concern with the critical validity of 'value statements' or opinions. No account is immune to such questions (Maxwell, 2002)

Table 9.5 Symptoms of truth

Condition	Demands
It must be exact so that no unnecessary ambiguity exists	Reader must not be left in any doubt as to what is intended
It must be economical so that it forces us to make the minimum number of assumptions and still explain the data	Elegance becomes a consideration
It must be mutually consistent so that no assertion contradicts another	The investigator must be aware of any new ideas and insights that could change the structure of the explanation
It must be externally consistent so that it conforms to what we independently know about the subject matter	Does this conform to what I otherwise think about cultural and social phenomena?
It must be unified so that assertions are organised in a manner that subsumes the specific within the general, unifying where possible, discriminating when necessary	Intellectual architecture must be good – with strong foundations, with clear, balanced, harmonious structure
It must be powerful so that it explains as much of the data as possible without sacrificing accuracy	Is there any way of explaining these data that is more comprehensive but not more complicated?
It must be fertile so that it suggests new ideas, opportunities for insight	Does this explanation help me to see the world more clearly? Does it give me a lens with which to examine the world?

Source: based on McCracken (1988, pp. 50–52).

See Chapter 8 for detailed information with regard to the appropriate processes for deductive research.

9.2.2 Rigour in Interpretation

The second consideration for interpretive researchers is rigour in interpretation (again, see Chapter 8 for a detailed analysis of methods appropriate for deductive research). McCracken (1988) maintains, based on the work of Bunge (1961), that an explanation of qualitative data must exhibit a number of conditions, or 'symptoms of truth', as detailed in Table 9.5.

Of course, the reader of any research will ultimately determine whether these symptoms of truth are in existence in any research project. Researchers should consider whether research projects follow these conditions and demands: (1) the use of an analytical framework (for example, the system views of creativity proposed by Csikszentmihalyi, 1988), theoretical lens (for example, social exchange theory) and methodology (for example post-positivism, or critical theory) to ensure an alignment of research strategy and interpretation; (2) the presentation of data, independent of any theoretical analysis (that is, presented as historical events) to improve the external consistency of the data (George and Bennett, 2004); and (3) the development of parsimonious theory that is rich in insights and new ideas.

9.3 CONCLUSION

This short chapter introduces some of the most complex and confusing aspects of research, something that is typically treated as though a 'black box' or magic alchemy, and focusses specifically on the issues associated with verifying conclusions from inductive and inductive research. The chapter should be read in conjunction with the chapters in Parts III and IV, as both address the issues associated with 'insight'.

NOTE

1. Hypothesis, or abduction, is variously described as retroduction, presumption and originary argument (Harrowitz, 1988). Abductive reasoning is considered to be the first stage of all inquiries, a necessary part of perception and memory (Fann, 1970; Magnani, 2001; Peirce, c1870/1950).

REFERENCES

Bunge, M. (1961). The weight of simplicity in the construction and assaying of scientific theories. *Philosophy of Science* **28**(2), 120–149.

Cronbach, L.J. (1975). Beyond the two disciplines of scientific psychology. *American Psychologist* **30**(2), 116–127.

Csikszentmihalyi, M. (1988). Society, culture, and person: a systems view of creativity. In R.J. Sternberg (ed.), *The Nature of Creativity: Contemporary Psychological Perspectives*. Cambridge, Cambridge University Press, pp. 325–339.

Eco, U. and T.A. Sebeok (eds) (1988). *The Sign of Three: Dupin, Holmes, Peirce. Advances in Semiotics*. Bloomington and Indianapolis, IN: Indiana University Press.

Fann, K.T. (1970). *Peirce's Theory of Abduction*. The Hague, The Netherlands: Martinus Nijhoff.

George, A.L. and A. Bennett (2004). *Case Studies and Theory Development in the Social Sciences*. Cambridge, MA, USA and London, UK: MIT Press.
Gomm, R., M. Hammersley and P. Foster (2000). Case study and generalization. In R. Gomm, M. Hammersley and P. Foster (eds), *Case Study Method*. London: Sage Publications, pp. 98–116.
Harrowitz, N. (1988). The body of the detective model: Charles S. Peirce and Edgar Allen Poe. In U. Eco and T.A. Sebeok (eds), *The Sign of Three: Dupin, Holmes, Peirce*. Bloomington and Indianapolis, IN: Indiana University Press, pp. 179–197.
Holbrook, M.B. and E.C. Hirschman (1993). *The Semiotics of Consumption: Interpreting Symbolic Consumer Behavior in Popular Culture and Works of Art*. Berlin: Mouton de Gruyter.
Hoyle, R.H., M.J. Harris and C.M. Judd (2002). *Research Methods in Social Relations*. Singapore: Wadsworth, Thomson Learning.
Lincoln, Y.S. and E.G. Guba (2003). Paradigmatic controversies, contradictions, and emerging confluences. In N.K. Denzin and Y.S. Lincoln (eds), *The Landscape of Qualitative Research: Theories and Issues*. Thousand Oaks, CA: Sage Publications, pp. 253–291.
Magnani, L. (2001). *Abduction, Reason, and Science: Processes of Discovery and Explanation*. New York: Kluwer Academic/Plenum Publishers.
Maxwell, J.A. (2002). Understanding and validity in qualitative research. In M. Huberman and M.B. Miles (eds), *The Qualitative Researcher's Companion*. Thousand Oaks, CA: Sage Publications, pp. 37–64.
McClintock, C.C., D. Brannon and S. Maynard-Moody (1979). Applying the logic of sample surveys to qualitative case studies: the case cluster method. *Administrative Science Quarterly* **24**(4), 612–629.
McCracken, G. (1988). *The Long Interview: Qualitative Research Methods*. Newbury Park, CA: Sage Publications.
Misak, C. (1988). Charles Sanders Peirce (1839–1914). In C. Misak (ed.), *The Cambridge Companion to Peirce*. Cambridge: Cambridge University Press, pp. 1–26.
Mitchell, J.C. (2000). Case and situation analysis. In R. Gomm, M. Hammersley and P. Foster (eds), *Case Study Method*. London: Sage Publications, pp. 165–186.
Peirce, C.S. (c1870/1950). Abduction and induction. In J. Buchler (ed.), *Philosophical Writings of Peirce*. New York: Dover Publications, pp. 150–156.
Peirce, C.S. (1878/1992). Deduction, induction, and hypothesis. In N. Houser and C. Kloesel (eds), *The Essential Peirce: Selected Philosophical Writings Volume I (1967–1893)*. Bloomington and Indianapolis, IN: Indiana University Press, pp. 186–199.
Peirce, C.S. (1903/1992). Pragmatism as the logic of abduction. In N. Houser and A.C. Lewis (eds), *The Essential Peirce: Philosophical Writings Volume II (1893–1913)*. Bloomington and Indianapolis, IN: Indiana University Press, pp. 226–241.
Richardson, L. (2003). Writing: a method of inquiry. In N.K. Denzin and Y.S. Lincoln (eds), *Collecting and Interpreting Qualitative Materials*, Vol. 2. Thousand Oaks, CA: Sage Publications, pp. 499–541.
Robinson, W.S. (2000). The logical structure of analytic induction. In R. Gomm, M. Hammersley and P. Foster (eds), *Case Study Method*. London: Sage Publications, pp. 187–195.
Shadish, W.R. (1995). The logic of generalization: five principles common to experiments and ethnographies. *American Journal of Community Psychology* **23**(3), 419–426.
Truzzi, M. (1988). Sherlock Holmes: applied social psychologist. In U. Eco and T.A. Sebeok (eds), *The Sign of Three: Dupin, Holmes, Peirce*. Bloomington and Indianapolis, IN: Indiana University Press, pp. 55–80.
Yin, R.K. (1981). The case study crisis: some answers. *Administrative Science Quarterly* **26**(1), 58–65.
Yin, R.K. (2003a). *Applications of Case Study Research*. Thousand Oaks, CA: Sage Publications.
Yin, R.K. (2003b). *Case Study Research: Design and Methods*. Thousand Oaks, CA: Sage Publications.

PART IV

VOICE

Having focussed on the first three parts of this *Handbook*, it is hoped that you will have the tools and insights necessary to develop valuable and insightful research projects. However, the challenge remains, no matter how good these projects may be, to find a voice for the research. Part IV of the *Handbook* sets out the challenges for a researcher in finding their voice within the academic community.

In the context of social entrepreneurship, some of these challenges are reviewed in Chapter 10. Aaron McKenny, Jeremy Short and Tyge Payne from Texas Tech University have written a useful and informative chapter that should, perhaps, have been the first chapter of this *Handbook*. It provides a detailed overview of the challenges facing researchers in the field. Indeed, as they note, if we are considered to be 40 years behind the work being conducted in the fields of strategic management and organisational behaviour, we indeed have much work to do. The chapter certainly provides an appropriate conclusion for the *Handbook*: it is a call for *your* action.

Note, this call for action and its framing within an academic 'system' that strives for research publication and promotion in top academic journals should remain just one of your projects. You should also be seeking to develop your research networks, infuse your teaching with research, develop your personal understandings, and positively impact communities and people through your outreach activities (quite a list of challenges).

Social entrepreneurship, perhaps more than any other field of business research, provides a platform for all of these challenges, but clearly calls for our care as well as our ability. The best of luck with your research endeavours, and I hope that this *Handbook* is a valuable resource for you.

10 The challenge for researchers

Aaron F. McKenny, Jeremy C. Short and G. Tyge Payne

Social entrepreneurship, with its focus on the creation of new value with an emphasis on solving social problems, has been of increasing academic interest in the last 20 years (Austin et al., 2006; Short et al., 2009b).

Unfortunately, the rigour and diversity of research methods used in social entrepreneurship research remain in an embryonic state compared to more established fields such as entrepreneurship and strategic management (Short et al., 2009).

Research in social entrepreneurship, to date, has been generally associated with a number of empirical challenges that parallel the growing pains in the development of the strategic management and entrepreneurship fields. A recent study of the social entrepreneurship literature indicates that only 8 percent of empirical articles used formal propositions or hypotheses and over 60 percent used a case-based approach (Short et al., 2009b). An early review of research methods in the entrepreneurship literature yielded similar findings, causing the research community to call for more emphasis on hypothesis testing and more sophisticated analyses (Low and MacMillan, 1988). Over 20 years later, the entrepreneurship literature has made marked improvements, but still lags behind that of the strategic management and organizational behavior peer fields in terms of methodological sophistication (Dean et al., 2007; Short et al., 2010b). If social entrepreneurship research progresses at a similar rate, these studies indicate that social entrepreneurship research is approximately 40 years behind strategic management and organizational behavior. Given the inherent difficulty of publishing in top-tier research outlets, closing this methodology gap rapidly may play a pivotal role in the legitimization of social entrepreneurship as a field of academic inquiry.

To facilitate the advancement of the social entrepreneurship literature, this chapter identifies and explicates a number of current challenges faced by social entrepreneurship scholars. While many of these challenges mirror those faced in the development of the entrepreneurship literature, others are idiosyncratic to the social entrepreneurship context. In identifying the most salient challenges, we pay closest attention to those important to researchers attempting to publish empirical work in the top-tier management and entrepreneurship journals.

This chapter makes three contributions to the social entrepreneurship research community. First, we review extant social entrepreneurship articles in the top-tier management and entrepreneurship journals to assess the current state of the literature and identify areas where further development is needed. Second, we identify key challenges that will likely be faced by social entrepreneurship researchers in the development and maturation of the literature. Finally, we identify several statistical techniques that can be used with the research methods from Part III of this volume to ask questions of interest to social entrepreneurship scholars. In short, this chapter looks at the challenges faced by social entrepreneurship scholars with the goal of helping to legitimize our literature by reducing the gap between the methods used in extant social entrepreneurship research and the methods common to the more established fields of entrepreneurship, strategic management and organizational behavior.

10.1 SOCIAL ENTREPRENEURSHIP IN TOP-TIER MANAGEMENT AND ENTREPRENEURSHIP JOURNALS

Social entrepreneurship research has drawn considerably from the management and entrepreneurship literatures. In the past 20 years, journals embracing these two literatures have published 38 percent of extant social entrepreneurship articles and make up 30 percent of studies citing social entrepreneurship articles (Short et al., 2009b). Further, by cross-referencing the 2008 ISI Web of Knowledge journal citation report data with Short et al.'s (2009b) review of the social entrepreneurship literature, we found that the top four journals publishing social entrepreneurship research, in terms of five-year impact factor, are all management journals (that is, *Academy of Management Journal*: 7.7, and *Academy of Management Review*: 8.2) and entrepreneurship (that is, *Journal of Business Venturing*: 3.9, and *Entrepreneurship: Theory and Practice*: 3.3) (Short et al., 2009b; Thomson Reuters, 2010). Given the demonstrated receptiveness of top-tier journals in these fields to publishing social entrepreneurship research, and the importance to a researcher's career prospects of publishing influential research (Pfeffer, 1993), understanding the gaps between the methodological expectations of these journals and the current methodology used in social entrepreneurship research is of practical significance to researchers in this field.

To explore gaps between current social entrepreneurship research methods and those common to top-tier journals in management and entrepreneurship, we compare findings from a recent comprehensive review of social entrepreneurship literature research methodology (that is, Short et al., 2009b) with the methodology used in extant social entrepreneurship studies in the top-tier journals. Specifically, we draw insights from studies examining the methodological progression of the entrepreneurship literature (for example Chandler and Lyon, 2001; Crook et al., 2010; Dean et al., 2007; Low and MacMillan, 1998; Short et al., 2010b). Our goal is to compare and contrast the research methods used in social entrepreneurship through May 2010 with methods commonly utilized in the greater entrepreneurship literature.

To identify social entrepreneurship articles in top-tier management and entrepreneurship journals, we used EBSCO to search for all articles through May 2010 containing 'social entrepreneur (-s, -ship)', 'social venture (-s, -ing)', and 'social enterprise (-s)'. An article was deemed to be relevant to social entrepreneurship if one of these phrases was contained in the article title, abstract or key words. To identify those studies published in top-tier management journals, we relied on Tahai and Meyer's (1999) list of the most influential management journals. This list included *Academy of Management Journal*, *Academy of Management Review*, *Administrative Science Quarterly*, *Journal of Management*, *Management Science*, *Organization Science* and *Strategic Management Journal*. To expand our search to include key entrepreneurship outlets we included *Journal of Business Venturing*, *Entrepreneurship: Theory and Practice*, and *Strategic Entrepreneurship Journal* (See Short et al., 2009). We also examined each journal's website to identify any in-press articles relating to social entrepreneurship. Our search yielded 11 social entrepreneurship articles that incorporate research methods either through case studies or other analytic techniques. Table 10.1 presents a brief review of these articles as well as an overview of the methods used in each paper.

10.2 EXAMINING METHODS IN SOCIAL ENTREPRENEURSHIP RESEARCH

We identified three key areas where the current methodological practices of the social entrepreneurship literature mirrored issues criticized in the general entrepreneurship literature: testing of a priori hypotheses, level of sophistication of analytical techniques, and small sample sizes. Each article was coded to highlight these aspects and compared to practices in the broader social entrepreneurship literature (that is, Short et al., 2009b) and with early entrepreneurship studies (that is, Chandler and Lyon, 2001; Low and MacMillan, 1988).

Table 10.1 Empirical social entrepreneurship articles in top-tier management and entrepreneurship journals

Article title	Author, year, journal	Study type	Data collection technique	Sample	Analytical technique
How opportunities develop in social entrepreneurship	Corner and Ho (2010), ET&P	Qualitative	Case study: Interviews Archival documents	1 company	N/A
Social bricolage: theorizing social value creation in social enterprises	Di Domenico et al. (2010), ET&P	Qualitative	Case study: Interviews Site visits Observations Documents	16 informants from 8 companies	N/A
Community-led social venture creation	Haugh (2007), ET&P	Qualitative	Case study: Interviews Participant observation Secondary data Electronic data	5 informants	N/A
The interplay of form, structure, and embeddedness in social intrapreneurship	Kistruck and Beamish (2010), ET&P	Qualitative	Case study: Documents Direct observation Interviews	10 companies	N/A
Institutional entrepreneurship in emerging fields: HIV/AIDS treatment advocacy in Canada	Maguire et al. (2004), AMJ	Qualitative	Case study: Interviews Observations Documents	29 individuals	N/A

Entrepreneurship in and around institutional voids: a case study from Bangladesh	Mair and Marti (2009), JBV	Qualitative	Case study: Interviews Observation Archival data	1 company	N/A
Social ventures from a resource-based perspective: an exploratory study assessing global Ashoka fellows	Meyskens et al. (2010), ET&P	Qualitative and quantitative	Content analysis: Profiles	70 individuals	Correlation analysis
Assessing mission and resources for social change: an organizational identity perspective on social venture capitalists' decision criteria	Miller and Wesley (2010), ET&P	Quantitative	Survey	44 individuals	Policy capturing, multiple regression and hierarchical linear modeling
Dual identities in social ventures: an exploratory study	Moss et al. (2011), ET&P	Quantitative	Content analysis: Mission statements	118 companies	MANOVA
Entrepreneurial orientation and the performance of religious congregations as predicted by rational choice theory	Pearce et al. (2010), ET&P	Quantitative	Survey	252 congrega-tions	Regression
Toward a theory of social venture franchising	Tracey and Jarvis (2007), ET&P	Qualitative	Case study: Participant observation Interviews	1 company	N/A

10.2.1 Testing of a Priori Hypotheses

Hypotheses are statements asserting a relationship between two or more variables and are important for the advancement of scientific knowledge (Kerlinger and Lee, 2000). Early research in the entrepreneurship domain was characterized by exploratory case analyses and posteriori statistical analyses designed to describe phenomena rather than to test hypotheses (Low and MacMillan, 1988). While these descriptive studies are valuable and help to develop a field's theoretical base, as the field progresses it becomes equally important to test these theories empirically.

Social entrepreneurship research has also been slow to incorporate formal, theory-driven hypotheses into empirical efforts. Indeed, a recent census of the social entrepreneurship literature identified only two studies (3 percent of all empirical studies) with testable, operational hypotheses (Short et al., 2009b). Empirical papers relying on qualitative methodology more commonly pose inductively generated propositions. Only four social entrepreneurship studies (5 percent of all empirical studies) presented formal propositions (Short et al., 2009b).

By contrast, we find that among extant social entrepreneurship articles in top-tier journals, 18 percent formally state and test one or more hypotheses and 27 percent pose formal propositions. Of the three quantitative studies in our sample, two presented formal hypotheses. For example, Pearce et al. (2010) pose and test eight hypotheses looking at the relationship between the entrepreneurial orientation and performance of religious congregations in a sample of 252 Lutheran congregations. The one study that did not pose formal hypotheses did state a formal research question in the examination of how award-winning social ventures exhibit elements of normative and utilitarian identities (Moss et al., 2011).

To move the social entrepreneurship literature forward, we urge scholars conducting quantitative research formally to develop, state and test theory-driven hypotheses. Similarly, those conducting qualitative research should pose formal, testable propositions where reasonable. This forces researchers to communicate explicitly and concisely the proposed and tested relationships from their studies, and provides a foundation upon which future studies can build.

10.2.2 Sophistication and Diversity of Research Methods

While both qualitative and quantitative studies can be found throughout the development of a research domain, qualitative research tends to flourish in the early stages when domain-specific theory is sparse. A study looking at the entrepreneurship literature between 1989 and 1999 found that 18 percent of empirical studies used qualitative techniques, and that there had not been a significant change over that period (Chandler and Lyon, 2001). By contrast, 74 percent of empirical studies in the social entrepreneurship field use qualitative methods (Short et al., 2009). This lopsided distribution in favor of qualitative methods suggests that the social entrepreneurship literature is still in its infancy. We advocate an increased emphasis on quantitative studies to establish a better balance between inductive theory generation and deductive hypothesis testing.

As quantitative studies become more common, hypothesized relationships should become more complex to account for the complexity of the relationships that social entrepreneurship scholars study. Further, the methods used to study these relationships should follow suit – becoming more sophisticated to test hypotheses accurately (Low and MacMillan, 1988). Early entrepreneurship research was principally concerned with describing the entrepreneurship phenomenon, and accordingly over 50 percent of the hypotheses tested during this period relied on descriptive statistics to do so (Dean et al., 2007). However, as the field began testing more complex hypotheses, the methods used evolved as well. Now hierarchical, simple and multiple regression are the three most common methods for hypothesis testing in entrepreneurship (Dean et al., 2007).

The diversity of quantitative methods used in extant social entrepreneurship research is reminiscent of the early entrepreneurship literature. Of all empirical social entrepreneurship studies, 19 percent report descriptive statistics, 8 percent report correlations, 3 percent reported some form of regression analysis, 3 percent used structural equation modeling, and t-tests, ranking and cluster analysis were each used in 2 percent of extant studies (Short et al., 2009). However, in the top-tier journals a different story is told: each quantitative study reported descriptive statistics, correlations and between one and three more complex analyses.

Miller and Wesley (2010) use hierarchical linear modeling in their policy capture study investigating how social venture capitalists evaluate the probability of a social venture's future effectiveness. They also use analyses of variance (ANOVA) to assess the reliability of their measures. Pearce et al. (2010) use three statistical techniques beyond the baseline descriptive statistics and correlation matrix in their study of Lutheran congregations. First, they use exploratory factor analysis to test for common method bias using Harmon's (1967) one-factor test. Second, they use confirmatory factor analysis to assess the psychometric properties of their survey instrument. Finally, they use multiple regression analyses to test their hypotheses regarding the relationship between entrepreneurial orientation and congregation performance. Pearce et al. (2010) also provide a rare example of a complex hypothesis, attempting to tease out the potential moderating role of environmental munificence in the entrepreneurial orientation–performance relationship among Lutheran congregations.

As we advocate for a more balanced emphasis between quantitative and qualitative studies, within each approach we also encourage the development of more sophisticated propositions and theory-driven hypotheses in order to understand better the complexities of social ventures. For instance, the strategic management and entrepreneurship literatures both suggest that introducing contingency models into our research may provide useful insights about these complexities. Both fields have commonly used Dess and Beard's (1984) dimensions of organizational task environments – munificence, complexity and dynamism – as potential moderators (for example Ensley et al., 2006; Goll and Rasheed, 1997, 2004). The role of these and other potential mediators/moderators could similarly be incorporated into the social entrepreneurship setting to test complex contingencies.

To test these more complex hypotheses, more sophisticated research methods and analytical techniques will be needed. Rather than simply describing social entrepreneurship using descriptive statistics and correlation matrices, multivariate techniques such as hierarchical regression and hierarchical linear modelling enable researchers to look for complex relationships. For example, hierarchical linear modelling is particularly well suited to examine how industry-level characteristics influence organizational-level relationships (Short et al., 2006). Hierarchical linear modelling allows models to incorporate variables at different levels of analysis (for example organizational and industry) while maintaining the statistical independence of observations when multiple organizations are nested within the same industry (Hofmann, 1997; Short et al., 2006), and has been used in entrepreneurship research to perform cross-level analyses with nested data (for example Monsen et al., 2010; Short et al., 2009a).

10.2.3 Sample Size

The larger the sample size, the more statistical power you will have and the more representative your sample will be of the overall population (Cohen, 1992; Kerlinger and Lee, 2000). Unfortunately, sampling has been a perennial problem in the entrepreneurship literature (Busenitz et al., 2003; Short et al., 2010b), with a number of sampling challenges also present in the strategic management research examining firm performance (Short et al., 2002). Given survivorship issues among entrepreneurial ventures (Cassar, 2004), the low response rate of entrepreneurs to surveys (Dennis, 2003) and few archival data sources (Chandler and Lyon, 2001), sample sizes in entrepreneurship research have been low compared to other fields.

This has been shown to be true of the social entrepreneurship literature as well. A report on strategic management research reveals a median sample size of 215, whereas social entrepreneurship has a median of only five (Boyd et al., 2005; Short et al., 2009b). The social entrepreneurship articles in the top-tier journals tell a similar story, with a median sample size of eight. However, when looking only at the quantitative studies, the social entrepreneurship articles in top-tier journals fare better. Pearce et al. (2010) collected 252 usable surveys from religious congregations; Miller and Wesley (2010) collected 57 usable surveys from social venture capitalists; and Moss et al. (2011) used a sample of 104 venture mission statements in their analyses.

Fortunately, steps can be taken to increase sample sizes in the social entrepreneurship literature. First, increased public interest in social entrepreneurship has created new archival data sources for social entrepreneurship researchers. One particularly attractive database is the GuideStar-NCCS National Nonprofit Research Database (http://nccs-dataweb.urban.org). This database contains data and scanned IRS Form 990s for thousands of United States-based non-profit organizations over multiple years. The increased public interest may also increase mass media coverage and social venture-related organizations including Ashoka (see Meyskens et al., 2010), the Skoll Foundation (see Moss et al., 2011), the Social Venture Network, and the Alliance for Nonprofit Management. Research also indicates that social ventures may behave differently than commercial ventures in survey research, enabling researchers to take steps to cater their research design to the social venture context (see Berry et al., 2003; Hager et al., 2003). For instance, one study found that non-profit executives were more likely to respond to a survey if the survey was received via Federal Express rather than via standard mail, but that questionnaire complexity and monetary incentives did not influence their propensity to respond to the survey (Hager et al., 2003).

10.3 OTHER METHODOLOGICAL CHALLENGES

One of the defining characteristics of social entrepreneurship research is the focus on the organization's social impact (McDonald, 2007; Van de Ven et al., 2007). However, measuring 'performance' in terms of social impact in a way that is generalizable, enabling large-scale quantitative analysis, poses a unique problem: the social goals of different types of organizations vary. Further, if one includes for-profit organizations with a social agenda as examples of social entrepreneurship, the concept of 'performance' becomes yet more complex. These organizations are likely to have both financial and social goals, much as family businesses have financial/economic and family-related/non-economic goals (for example Tagiuri and Davis, 1992). Moss et al. (2011) examine mission statements to demonstrate how award-winning social ventures strive to accomplish both normative and utilitarian performance targets. Examining such organizational narratives provides one possible strategy for creating a large and comparable data set to assess differences in social ventures.

The entrepreneurship field has successfully moved from a predominance of cross-sectional data analyses to incorporating more longitudinal studies (Dean et al., 2007). In order to test for causality in a relationship between two variables, four conditions must be met: the cause must precede the effect; cause and effect must co-vary; the causal relationship between cause and effect must be theoretically supported; and alternative explanations must be exhausted (Hair et al., 2010). When researchers rely on cross-sectional data, it is impossible to test whether the cause preceded the effect, leading to ambiguity on the direction of causality. In the context of entrepreneurship and social entrepreneurship, collecting long-term longitudinal data can provide insights into strategic phenomena as firms and industries evolve (Low and MacMillan, 1988). None of the quantitative papers in our sample were coded as using longitudinal data, suggesting that this could represent a fruitful opportunity for future research in social entrepreneurship.

Finally, it is important to consider the reliability and validity of the measures used in our research (Chandler and Lyon, 2001; Crook et al., 2010). Reliability is defined as the extent to which multiple measurements using the same instrument will net the same or similar results (Kerlinger and Lee, 2000). Validity is defined as the extent to which the instrument measures what it is intended to measure (Kerlinger and Lee, 2000). Reliability and validity are important to entrepreneurship research, as with all research, because in the absence of either measurement, error is introduced – jeopardizing the results of statistical analyses (Kerlinger and Lee, 2000).

Meyskens et al. (2010) perform a content analysis of Ashoka Fellows's profiles to capture a broad range of information (funding sources, organizational structure, types of partners, innovativeness and knowledge transferability). A logical follow-up to this study would be to explore the individual dimensions more extensively in order to understand better how each influences social value creation. Such a study could leverage the process presented by Short et al. (2010a) by which computer-aided content analysis word lists for individual constructs can be systematically created and validated. These word lists can then be used with content analysis software to gather data rapidly and reliably from a large quantity of narratives (for example Ashoka Fellow profiles). One specific software package, DICTION, is particularly appealing as this content analysis package includes a measure of communitarian values relevant to social ventures (Moss et al., 2011; Short and Palmer, 2008).

10.4 IDEAS FOR FURTHER METHODOLOGICAL DEVELOPMENT

One of the most salient challenges in entrepreneurship research is the lack of rigorous methods (Short et al., 2010b). Part II of this book discussed several research methods that might help to investigate phenomena of interest to social entrepreneurship scholars. Here we present a number of broad categories of statistical techniques that can be used with these methods, as well as examples of research questions that could be addressed using the techniques (see Shook et al., 2003). Table 10.2 builds on the list of possible social entrepreneurship research questions developed by Short et al. (2009b) and proposes possible research methods and analytical techniques that could be used to test such questions of interest empirically.

10.4.1 Tests of Mean Differences

Among the simplest hypothesis testing techniques are t-tests. T-tests generally look for a difference in a single dependent variable between two samples (Hair et al., 2010). For instance, an independent-samples t-test could be used to look for differences in levels of risk taking between social and commercial ventures. However, t-tests can also look for a difference between one sample mean and a test value specified by the researcher. For instance, using a one-sample t-test one could identify whether the average growth rate of social ventures is significantly different than some prespecified benchmark (for example, 3 percent).

10.4.2 General Linear Models

General linear models (GLMs) are estimation procedures based on a variate – a probability distribution specified by the researcher and a function relating the two (Hair et al., 2010). GLM analyses are the most common statistical techniques for testing hypotheses in the broader entrepreneurship literature (Dean et al., 2007). There are two broad categories of GLM techniques: analyses of variance (ANOVA) and regression.

Table 10.2 Social entrepreneurship research opportunities

Potential research focus on social entrepreneurship	Possible research questions	Data collection technique	Analytical technique
Social value creation	Which entrepreneurial and strategic processes are most effective for creating social value across different social entrepreneurship activities?	Discourse analysis of press releases	Regression
	What characteristics of individuals and/or TMTs are most effective in creating social value?	Survey of social entrepreneurs or experiment	Partial Least Squares, SEM, and Regression
Opportunity creation and discovery	Does the unique experience of a social venture foster the creation of new opportunities?	Discourse analysis of business plans	Regression
	Do social entrepreneurs use opportunity discovery processes in the same ways as commercial entrepreneurs?	Survey of social and commercial entrepreneurs	ANOVA/MANOVA
Risk taking in social ventures	Do social ventures hold more conservative stances toward risk than commercial ventures?	Interviews	t-tests/ANOVA
	What factors play a role in enabling social entrepreneurs to take on greater risk?	Experimental designs	ANOVA/MANOVA
Innovation management in social ventures	Can social entrepreneurs create disruptive innovations in the commercial sector?	Case studies	N/A
	Do the same factors that promote concurrent incremental and revolutionary changes in commercial ventures apply in social ventures?	Discourse analysis of historical documents	Logistic regression

Effects of change processes on social ventures	In what ways do social innovation processes change the ventures creating the innovations?	Ethnography of known innovative social enterprises	N/A
	What factors contribute to growth in social ventures and are they similar to growth factors in commercial ventures?	Longitudinal analysis of archival data (e.g., GuideStar-NCCS database)	Hierarchical linear modeling
Role of technology in creating social value	In what ways do technologies provide competitive advantages in social ventures?	Action research	N/A
	What elements of effective technology utilization do social ventures have in common with commercial ventures?	Semi-structured interviews and surveys of IT officers of social ventures	Regression
Diffusion of social innovations	Do social ventures view diffusion differently than commercial ventures?	Semi-structured interviews of social and commercial entrepreneurs	ANOVA/MANOVA or t-tests
	What conditions most influence social ventures' efforts to erect barriers to diffusion?	Network analysis	Regression
Processes underlying social venture formation	Are the motivations/drivers of social venture creation the same as or different from those of traditional venture creation?	Survey of social entrepreneurs	Conjoint analysis
	Which dimensions or patterns of an entrepreneurial orientation are key to effective social venturing?	Discourse analysis of webpage content and press releases	Cluster analysis and ANOVA/ MANOVA

Source: Extends a table presented by Short et al. (2009b).

Similar to the t-test, the ANOVA category looks for differences in means of some dependent variable among a discrete set of groups. However, unlike the t-test, the ANOVA category of analyses can control for co-variates (ANCOVA), look at relationships with multiple dependent variables simultaneously (MANOVA), or both (MANCOVA). For instance, one might use ANCOVA in a study looking at whether social entrepreneurs use opportunity discovery processes differently than commercial entrepreneurs.

Regression is the second major category of GLM techniques. Regression is very similar to ANOVA, except that instead of looking for differences in the dependent variable among discrete groups, regression allows the independent variable to be continuously modeled such that the equation $y = a + \sum(bnxn)$ is satisfied, where y is the dependent variable and xn are either control or independent variables. A regression model might be useful in a study looking at identifying which entrepreneurial and strategic processes are most effective for creating social value across different social entrepreneurship activities.

10.4.3 Longitudinal Data Methods

Hierarchical linear modeling is a regression-based analytical tool that gets around the level of analysis issues encountered when incorporating variables from multiple levels of analysis within one statistical technique (Raudenbush and Bryk, 2002). For example, Miller and Wesley's (2010) social entrepreneurship article used hierarchical linear modeling to account for multiple observations nested within each individual. Using normal regression with such data would violate the independence of observations assumption, but hierarchical linear modeling ameliorates this issue. One social entrepreneurship study that would be particularly well suited for hierarchical linear modeling might be to investigate the firm- and industry-level determinants of social venture performance, thereby extending a key research stream germane to research in strategic management and entrepreneurship (see Short et al., 2009a; 2010). Hofmann (1997) provides a good starting point and theoretical primer to the hierarchical linear modeling technique.

10.4.4 Discrete Events Methods

Event studies are a common method to examine how a specific occurrence of importance (for example initial public offering – IPO, merger, leadership change) impacts the firm financially (Binder, 1998; McWilliams and Siegel, 1997). For example, in the entrepreneurship literature, Davila et al.

(2003) use an event study to look at the impact of venture capital financing on the growth of the business. If the researcher's definition of social entrepreneurship includes for-profit organizations with a social agenda, then an event study in the social entrepreneurship context could investigate how pursuing goals related to the social side of the organization influences the stock price of the organization.

10.4.5 Methods Explicitly Accounting for Firm Heterogeneity

A configurational approach to the study of organizations is commonly used in the strategy and entrepreneurship literatures (for example Wilklund and Shepherd, 2005; Payne, 2006; Payne et al., 2009). Among the many configurations-based studies, cluster analysis is a commonly used technique (Short et al., 2008). Cluster analysis allows the researcher to group objects based on their characteristics (Hair et al., 2010). After identifying these clusters, the researchers can then use GLM techniques (for example ANOVA, regression) to identify differences in non-clustered variables among the clusters (Payne, 2006; Short et al., 2008).

Zahra et al. (2008) identified five key attributes of social opportunities: prevalence, relevance, urgency, accessibility and radicalness. In this paper, Zahra et al. tied patterns of these five attributes to four different internationalization implications (social opportunity, commercial opportunity, internationalization at inception and international geographic scope of the venture). After collecting data on the attributes of a number of different opportunities, cluster analysis could be applied to assign each opportunity to the closest related internationalization implication based on its attributes. The researcher could then test empirically the implications of each pattern attributes. Ketchen and Shook (1996) provide a review and critique of the cluster analysis procedure and its methodological considerations from a strategic management perspective that serves as a useful introduction to the method.

10.4.6 Methods to Analyze Decision-Making

Conjoint analysis is a technique that requires study participants to evaluate different configurations of attributes of a certain object in order to understand the participants' cognitive decision-making structures (Louviere, 1988; Shepherd and Zacharakis, 1997). Conjoint analysis has been used in the management literature to look at top managers' strategic decision-making processes (Priem, 1992), and in the entrepreneurship literature to assess whether venture capitalists' assessment of a company predicts the company's survival (Shepherd, 1999). In the context of social entrepreneurship, conjoint analysis could be used to help understand the motivations and drivers of social venture creation and whether these differ from the motivations to start a commercial enterprise. See Shepherd and Zacharakis's (1997) introduction to conjoint analysis and how it might be applied to an entrepreneurship setting.

10.5 CONCLUSION

To begin to close the gap between the current state of social entrepreneurship research methodology and the expectations of top-tier journals, this chapter makes three contributions to the social entrepreneurship literature. First, we review empirical social entrepreneurship studies published in top-tier management and entrepreneurship journals and contrast them with the broader social entrepreneurship literature. Second, we identify several methodological challenges that the social entrepreneurship field will likely need to address as the field works toward legitimacy. Finally, we briefly identify statistical techniques that may be used as the social entrepreneurship literature develops, to test increasingly complex hypotheses.

REFERENCES

Austin, J., H. Stevenson and J. Wei-Skillern (2006). Social and commercial entrepreneurship: same, different, or both? *Entrepreneurship: Theory and Practice* **30**, 1–22.

Berry, J.M., D.F. Arons, G.D. Bass, M.F. Carter and K.E. Portney (2003). *Surveying Nonprofits: A Methods Handbook*. Washington, DC: Aspen Institute.

Binder, J.J. (1998). The event study methodology since 1969. *Review of Quantitative Finance and Accounting* **11**, 111–137.

Boyd, B.K., S. Gove and M.A. Hitt (2005). Construct measurement in strategic management research: illusion or reality? *Strategic Management Journal* **26**, 239–257.

Busenitz, L.W., G.P. West III, D. Shepherd, T. Nelson, G.N. Chandler and A. Zacharakis (2003). Entrepreneurship in emergence: past trends and future directions. *Journal of Management* **29**, 285–308.

Cassar, G. (2004). The financing of business start-ups. *Journal of Business Venturing* **19**, 261–283.

Chandler, G.N. and D.W. Lyon (2001). Issues of research design and construct measurement in entrepreneurship research: the past decade. *Entrepreneurship: Theory and Practice* **25**, 101–113.

Cohen, J. (1992). A power primer. *Psychological Bulletin* **112**, 155–159.

Corner, P.D. and M. Ho (2010). How opportunities develop in social entrepreneurship. *Entrepreneurship: Theory and Practice* **34**, 635–659.

Crook, T.R., C.L. Shook, M.L. Morris and T.M. Madden (2010). Are we there yet? An assessment of research design and construct measurement practices in entrepreneurship research. *Organizational Research Methods* **13**, 192–206.

Davila, A., G. Foster and M. Gupta (2003). Venture capital financing and the growth of startup firms. *Journal of Business Venturing* **18**, 689–708.

Dean, M.A., C.L. Shook and G.T. Payne (2007). The past, present, and future of

entrepreneurship research: data analytic trends and training. *Entrepreneurship: Theory and Practice* **31**, 601–618.
Dennis Jr., W.J. (2003). Raising response rates in mail surveys of small business owners: results of an experiment. *Journal of Small Business Management* **41**, 278–295.
Dess, G.G. and D.W. Beard (1984). Dimensions of organizational task environments. *Administrative Science Quarterly* **29**, 52–73.
Di Dominico, M.L., H. Haugh and P. Tracey (2010). Social bricolage: theorizing social value creation in social enterprises. *Entrepreneurship: Theory and Practice* **34**, 681–703.
Ensley, M.D., C.L. Pearce and K.M. Hmieleski (2006). The moderating effect of environmental dynamism on the relationship between entrepreneur leadership behavior and new venture performance. *Journal of Business Venturing* **21**, 243–263.
Goll, I. and A.A. Rasheed (1997). Rational decision-making and firm performance: the moderating role of environment. *Strategic Management Journal* **18**, 583–591.
Goll, I. and A.A. Rasheed (2004). The moderating effect of environmental munificence and dynamism on the relationship between discretionary social responsibility and firm performance. *Journal of Business Ethics* **49**, 41–54.
Hager, M.A., S. Wilson, T.H. Pollak and P.M. Rooney (2003). Response rates for mail surveys of nonprofit organizations: a review and empirical test. *Nonprofit and Voluntary Sector Quarterly* **32**, 252–267.
Hair, Jr., J.F., W.C. Black, B.J. Babin and R.E. Anderson (2010). *Multivariate Data Analysis*, 7th edn, Upper Saddle River, NJ: Pearson Education.
Harmon, H. (1967). *Modern Factor Analysis*. Chicago, IL: University of Chicago Press.
Haugh, H. (2007). Community-led social value creation. *Entrepreneurship: Theory and Practice* **31**, 161–182.
Hofmann, D.A. (1997). An overview of the logic and rationale of hierarchical linear models. *Journal of Management* **23**, 723–744.
Kerlinger, F.N. and H.B. Lee (2000). *Foundations of Behavioral Research*, 4th edn. Orlando, FL: Wadsworth-Thomson Learning.
Ketchen Jr., D.J. and C.L. Shook (1996). The application of cluster analysis in strategic management research: an analysis and critique. *Strategic Management Journal* **17**, 441–458.
Kistruck, G.M. and P.W. Beamish (2010). The interplay of form, structure, and embeddedness in social intrapreneurship. *Entrepreneurship: Theory and Practice* **34**, 735–761.
Louviere, J.J. (1988). Analyzing decision making: metric conjoint analysis. Sage University Paper series on Quantitative Applications in the Social Sciences 07-067. Beverly Hills': Sage Publications.
Low, M.B. and I.C. MacMillan (1988). Entrepreneurship: past research and future challenges. *Journal of Management* **14**, 139–162.
Maguire, S., C. Hardy and T.B. Lawrence (2004). Institutional entrepreneurship in emerging fields: HIV/AIDS treatment advocacy in Canada. *Academy of Management Journal* **47**, 657–679.
Mair, J. and I. Marti (2009). Entrepreneurship in and around institutional voids: a case study from Bangladesh. *Journal of Business Venturing* **24**, 419–435.
McDonald, R. (2007). An investigation of innovation in nonprofit organizations: the role of organizational mission. *Nonprofit and Voluntary Sector Quarterly* **36**, 256–281.
McWilliams, A. and D. Siegel (1997). Event studies in management research: theoretical and empirical issues. *Academy of Management Journal* **40**, 626–657.
Meyskens, M., C. Robb-Post, J.A. Stamp, A.L. Carsrud and P.D. Reynolds (2010). Social ventures from a resource-based perspective: an exploratory study assessing global Ashoka fellows. *Entrepreneurship: Theory and Practice* **34**, 661–680.
Miller, T.L. and C.L. Wesley II (2010). Assessing mission and resources for social change: an organizational identity perspective on social venture capitalists' decision criteria. *Entrepreneurship: Theory and Practice* **34**, 705–733.
Monsen, E., H. Patzelt and T. Saxton (2010). Beyond simple utility: incentive design and trade-offs for corporate employee-entrepreneurs. *Entrepreneurship: Theory and Practice* **34**, 105–130.

Moss, T.W., J.C. Short, G.T. Payne and G.T. Lumpkin (2011). Dual identities in social ventures: an exploratory study. *Entrepreneurship: Theory and Practice* **35**, 805–830.

Payne, G.T. (2006). Examining configurations and firm performance in the suboptimal equifinality context. *Organization Science* **17**(6), 756–770.

Payne, G.T., K.H. Kennedy and J.L. Davis (2009). Competitive dynamics among service SMEs. *Journal of Small Business Management* **46**(4), 421–442.

Pearce II, J.A., D.A. Fritz and P.S. Davis (2010). Entrepreneurial orientation and the performance of religious congregations as predicted by rational choice theory. *Entrepreneurship: Theory and Practice* **34**, 219–248.

Pfeffer, J. (1993). Barriers to the advance of organizational science: paradigm development as a dependent variable. *Academy of Management Review* **18**, 599–620.

Priem, R. (1992). An application of metric conjoint analysis for the evaluation of top managers' individual strategic decision making processes: a research note. *Strategic Management Journal* **13**, 143–151.

Raudenbush, S.W. and A.S. Bryk (2002). *Hierarchical Linear Models: Applications and Data Analysis Methods*, 2nd edn. Thousand Oaks, CA: Sage.

Shepherd, D.A. (1999). Venture capitalists' assessment of new venture survival. *Management Science* **45**, 621–632.

Shepherd, D.A. and A. Zacharakis (1997). Conjoint analysis: a window of opportunity for entrepreneurship research. In J. Katz (ed.), *Advances in Entrepreneurship, Firm Emergence and Growth*, Vol. 3. Greenwich, CT: JAI Press, pp. 203–248.

Shook, C.L., D.J. Ketchen Jr., C.S. Cycyota and D. Crockett (2003). Data analytic trends and training in strategic management. *Strategic Management Journal* **24**, 1231–1237.

Short, J.C., J.C. Broberg, C.C. Cogliser and K.H. Brigham (2010a). Construct validation using computer-aided text analysis (CATA): an illustration using entrepreneurial orientation. *Organizational Research Methods* **13**, 320–347.

Short, J.C., D.J. Ketchen Jr., N. Bennett and M. du Toit (2006). An examination of firm, industry, and time effects on performance using random coefficients modeling. *Organizational Research Methods* **9**, 259–284.

Short, J.C., D.J. Ketchen Jr., J.G. Combs and R.D. Ireland (2010b). Research methods in entrepreneurship: opportunities and challenges. *Organizational Research Methods* **13**, 6–15.

Short, J.C., D.J. Ketchen and T.B. Palmer (2002). The role of sampling in strategic management research on performance: a two-study analysis. *Journal of Management* **28**, 363–385.

Short, J.C., A. McKelvie, D.J. Ketchen Jr. and G.N. Chandler (2009a). Firm and industry effects on firm performance: a generalization and extension for new ventures. *Strategic Entrepreneurship Journal* **3**, 47–65.

Short, J.C., T.W. Moss and G.T. Lumpkin (2009b). Research in social entrepreneurship: past contributions and future opportunities. *Strategic Entrepreneurship Journal* **3**, 161–194.

Short, J.C. and T.B. Palmer (2008). The application of DICTION to content analysis research in strategic management. *Organizational Research Methods* **11**, 727–752.

Short, J.C., G.T. Payne and D.J. Ketchen Jr. (2008). Research on organizational configurations: past accomplishments and future challenges. *Journal of Management* **34**, 1053–1079.

Tagiuri, R. and J.A. Davis (1992). On the goals of successful family companies. *Family Business Review* **5**, 43–62.

Tahai, A. and M.J. Meyer (1999). A revealed preference study of management journals' direct influences. *Strategic Management Journal* **20**, 279–296.

Thomson Reuters (2010). ISI web of knowledge: journal citation reports. http://admin-apps.isiknowledge.com.lib-e2.lib.ttu.edu/JCR/JCR (accessed 1 June 2010).

Tracey, P. and O. Jarvis (2007). Toward a theory of social venture franchising. *Entrepreneurship: Theory and Practice* **31**, 667–685.

Van de Ven, A.H., H.J. Sapienza and J. Villanueva (2007). Entrepreneurial pursuits of self- and collective interests. *Strategic Entrepreneurship Journal* **1**, 353–370.

Wiklund, J. and D. Shepherd (2005). Entrepreneurial orientation and small business performance: a configurational approach. *Journal of Business Venturing* **20**, 71–91.
Zahra, S.A., H.N. Rawhouser, N. Bhawe, D.O. Neubaum and J.C. Hayton (2008). Globalization of social entrepreneurship opportunities. *Strategic Entrepreneurship Journal* **2**, 117–131.

Index

abductive conclusion 220–22
Abolafia, M.Y. 16
academic journal coverage 232–3, 234–5
acquiescence bias 175–6
action 85, 95–6
action research (AR) 79, 82, 101–2
  perspective of 82–4
  strengths and weaknesses 100–101
action research cycle (ARC) 79–80, 84–5, 90–91
  ebb and flow dynamics 88–90
  episodes of cycle 85–8
adaptability of method 99–101
adjacency data matrix 155, 156
administrative error 177–8
Ahmad, N. 9, 16, 18, 81
Al-Laham, A. 150
Albaum, G.S. 35
Aldrich, H. 150, 151, 164
Alter Eco 131–7
Alter, S.K. 13, 16
Alvesson, M. 70, 119, 129
Alvord, S.H. 5
Amabile, T.M. 7, 40
ambiguity in questionnaires 200
Amit, R. 18, 27, 40
analysis of variance (ANOVA) 211–13, 244
analytic induction 221
analytical generalisation 220, 221
Anderson, A. 164
Anderson, R.B. 11
Andreasen, A.R. 170
ANT (actor network theory) 68–9
Appadurai, A. 55
Arendt, H. 12
Armstrong, P. 17
Arndt, J. 176
Arnold, S.J. 26
assumptions in questionnaires 201–2
attitude scales 190–91
auspices bias 177
Austin, J.E. 5, 18, 19, 81, 151, 231
Australian Bureau of Statistics (ABS) 182
Australian Market and Social Research Society 181, 184
authenticity 223
axiology 30

Bagozzi, R.P. 15
Baines, S. 150
Baker, K.G. 35
Barclay, I. 35
Barczak, G. 171
Baron, D.P. 5
Baron, R.A. 150
Barron, F. 37
Barthes, R. 132
Baumann, S. 37
Baumgartner, H. 176
Beamish, P.W. 151, 165, 234
Beard, D.W. 238
Beckert, J. 27
Belk, R.W. 17
Belso-Martínez, J.A. 150
Bennett, A. 107, 108, 109, 116, 222, 227
Bennett, R.C. 35
Bentham, J. 21
Berkowitz, L. 82, 84
Berkowitz, S.D. 151
Berkun, S. 99
Berman, E. 188, 206
Berry, J.M. 239
betweenness 161
Bhagavatula, S. 150
Binder, J.J. 244
Birley, S. 150, 162
bivariate analysis of association 213–16
bivariate analysis of difference 209–13
Blackburn, R. 74
Bochner, A.P. 70
Boddice, R. 66
Boer, P. 151

Boje, D.M. 52, 59, 61
Boland, R.J. 58
Bonnacich, P. 159
Borda, O.F. 82
Borgatti, S.P. 151, 158
Bornstein, D. 5, 55, 66
Boschee, J. 16
Bouwen, R. 51, 54, 58
boxplots 209–10
Boyd, B.K. 239
Bradbury, H. 83, 85
Brinckerhoff, P.C. 16
Brockhaus, R. 38
Brown, A. 13
Brown, A.D. 64, 73
Brown, L.D. 5
Bruner, J.S. 53, 55
Bruyat, C. 18–19, 27, 40
Bryk, A.S. 244
Bunge, M. 226
Burke, P. 63
Burns, A. 84
Burt, R.S. 34, 40, 41, 154, 161
Busenitz, L.W. 238
business researchers 31

Calás, M.B. 75
Caldwell, B. 30, 34
Callari, A. 17
Campbell, D.T. 84
Capra, F. 27
CAQDAS (computer-assisted qualitative data analysis software) 117–20
Carson, D. 26
Carsrud, A.L. 41
Cartesian concepts 27
case selection
  in case study research 110–12
  in discourse analysis 137–8
case studies 106–9
case study research 110–21
Cassar, G. 238
Casson, M. 35, 36
Cateora, P. 204
Caust, J. 41
Caves, R.E. 17, 37
centrality measures 159, 161
Chandler, G.N. 233, 237, 238, 240
Chase, S.E. 53
Checkland, P. 84
Chell, E. 150
Cherry, N. 85
chi-square 213–14
Chia, R. 57
Cho, A.H. 5, 11, 14, 16, 56, 66, 81
Christensen, C.M. 7
CIA (Central Intelligence Agency) 183
Cieslik, J. 172
classic studies 31
clique analysis 159, 160
Clohesy, S. 5
closeness 161
clustering 158–9
  hierarchical 162, 163
Cobley, P. 53, 73
Cohen, J. 238
cohesion 158–9
Colbert, F. 36
Coleman, J.S. 158
Collins, O.F. 17, 38
communicative arenas (CAs) 85–8
conclusions
  abductive conclusion 220–22
  deduction 218–19
  induction 218–19
  logical processes of 218–22
  verifying 222–7
confidence intervals 212
construct validity 192–3, 224
Cook, T.D. 84
Cooke, P. 150
Cooper, R.G. 35, 42
Corner, P.D. 234
correlation 214–16
Coupland, N. 130
Court, D. 89
Coyne, R. 27, 40
Crane, E. 176
Crawford, C.M. 18, 27, 35, 40
creativity 7
Creswell, J.W. 114, 119
criterion validity 192
critical discourse analysis 130
critical linguistic analysis 130–31
Cronbach, L.J. 220
Crook, T.R. 233, 240
cross-sectional studies 171–2
cross-tabulation 213–14
Crotty, M. 107

crystal metaphor 223
Csikszentmihalyi, M. 7, 88, 227
culture-bound response bias 177
Curasi, C.F. 17
Czarniawska-Joerges, B. 58, 64

Dacin, P.A. 5, 6
Daston, L. 32
data analysis
  in case study research 116–17
  in discourse analysis 139–42
  in survey analyses 206–16
data collection
  in case study research 112–16
  in discourse analysis 138
  network 153–4
data-processing error 178
data reduction 117
Davidsson, P. 150
Davila, A. 245
Davis, J.A. 240
Davis, S.N. 27
De Carolis, D.M. 150
De Cock, C. 127
De Fina, A. 74
Dean, M.A. 231, 233, 237, 240, 241
decision-making analysis 245–6
deduction 218–19
Dees, J.G. 11, 13–14, 66
Deetz, S. 119
Defoe, D. 38
degree centrality 159, 161
Dempsey, S.E. 58, 67
Dennis, W.J., Jr. 238
density 158–9
Denzin, N.K. 26
Descartes, R. 27
descriptive analysis 206–9
descriptive validity 223, 224
Dess, G.G. 18, 238
determinants 8
Devendra, P. 172
Dewey, J. 82
Dey, P. 56, 66, 67, 68–9, 70
Dholakia, N. 15
Dick, P. 127, 128
Dilthey, W. 39, 40
DiMaggio, P. 164
discourse analysis 127–8
  corpus of analysis 138–9
  critical discourse analysis 130
  critical linguistic analysis 130–31
  data analysis 139–42
  data collection 138
  diversity of approaches to 129–31
  multimodal aspect of 131–7
  researcher's toolbox 145–7
  topic and case selection 137–8
  value in social entrepreneurship
      context 128–9
  writing up data analysis 142–5
discrete events methods 244–5
document analysis 114
Donckels, R. 150
Donnelly-Cox, G. 81
Donnerstein, E. 82, 84
door-to-door interviews 185–6
Doreian, P. 158
Douglas, H. 171
Dowling, M. 162
Down, S. 61, 62
Drapal, K. 184, 187
Drayton, B. 11, 18

ebb and flow dynamics 86, 88–90, 98–9
Ebbutt, D. 83
Eckhardt, J.T. 11, 15, 34
Eckkrammer, E.M. 131, 138
Eco, U. 218, 221
economic activity 14–17, 20
Economy, P. 11, 13
Eikenberry, A. 184, 187
Eisenhardt, K.M. 106, 108, 110, 111,
    121
Elias, J. 13
Elias, N. 40
Elliott, J. 83
Ellis, C. 70
Elsbach, K.D. 36
embeddedness 164–5
embedding narratives 65–6
Emerson, J. 5, 13–14
Emerson, R.M. 12
empirical inference 219–20
Ensley, M.D. 238
enterprising human action 10–12, 20
entrepreneurial activity, defining 6–9
entrepreneurs 37–8
entrepreneurship, defining 8–9
epistemology 26, 30, 53–6

Eraut, M. 89
Essers, C. 69
Eugene, K. 172
evaluative validity 223, 225
Evans, D.S. 33
Even, R. 37
Evered, R.D. 82
external validity 223, 225
extremity bias 176

Fairclaugh, N. 127
Fairclough, N. 127, 128
Fann, K.T. 218, 219, 220, 227
Faust, K. 151
Feldman, D.H. 7
Fernhaber, S.A. 150
fieldwork and editing 205
Fischer, C. 154
Fischer, E. 26
Fletcher, G.J.O. 41
fluidity of method 99–101
Fontana, A. 114
Fowler, A. 16
Freeman, L.C. 155, 159
Frey, J.H. 114
fundamental themes 85, 92–4

Gabriel, Y. 58, 59–60
Galaskiewicz, J. 153
Galbraith, J.K. 17
Galison, P. 32
Gans, H.J. 37
Gardner, H. 18, 40
Gartner, W.B. 51, 74
Gassenheimer, J.B. 10, 15, 16
Geertz, C. 54
Gellynck, X. 150
general linear models (GLMs) 241, 244
generalisation 109
Georgakopoulou, A. 74
George, A.L. 107–9, 116, 222, 227
Ghauri, P. 106–9, 111–13, 116
Gillespie, J.J. 164
Giorgi, A. 39, 41, 42
Goddard, H. 51
Golafshani, N. 118
Goll, I. 238
Gomm, R. 220
Goodman, J.P. 40
Graebner, M.E. 108, 110, 111
Granovetter, M. 40, 41, 164
Grant, D. 127, 128, 130
Grant, P. 31, 32
graphs 155–8, 207, 208
Greene, J.C. 115
Greenwood, D.J. 83, 84, 85, 87–8
Grisar-Kasse, K. 115
Grocer 137
Gruber, H.E. 27, 40, 108
Grundy, S. 85
Guba, E.G. 26, 30, 106, 109, 118, 222, 223
Gubrium, J.F. 59, 60
Guignon, C.B. 27
Gupta, A.K. 36
Gustavsen, B. 87

Hage, P. 155
Hager, M.A. 239
Hair, J.F., Jr. 240, 241, 245
Hall, S. 85
Hallen, B.L. 150
Halliday, M.A.K. 131, 132
Hanneman, R. 151
Harary, F. 155
Hardy, C. 127–31
Harmon, H. 237
Harrington, A. 43
Harrington, D.M. 37
Harrowitz, N. 220, 221, 227
Hart, S. 35
Hartley, J.F. 107, 108
Haugh, H. 5, 16, 81, 151, 234
Hausman, C.R. 18, 27, 40
Heidegger, M. 40
Hekman, S. 42
Henry, E. 5, 81
Herman, D. 54
Hesterly, W.S. 150
heterogeneity in organisations 245
hierarchical clustering 159, 162, 163
hierarchical linear modelling 244
Hingley, M.K. 150
Hirsch, P.M. 37
Hirschman, E.C. 17, 26, 36, 218
histograms 209–10
historical accounts 116
Hite, J.M. 150, 164
Hjorth, D. 51, 55, 74
Ho, M. 234

Hofmann, D.A. 238, 244
Hohenthal, J. 115
Holbrook, M.B. 218
Holstein, J.A. 59, 60
Holwell, S. 84
Honig, B. 150
Hopkins, D.J. 83
Hoppe, H.-H. 17
Horowitz, P. 38
Houston, F.S. 10, 15, 16
Hoyle, R.H. 224, 225
Huberman, A.M. 85
Hughes, J. 182
Huizinga, J. 11
Hume, D. 27
hypertextual environment 133–7
hypothesis 218–19, 221, 227
hypothesis testing 236, 238

identity formation 62–4
image-text interactions 131–7
impact 9
induction 218–19
inferences 218–21
innovation 8, 39
internal validity 224
internet surveys 185–6
interpretation, rigour in 226–7
interpretive structuralism 130, 131
interpretive validity 223, 224
intertextuality 65–6
interval-scaled data 209
interviewer bias 176
interviewer cheating 178
interviewer error 178
interviews 113–14
  personal 180, 185–6
  storytelling 59–60
  telephone 180–82, 185–6

Jack, S.L. 150, 164
Jacobson, R. 37
Jäger, S. 145
Jain, S. 204
Jameson, F. 66
Janssen, S. 37
Jarillo, J.C. 10
Jarvis, O. 235
Jaspers, K. 27
Jaworski, A. 130
Jensen, M.C. 17
Johannisson, B. 70
Johansson, A.W. 60, 62
Johansson, J.K. 36
Jones, R. 62, 63, 81
Jovanovic, B. 33
Julien, P.-A. 18–19, 27, 40

Kariv, D. 150
Karreman, D. 129
Katz, J. 75, 159
Katz, L. 159
Kelley, T. 36
Kellior, B. 177
Kemmis, S. 83, 85, 87
Kerlinger, F.N. 236, 238, 240
Ketchen, D.J., Jr. 245
Khan, S. 107
Kichwa language 79–81
Kihlstrom, R.E. 33
Kilduff, M. 165
Killworth, P.D. 154
Kim, P. 150, 151, 164
Kimble, G. 42
King, N. 113, 114
Kirzner, I.M. 33, 34, 37, 38
Kistruck, G.M. 151, 165, 234
Kloosterman, R.C. 150
knowledge-based approach 35
Kor, Y.Y. 150
Korosec, R. 188, 206
Kotler, P. 15
Kovalainen, A. 74
Krackhardt, D. 154, 165
Kramer, R.M. 36
Kress, G. 131, 132, 133, 138, 146
Krueger, N.F. 41

Laffont, J.-J. 33
Lamb, H. 139
Lambrecht, J. 150
Langley, A. 116, 118
language complexity in questionnaires 197, 198
Larson, A. 150, 162
Latour, B. 55, 68, 71
Lauglaug, A.S. 36
Lavidge, R. 216
Law, J. 52, 69, 70
Le Breton-Miller, I. 150

Lechner, C. 162
Lecomte, T. 137
Lee, D. 150
Lee, H.B. 236, 238, 240
Lee, S. 172
Leech, N.L. 115
Legard, R. 113, 114
Leger, Y.A. 170
Leinbach, C. 36
Lemke, J.L. 131
Leonard, D. 27, 36, 40
Lepak, D.P. 12
Lerner, M. 5
Leroux, K. 171, 184, 187, 188
Lester, R.K. 19
Levin, M. 83, 84, 85, 87–8
Levy, S.J. 15
Lewin, K. 82
Lewis, J. 111, 113, 117, 118, 119
Lincoln, Y.S. 26, 30, 106, 109, 118, 222, 223
Lindgren, M. 66
Liu, T.-H. 108
Locke, J. 27
logical inference 220, 221
Lombardo, A.P. 170
longitudinal data methods 244
longitudinal studies 172, 240
Lorrain, F. 161
Louviere, J.J. 245
Low, M.B. 231, 233, 236, 237, 240
Lubart, T.I. 7
Luce, R.D. 159
Ludema, J.D. 87
Lumpkin, G.T. 18
Lyon, D.W. 233, 237, 238, 240
Lyons, W. 27
Lyotard, J.F. 53, 67, 68

MacMillan, I.C. 231, 233, 236, 237, 240
Madison, G.B. 38
Magnani, L. 219, 222, 227
Maguire, S. 128, 234
Mahajan, V. 35, 42
Maier, F. 145
mail intercept interviews 185–6
mail surveys 185–6
Mair, J. 11, 16, 151, 165, 235
management activity
  implications for researcher 36
  knowledge-based approaches to 35
  non-analytic approaches to 35–6
Marietta, D.E. 14
Marino, L.D. 150
markets 17–18, 36–7
Marsden, P.V. 152
Marshak, R.J. 127, 128
Martens, M.L. 74
Marti, I. 5, 11, 16, 151, 165, 235
Martin, R.L. 13
Martinec, R. 131, 132, 133, 146
Martínez-Fernández, M.A.T. 150
Maxwell, J.A. 220, 223, 224, 225
McCallister, L. 154
McCarty, C. 153
McClelland, D. 32
McClintock, C.C. 220
McCracken, G. 36, 118, 222, 226
McDonald, R. 239
McGregor, D. 17
McHale, B. 53
McLean, M. 11, 16, 151
McNiff , J. 85
McTaggart, R. 83, 85
McWilliams, A. 244–5
mean differences, tests of 241
measurement 184
  attitude scales 190–91
  evaluation of measures 192–3
  levels of 189
  method of 187
  number of measures 188–90
  object of 187
  rule of measurement 187–8
Meckling, W.H. 17
Metcalf, J.S. 19
method
  adaptability and fluidity 99–101
  rigour in application of 222–6
methodological development 241–6
methodology 26–7, 30
Meyer, J.-A. 28, 31, 32, 37
Meyer, M. 130
Meyer, M.J. 233
Meyskens, M. 235, 239, 240
Mickunas, A. 37
Miczo, N. 12
Milanov, H. 150
Miles, M.B. 85

Milgram, S. 164
Miller, D. 150
Miller, D.L. 119
Miller, T.L. 235, 237, 239, 244
Mintzberg, H. 17
Misak, C. 221
Mitchell, J.C. 220
mixed data collection 115–16
Mizruchi, M.S. 153
Mohan, L. 172
Molina-Morales, F.X. 150
Monsen, E. 238
Moreno, J.L. 155
Morgan, G. 31, 32, 129
Morse, E.A. 150
Mort, G.S. 5, 81, 108, 164
Moss, T.W. 235, 236, 239, 240, 241
multimodal discourse analysis 133–7
multiple-case design 111–12
multiple, representing the 68–9
Mushuk Muyu project 79–81, 90–100

Narotzky, S. 36
narrating genres 66–8
narrative analysis
  embedding narratives 65–6
  genres of narrating 66–8
  narrative processes of identity formation 62–4
  stories and the researcher 71–3
  writing and changing stories 68–71
narrative approaches 51–2
  applying to research 52–4
  generating narrative data 57–61
  ontological & epistemological dimensions 53–6
  reasons to invest in 73–5
  researcher's dilemma 56–7
network theories
  embeddedness 164–5
  small-world phenomenon 164
  strength-of-weak-ties theory 162, 163
networks, types of 152–3
'new'
  products, processes, markets 17–18
  understanding 'social' in 18–19
Newman, H.K. 5
Newspoll News 199
Nicholls, A. 5, 11, 14, 16, 55, 66, 81
Noel, E. 85
non-analytic approaches 35–6
Nonaka, I. 36
Noorderhaven, N.G. 26

objectivist approaches 31, 32
  implications of prioritisation 42
  weaknesses 39–41
O'Connor, E. 65
O'Connor, I. 117
OECD 8, 137
O'Halloran, K.L. 132
O'Neill, H. 173, 181
ontology 26, 30, 53–6
Onwuegbuzie, A.J. 115
opportunity 33–5
Osberg, S. 13
Osmond, J. 117
Osteen, M. 17
Oxford English Dictionary (OED) 12, 13, 33
Özcan, G.B. 150
Ozgen, E. 150

Packendorff, J. 66
Packer, M.J. 39
Padmanabhan, K.P. 67
Palmer, T.B. 241
Pandya, A. 15
Parker, I. 128
Patton, M.Q. 111, 112, 117, 118
Patzelt, H. 150
Payne, G.T. 245
Payne, S. 198, 201
Pearce, J. 81
Pearce, J.A., II 235, 236, 237, 239
Pearson's r 214–15
Peirce, C.S. 218, 219, 221, 227
Penrose, E.T. 18, 31, 32, 39
Peredo, A.M. 11, 16, 151
performance 9
  measuring 239–40
Perren, L. 31, 32
Perrini, F. 11, 16, 81
Perry, A.D. 159
Perry, C. 26
personal interviews 180, 185–6
Pettigrew, A.M. 31, 33
Pfeffer, J. 232
Phelan, J. 51, 55

Phillips, N. 127, 128, 130
philosophy of science 27–9
pie charts 207, 208
Piekkari, R. 107
Piore, M.J. 19, 27, 35, 39, 40
Pirolo, L. 150
Polanyi, K. 164
Polletta, F. 64
Poolton, J. 35
Porter, J.E. 65
Porter, M.E. 31, 32
positivism 29, 30, 43, 222
Prasad, P. 26–7, 52
pre-test questionnaire 204
Presutti, M. 150
Priem, R. 245
problem arena 85, 91–2
processes and products, new 17–18, 20
projected vision 90
Punch, K.F. 85

qualitative data collection
  document analysis 114
  interviews 113–14
  reflective journals 114–15
qualitative research 236–7
qualitative software 117
quantitative data collection 115
quantitative research 237
questionnaire design 193–4
  content of questions 194–5
  form of response 195–7
  information sought 194
  physical characteristics 203
  pre-test questionnaire 204
  question sequence 202–3
  re-examination and revision 203–4
  type of questionnaire 194
  wording 197–202
questions, wording
  ambiguity 200
  burdensome questions 202
  complexity of language 198
  double-barrelled items 201
  leading and loaded 197–200
  making assumptions 201–2
questions, wording of
  complexity of language 197
  structured and disguised 179–80

Rabinowitz, P.J. 51
Race, P. 83, 85
Ragin, C.C. 119
Ramachandran, V.S. 111
random sampling error 172–3
Rasheed, A.A. 238
Raudenbush, S.W. 244
reachability 158
reality, researcher's view of 31
Reason, P. 83, 85
reflection-in-action 89
reflection-on-action 85, 97–8
reflective journals 114–15
regression 237–8, 244
regular equivalence 161–2
Reis, T. 5, 16
Reitz, K.P. 161
relational data matrix 155, 156
reliability 118–19, 120, 192, 223, 225, 240
research methods, sophistication and diversity 236–8
researchers
  best practice checklist for 120–21
  challenges faced by 231–41
  grounding in action research (AR) 83
  opportunities for 242–3
  toolbox for 145–7
respondent error
  deliberate falsification 174–5
  non-response error 173–4
  types of response bias 175–7
  unconscious misrepresentation 175
response bias 174, 175–7
response, determining form of 195–7
Rhodes, C. 73
Rhodes, M.L. 81
Richards, R.J. 27
Richardson, L. 223
Rickman, H.P. 40
Riddle, M. 151
rigour
  in application of method 222–6
  in interpretation 226–7
Rindova, V. 75
Ritchie, J. 118, 119
Roberts, G. 176
Robinson, J. 5, 16

Robinson, W.S. 220, 221
robustness 118
Rogers, E.M. 36, 158
role equivalence measures 161–2
Ronchi, D. 154
Rosen, S. 34
Rothenberg, A. 18, 27, 40
Rubin, J. 181
Ruth, J.A. 12
Rutledge, D. 11

Salway, A. 131, 132, 133, 146
sample-selection error 178
sample size 205, 238–9
sampling 204–5
Sanders, M.L. 58, 67
scatterplots 214–15
Schön, D.A. 85, 89, 97
Schumpeter, J.A. 7, 18, 35, 36, 40
Schutz, A. 83
Scott, J. 151
Sebeok, T.A. 218, 221
Seelos, C. 16
Seidman, I.E. 114
self-administered surveys/
questionnaires 182–4
sensitivity 193
Seymour, R.G. 9, 15, 16, 18, 39, 81
Shackle, G.L.S. 12–13, 14
Shadish, W.R. 220
Shane, S.A. 11, 15, 16, 33, 34, 41
Shapero, A. 38
Shapiro, I. 32
Sharir, M. 5
Shepherd, D.A. 245, 246
Shook, C.L. 241, 245
Short, J.C. 108–9, 231–3, 236–41,
243–5
Siegel, D. 244–5
Siggelkow, N. 111
single-case design 110–11
Skinner, B.F. 42
Skjervheim, H. 31
small-world phenomenon 164
Smircich, L. 28, 31, 32, 129
Smith, C. 12
Smith, D. 172
Snape, D. 107
Snodgrass, A. 27, 40
social desirability bias (SDB) 177
social entrepreneurship
as challenging research setting
81–2
coverage in journal literature 232–3,
234–5
defining concepts 5–9
overview 3–4
research opportunities 242–3
and the researcher 10–19
working definitions 19–20
social linguistic analysis 130
social network analysis 150–51
graphs 155–8
network data collection 153–4
network measures 158–62
network theories 162–5
relational data matrix 155, 156
social network approach 151–3
'social', understanding of
in economic activity 16–17
in enterprising human action
11–12
in entrepreneurship research 5–6
in 'new' 18–19
in value generation 14
social value production 89–90
Somers, M.R. 55, 62
Sorenson, R.L. 150
Souitaris, V. 150
Spencer, L. 107
Spinosa, C. 66
Srinivasan, V. 36
Stake, R.E. 106–9, 111, 114, 121
Starr, J.A. 150, 162
statistical generalisation/inference
219–20
Steenkamp, J.E.M. 176
Steier, L.P. 150
Sternberg, R.J. 7
Stevenson, H.H. 10
Stewart, D. 37
Steyaert, C. 51, 54–6, 58, 60, 62, 66–70,
74–5
Stone, W. 182
story writing and changing 68–71
storytelling *see* narrative approaches
strategic action planning (SAP) 85,
94–5
Straus, S. 36
strength-of-weak-ties theory 162, 163

Stringer, R. 7
structural equivalence 161
Styles, C. 15
subjective-objective debate 27–9
subjectivist approaches 31, 32–3
  implications of prioritisation 42
  weaknesses 39, 41–2
subjects (of research) 83
Suchman, M.C. 65
Sundaramurthy, C. 150
survey error, reducing 178–9
surveys
  errors in survey research 172–9
  measurement 184, 187–93
  method advantages/disadvantages 184, 185–6
  methods of conducting 179–84
  nature of 171–2
  survey design 170–71
Susman, G.I. 82
Swedberg, R. 18, 27, 40
symptoms of truth 226
systematic error 173–8

t-tests 210–11, 241
Taba, H. 85
Tacchi, J.A. 84, 85
Tagiuri, R. 240
Tahai, A. 233
Tapsell, P. 5, 81
Taylor, M. 159
telephone interviews 180–82, 185–6
Tenkasi, R.V. 58
tests of mean differences 241
theoretical inference 220, 221
theoretical validity 223, 224
Thisted, L.N. 60
Thomson Reuters 232
Tierney, W.G. 70
Tönnies, F. 17
Tracey, P. 235
Truzzi, M. 218
Tsang, E. 150
Tsoukas, H. 57
Tuckel, P. 173, 181
Twersky, F. 5

univariate analysis 206–9
Urry, J. 70
Uzzi, B. 164, 165

validity 119, 192–3, 222–6, 240–41
value generation 12–15, 20
van de Ven, A.H. 239
van der Poel, M.G.M. 154
van Leeuwen, T. 131, 132, 133, 138, 146
van Manen, M. 89
van Slyke, D.M. 5
van Wynsbeghe, R. 107
Venkataraman, S. 11, 33
Vennesson, P. 107
Verschuren, P. 107, 109
Voelcker, J. 18
von Hayek, F.A. 31, 33, 34, 37, 40
von Mises, L. 10, 11, 31, 33, 38
Vurro, C. 11, 16, 81

Walker, E. 13
Wallace, D.B. 40, 108
Wasserman, S. 151
Watts, D.J. 164
Webb, G. 83
Webster, C.M. 154
Weerawardena, J. 5, 81, 108, 164
Weinberg, D. 29
Weiner, A. 17
Weitzman, E.A. 117
Weller, S.C. 154
Wellman, B. 151
Wesley, C.L., II 235, 237, 239, 244
White, D.R. 161
White, H.C. 161
White, J.B. 64
Whitfield, T.W.A. 11
Widdershoven, G. 60
Wilkinson, I. 114
Wills, D. 150
Wind, J. 35, 42
Winter, R. 87
Wodak, R. 127, 130
Woods, C. 5, 81
writing up data analysis
  in case study research 118–20
  in discourse analysis 142–5
Wu, L.-Y. 150

Yin, R.K. 106–8, 111, 113–14, 121, 222–5
Young, D. 5

Young, L. 114
Young, R. 5, 13, 16, 90

Zacharakis, A. 245, 246
Zahra, S.A. 245
Zikmund, W.G. 186, 191
Zuber-Skerritt, O. 83
Zucker, D.M. 106, 110, 121
Zukin, S. 164